NORWICH 915.04 CARR
Carroll, Charlie,
Peaks on the horizon :

FEB 1 4 2015

GUERNSEY MEMORIAL LIBRARY
0 00 04 0269824 5

Peaks

ON THE

Horizon

D0720804

Guernsey Memorial Library
3 Court Street
Norwich, NY 13815
www.guernseymemoriallibrary.org

Peaks ON THE Horizon

TWO JOURNEYS IN TIBET

CHARLIE CARROLL

Soft Skull Press
an imprint of COUNTERPOINT

Copyright © 2015 Charlie Carroll

All rights reserved under International and Pan-American
Copyright Conventions. No part of this book may be used or
reproduced in any manner whatsoever without written permission
from the publisher, except in the case of brief quotations embodied
in critical articles and reviews.

Library of Congress Cataloging-in-Publication Data Is Available

ISBN 978-1-61902-484-7

Soft Skull Press
An Imprint of COUNTERPOINT
2560 Ninth Street, Suite 318
Berkeley, CA 94710
www.softskull.com

Printed in the United States of America
Distributed by Publishers Group West

10 9 8 7 6 5 4 3 2 1

For my father
Barrie

Note from the Author

To protect the identities of all the Tibetans and Chinese who candidly spoke to me during my journey, and to prevent any possible incarceration which could result from their admissions to a writer, all names in this book have been changed.

At the time of my journey, £1 was worth approximately 10 yuan.

The Tibetan chapter titles are simply the phonetic spelling of the numbers one to fifteen ascending in the Tibetan language.

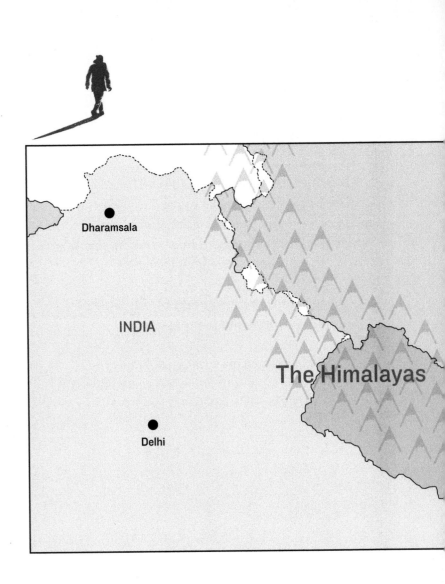

Peaks
ON THE
Horizon

TIBET

Lhasa

Zhangmuzhen

NEPAL

Kathmandu

BHUTAN

Contents

chig

Lobsang felt his mother's fingers curl around his skinny bicep as she gently shook his arm. He kept his eyes closed. It was customary for her to wake him for school in this way each morning, and customary for him to pretend he was still asleep. The rules of the game stated that his mother would shake him four times, repeat his name twice and then walk away from his bed to shout: 'Father! Our Lobsang has died in the night. We had better get a new Lobsang.' This was the child's cue to fling back his yak-hair blanket, leap to his feet and announce: 'I fooled you!' Then his mother would kiss him, the game would be over, and the new day would begin.

Once, he jumped from his bed and said: 'I fooled you! But get the new Lobsang so he can go to school for me.' His mother did not kiss him that morning, and he understood that he had broken the game's rules. From then on, he stuck to them religiously.

This time, it was his mother who was breaking the rules. She had shaken his arm a full eight times and repeated his name at least five. Then she said something unexpected: 'Lobsang, you must open your eyes, Lobsang.'

This he did, if only to reprimand her over her disrespect for their morning ritual, but the words stuck in his throat when he felt the cold outside his blanket. It was still early March, he knew that, but this was not a morning temperature. This cold meant something was wrong. Instead of reproaching his mother, he asked a simple: 'Why?'

'Later,' his mother said, stroking his forehead. 'Now, you must do what I say. No complaints.'

'OK!' he grinned, suddenly excited because he knew what his mother was up to. He leapt from the bed and performed a little dance on the floor to make his mother smile. She did not.

'Not so loud!' she whispered.

With pantomime-steps, he tiptoed across the room. 'Not so loud!' he whispered back, giggling at his impression and at his mother for trying to surprise him in this way. It was all too obvious. He grabbed at her hand and pulled her ear down towards his mouth. 'Are we going on a pilgrimage?' he breathed.

Lobsang's mother smiled at her youngest son. 'Yes,' she said. 'We're going on the best kind of pilgrimage. We're going to see Dorje.'

Dorje! For all Lobsang's guesswork, he had never supposed a visit to his eldest brother would be the surprise. He adored Dorje and had thrown tantrum after tantrum when his brother had left over a year ago. When the outbursts had not worked, Lobsang came to understand that he could only bring Dorje back by being good. And this he had been – *really* good – for a whole year. Now he was going to get his reward.

His mother led him out of their small house. A gigantic truck sat on the street with its lights off but its engine running. Following his mother's gestures, Lobsang climbed into the back of the truck and picked his way through the crates, boxes and bags to find in a corner his sister, Jamyang, and his brother, Chogyal. Jamyang held out her arms and Lobsang tripped into them.

'We're going on a pilgrimage to see Dorje!' he said.

'I know,' Jamyang replied, but she did not smile.

Chogyal said nothing and did not look at Lobsang as their mother and father climbed into the truck and sat with them. Their father took a thin but large cotton sheet from one of the crates and pulled it over them all. Lobsang felt disappointed that his father was coming on the pilgrimage (he had often wished that Dorje was his real father), but he at least seemed to know how to get the truck to start and stop. One bang of his fist on the wall behind them was enough to get the truck rolling; another brought it to a quick halt.

'Remember,' his mother told him as they bumped slowly out and along the streets of Lhasa. 'You must do what I say.'

Lobsang pressed his hands together in a gesture of prayer, bowed his head, and grinned. 'What must I do, mother?' he called above the roar of the engine.

She smiled back at him, reached out one hand and stroked his forehead. 'For now? Sleep.'

He felt aggrieved. Sleep? He had just woken up!

'The more you sleep,' his mother remonstrated, 'the quicker time will pass, and you'll get to see Dorje sooner than if you stay awake the whole time.'

Such logic had an immediate effect, and Lobsang closed his eyes without another word.

Though the truck bounced and its interior fluctuated between searing heat and numbing cold, Lobsang slept, and, when he didn't, he pretended he did. Sometimes, his mother or Jamyang nudged him and told him to eat. He would groan and mutter 'I am asleep', though he made sure to chew on the *tsampa* or the cubes of cheese gently nudged between his lips. He opened his eyes to greedily accept any offer of sweet, milky tea, but made sure they remained shut and his mouth remained mute whenever yak-butter tea took its place. He had never liked yak-butter tea, and never would, even though – years later – he would drink at least five cups a day and proclaim its benefits to anyone listening.

Lobsang was young and he knew it. He had spent enough time with the ageing monks who regularly came to visit his home – some family, most not – to recognise what the creases in their faces denoted, and then recognise with his own hands what his own smooth complexion suggested. For Lobsang, there was young (himself), adult (his sister and brother, though they were only fifteen and eighteen respectively), old (Dorje, his mother and father) and *very* old (the monks). And this meant that Lobsang understood time: for the young like him, they had so much of it they grew easily bored; but for the old like Dorje, his mother, father and the monks, time was something to be continually remarked upon and pointed out. Old people, Lobsang knew, obsessed over time because they did not have much of it left.

And so when, five days into their pilgrimage and still in the back of the truck, Lobsang's was the only excitement left among his family, he understood why. He was prepared to sacrifice as much time as was needed – he had so much of it! – to see Dorje again, but his mother and father, Chogyal and Jamyang were growing increasingly irritable with each passing hour. One morning, after they had played hide-and-seek in the clefts of a dusty hillock for four hours, Chogyal had hit Lobsang in the face for hiding too well and not appearing when his name was called. Lobsang knew Chogyal had broken the rules of the game, and his cheek stung from the swipe of his brother's knuckles, but he forgave Chogyal anyway, because he knew that Chogyal's time was running out, and he would rather not waste it chasing his younger brother through brown caves.

Most nights they all slept together in the truck while it bounced, and Lobsang loved this, but occasionally they stopped in small villages when the stars were brightest to sit in a room with a fire and other old people. When this happened, Lobsang had to lie in a corner of the room with his sister while she expertly flipped him on his side and pulled his back into her stomach. Lobsang tried to stay awake during those nights because he knew that sleeping on the truck would bring him to Dorje quicker. When their hosts went to their own corners to sleep, Lobsang would listen to his mother, father and Chogyal talk over the embers of the fire.

'I want to go back.'

'Don't you understand what would have happened if we'd stayed?'

'Think of your sister, of your brother.'

'Jamyang agrees with me. She would have come to the protest if you had let her.'

'They already have one brother missing. It would not be fair to have two.'

'Dorje chose to leave, and he is happy. Let me make my own choices and be happy with them.'

'Dorje's choice was to live and work in Nepal. To make money. Money which has helped us live. What was your choice? To be arrested?'

'Men are arrested for crimes. I committed no crime.'

'Listen to your father. You would have been arrested.'

'For what? Waving a flag in the Barkhor? That's not a crime. It's a belief.'

'I understand. I do.'

'Your mother is too soft on you. Do you know what we had to do to protect you? Three days we hid you, three days we lied. They would have taken you.'

'Let them take me.'

'They would have *killed* you!'

Lobsang recognised this final hiss as his mother's. Then, he recognised the sound of her crying softly.

'I will not lose a son. Not one.' This was his father's voice, delivered in a tone which Lobsang knew neither he nor his siblings could contest. 'What you did was right, Chogyal. What you *believe* is right. But I made a choice. When the police came the third time looking for you, they beat me. I would not tell them where you were. You are important to me, and you are important to your mother, to Dorje, to Jamyang and to Lobsang. We *must* leave.'

Chogyal did not complain for the rest of the pilgrimage, though he remained sullen and quiet. Lobsang's father stopped banging his fist on the wall of the truck, and

Lobsang's mother developed an unshakeable cough. One day, under a low and fierce sun, Jamyang took Lobsang out of the truck and down to the shoreline of a lake to wash him. The lake's green waters, Lobsang noticed, matched the jade amulet hanging from his sister's neck.

'Are we *really* going to see Dorje?' Lobsang asked.

Jamyang smiled. 'Yes. He is coming to meet us and take us to Nepal.'

'What's Nepal?'

'Another country.'

'But I like this country.'

'So do I. But it's not safe here for Chogyal anymore. He protested.'

Lobsang considered the word 'protested'. He did not understand it, but it sounded like fun.

'And now they have his name,' Jamyang continued. 'They want to put him in jail.'

'Protested' didn't sound like much fun anymore.

'You wouldn't see him for a long time. You miss Dorje, don't you?'

'I miss Dorje *lots*,' Lobsang said with some pride.

'Well, he's only been gone one year. Chogyal would be gone for maybe twenty.'

Lobsang tried to think what twenty years was like, but could not. Because of this, he began to cry. Jamyang clutched his naked shoulder and pulled him into her.

'It's all right, Lobsang – Dorje is going to walk over mountains to find us. And then he's going to take us to his home in Nepal. He has a wife. Imagine that! Another sister! And we'll all live together. One family. No one missing.'

Mountains. When their journey in the truck came to an end and they stepped from its belly for the final time, all Lobsang could see was mountains. They were white and smooth, never-ending, so tall some had clouds for hair. How could Dorje possibly walk over these? Lobsang tried, but tramping through the deep snow required muscles he had not developed, and the air became too cold and thin for him, so that Jamyang, Chogyal, his mother and his father took turns carrying him over the frozen passes. He did not need to try to sleep any longer: unconsciousness was too strong an opponent to fight off.

He awoke on the bare floor of a tiny monastery, a cup of steaming yak-butter tea pressed to his lips. For once, he did not push it away. A monk leered over him, chanting *Om mani padme hum*, and spat in his face. Lobsang instinctively shut his eyes tight. When he reopened them, the monk stuck his tongue out at him.

He awoke on the back of his father as they pushed onwards through snow, a blizzard around his ears, his family audible but not visible. His father patted his right leg and hollered a song into the storm.

He awoke on his mother's lap, her fingers caressing his forehead, nothing but Chogyal's nose discernible by the flickering flame of a single yak-butter candle.

He awoke to four shakes and his name called twice. 'Lobsang,' his mother cooed. 'Lobsang. We are here.'

She had broken the rules again, but he did not mind this time. Opening his eyes, he looked out upon green where there was once white, wood where there was once stone and ice.

'We're here,' his mother said. 'Dorje is coming.'

Across the flowered valley before him, in a warm mist devoid of sharp ice and bare rock, Lobsang watched the small figures of two men as they trekked upwards.

'Is that Dorje?' he asked.

'That,' his father said, pointing at the nearest of the two figures, 'is Dorje. And that...' his lone finger was joined by three more and a thumb as, palm outwards, he gestured at the expanse before them all, '... is Nepal.'

Lobsang rolled the word 'Nepal', his new home, around the contours of his mouth, testing its dimensions against his tongue and lips. He decided he liked it.

Six men appeared from the trees below. They wore uniforms that made it difficult for Lobsang to distinguish them from the ethereal foliage. *Hide-and-seek*, Lobsang thought. *They'll never beat Dorje. He's a master.*

The six men resolved themselves into a straight line, a border between Lobsang and Dorje. They walked towards the latter, and Dorje's companion emitted an echoing shriek before turning and running in the opposite direction, away from Lobsang.

We're over here! Lobsang wanted to call, but found he could not.

One of the six men raised his right arm. A piercing clap rang through the hills. Dorje's companion fell to the floor.

'No,' Lobsang's father whispered, his voice hoarse and terrified.

Dorje had not run. He continued to face the six men. Slowly, he dropped to his knees. The six men surrounded him. There was another clap.

Lobsang did not see what happened next, for his father had gathered him in his arms – Lobsang's face pressed tight against his father's chest – and was running. Lobsang was crying, and even thought he understood why he was crying, crying for Dorje, and crying for the fact that they were running back towards the snow.

My Snow
Leopard

|

The year Lobsang left Tibet, 1989, was the same year I discovered it. He was five; I was nine.

It was lunchtime, it was wet, and I had found shelter in my school's library. I was no stranger there, and I often liked to sit beneath the shelves of the 'Adult Reading' section because I thought this made me look clever. That afternoon, I found a copy of Heinrich Harrer's *Seven Years in Tibet*, bound in a yellow hardback cover with faded gold lettering, part of a set perhaps. I cannot precisely recall why I was drawn to it: the cover was bare apart from the title, and I had not heard of Tibet. I think I liked the author's strange name. No matter, what I do remember is opening to the frontispiece – a black and white photograph of a young man wearing a funny hat and holding up a bell while bald heads and frilly curtains surrounded him – and then flipping through the pages of tiny writing to find a hand-drawn map filled with mountainous peaks and ridges, and through them a long and dotted line of footsteps. Across the map were words even more unusual than the name of the writer and the faces on the photograph:

Lhasa, Shigatse, Gyabnak, Nanda Devi, Dehradun. I took the book home, read it slowly over the next two months, and then, to my later shame, never returned it to the school library.

As a child, I was obsessive in my fascinations. At that time, I wanted to be a paleontologist studying dinosaur fossils, and before that a marine biologist. Tibet became my new interest, and for the next few years all I wanted to be was a Tibetologist. I read whatever my mother could find me – most of it fantastical stories of flying monks and friendly snow lions – but some of it sound and factual, and I began to pride myself on being a little expert on the country. In secondary school, I never passed a library encyclopaedia without flicking to its Tibet entry; I used the geography CD-Roms on my school's computers to stare at photographs and drawings of the plateau; the assessed speeches I had to prepare for English lessons were always about Tibet.

I learned that Tibet was not even a country, but the Tibetan Autonomous Region (TAR) within China, yet ethnically Tibetans spread out across a far larger swathe of land known as Greater Tibet, which included not just the TAR, but also the areas of Kham and Amdo to the east, where nomads lived in gigantic tents, rode on horseback and fought with swords. I learned that Tibet's government did not even live in Tibet, but in India, in a small hill town in Dharamsala where they pitted their wits against the Chinese and demanded their country back. When it came to China itself, I became confused by the sheer volume of varying ethnicities, and so contented myself instead with the young teenager's predilection for sound bites. In China, the majority group were called the Han. They had stolen Tibet from the Tibetans in 1950. They had been led by an old man called Mao Tse-tung. I was confused about why the Chinese had done this, why they had invaded Tibet and, moreover, why they were still there. I yearned to find out for myself.

At least twice a year, I reread *Seven Years in Tibet*. Harrer's journey never failed to thrill me: it was the kind of adventure I craved in those days when I would gawp skyward at the planes which flew miles overhead, or spit from railway bridges on to the roofs of passing trains, giggling to myself that a piece of me was travelling elsewhere. One day, I told myself as I lay on my bed, propped up by my elbows and reading *Seven Years in Tibet* for the twelfth time, I would go to Tibet.

My obsession with Tibet lasted longer than its predecessors had, but it too eventually dissipated, at about the same time as I found music and alcohol. Yet it always lingered. When I left home at the age of eighteen to travel for the first time, I hoped it would be to Tibet, but I did not have the means, and never made it outside the limits of Europe. Throughout my early twenties, when I attended university and then became a schoolteacher, I travelled each summer, for this had in its own way become an obsession. For five years, I spent my Augusts roaming Asia, and though I always meant to, I never made it to Tibet, usually because the country was closed to tourists.

And then, of course, I fell in love, and I got married, and for a while I forgot about Tibet entirely.

I was, it seemed, not the only one. Perhaps my Tibet fascination coincided with the world's. Throughout the 1990s, its media presence was inescapable: the Dalai Lama was a household name; Free Tibet campaigns and organisations popped up everywhere; the Beastie Boys headlined benefit concerts; protests and riots and marches brought to light the atrocities the Tibetans had suffered at the hands of the Chinese; even Hollywood got involved – Martin Scorsese made *Kundun*, his biopic of the Dalai Lama; *Seven Years in Tibet* had been filmed with Brad Pitt as Heinrich Harrer; Richard Gere turned up in Dharamsala to publicly support the Dalai Lama. But, as the twentieth century came to a close, so too did the importance of Tibet's right to self-determination in the public eye.

And then, in 2008, the Beijing Olympics sparked a wave of pro-Tibet riots and demonstrations that arced across the globe, returning the Tibet issue to the world's attention and, with it, to mine. At the time, I was engrossed in writing my first book, but I used Tibet as a means to take my mind off the copious research on the English education system which I ploughed through each night. I bought and reread *Seven Years in Tibet* (I had donated my first copy to a charity shop a long time ago), and then did the same with other books about the country. The old obsession began to creep back in.

When I finished my first book, I allowed myself the luxury of six months off. I needed to leave England for a while, needed to travel, and there was no doubt that it had to be Tibet. I told a friend about my plans.

'You won't be able to get in,' he said.

'I've been looking into it. The borders were closed after the Olympic riots, but they're supposed to be open now. The trouble is, no one really knows. There's just no information coming out of Tibet. The only way is if I go to China and find out for myself.'

'You won't get in,' he repeated. 'Have you ever read that Peter Matthiessen book, *The Snow Leopard*?'

I had. In 1973, the writer Peter Matthiessen joined an expedition into a stretch of the Himalayas which forms the Tibetan-Nepali border. Led by the field-biologist George Schaller, and guided by a scant crew of Sherpas, Matthiessen set forth into the mountains at the beginning of an unforgiving winter. His primary goal was to observe and document the natural routines of a rare species of blue sheep, the bharal, specific only to that locale. Underlying that objective, however, was the potential of an even less hopeful opportunity – the sighting of a snow leopard. The snow leopard might be the most reclusive mammal on earth, a quiet and secretive creature with a natural habitat inhospitable to life and to blood. Few Westerners have ever seen a snow leopard in the wild, and Matthiessen hoped to be one of the first. Walking more than 250 miles from Pokhara to Crystal Mountain over some of the highest passes in the world, Matthiessen spent two months on his pilgrimage. After an arduous and frozen journey, living nomadically and ascetically with few Western comforts save his journal, he finally returned to America at the end of the year. He had not seen a single snow leopard.

'Tibet's gonna be your snow leopard,' my friend said. 'You'll chase it. You'll pursue it. But you'll never see it.'

2

If every country is unique, then every border is more so. Some borders reflect their country's desperation for tourism and can be crossed for ten dollars and a spare passport photo to affix to an entry form. Others make you wait, have to be sure that you are committed to your enterprise, and so divert you and your patience to an embassy and a five-day system of visa processing. Still others ask not only where you are going, but where you are from, and the difference between a British and an Indian passport can change your experience dramatically. And then there are the borders which do not care about your nationality, what your occupation is, how long you wish to stay, your state of health, or even your state of wealth. They remain as impenetrable as a chastity belt, impossible to breach either from without or within, and those who hold the key guard it jealously.

Tibet's many (disputed) borders seem to flit between all types. At some points in history it has been easy to pass into its confines, though at most times it has been near impossible, as a wealth of good literature will attest. Vikram Seth surfed lorries over flooding rivers to get into Tibet; the great Heinrich Harrer crossed the Himalayas on foot; and Paul Theroux had to enter the country with the assistance of an altitude-sick Chinese driver who crashed their car on the Tibetan Plateau and almost killed both of them.

Though the very early twenty-first century saw some freedom of movement across Tibet's borders, this dissolved during the 2008 Beijing Olympics and its ensuing pro-Tibetan-independence demonstrations. The borders were closed for the best part of a year, opened briefly, and then shut again. It is likely they will remain in this unpredictable state of flux for some time, and any traveller who can make it to Lhasa for even a day should count themselves very, very lucky. In Chengdu – one of the closest Chinese cities to the Tibetan Autonomous Region – stories abound of travellers who have crossed the border illegally, and then been shot.

I soon learned that, if I was to get to Tibet, my only chance was through China. I had researched the state of the borders with meticulous determination over the past months to be presented with scant, and often conflicting, information. I put off my departure time in the hope that something concrete would appear on the many online traveller forums I frequented, but it never did, and the weeks began to disappear. I vacillated for what felt an age, but my time was not indefinite, and I had already signed a contract to start teaching again in January. I ruminated on the consequences of travelling all the way to China only to find my entry to Tibet denied, and then weighed that against sitting in my study for the next four months in this continued state of uncertainty. With this in mind, I made my decision, and bought an open return ticket to Chengdu, the capital of Sichuan province. Exactly fifty years and six months after the 1959 'Lhasa Uprising' against Chinese rule, I boarded a train at Bristol and pushed out through the south of England, finally and eagerly on my journey to the east.

My backpack, too large to fit in the overhead rack, rested instead at the end of the carriage. I made sure to sit close to it and to have it in full view, for it contained expensive luxuries I was not used to taking with me on a journey. I had always been a miserly traveller. I never bought anything new for a trip but took only what I already owned: stubs of soap, half-used bottles of ten-year-old suncream, an old pair of trainers and two sets of expendable clothes which could be ripped, burnt or lost without worry.

But I stocked up for Tibet. While I waited for news on the state of the borders, in the few moments when I was not working or researching, I shopped. This was going to be a journey unlike any I had ever taken, and I needed to be prepared for it. The harsh terrain necessitated hiking boots, the harsh weather waterproofs and thick clothing, the harsh journeys Imodium. I bought my first ever Swiss army knife and my first ever iPod. I invested in a hideously lurid but warm ski-jacket and a sleeping bag with similar attributes. I put Lemsips in my first aid kit.

Aside from my research, my reading and my shopping, a different kind of preparation also filled my time. I set up a new email address to avoid rogue messages popping up on my Internet cafe screens (and, possibly, Chinese cybercensor screens) – 'How's Tibet? *Getting enough material for your book?*' I told all my friends and family I would not be calling them while I was away for exactly the same reason, and let them know my wife would be the only one to hear from me. I worried over which books to take with me, fearing incrimination should they be discovered in my backpack by a curious border guard: Solzhenitsyn was too critical of communism to consider; *A Fine Balance* was too critical of enforced states of emergency; and Rushdie was too critical in general. I even crossed Somerset Maugham's *Of Human Bondage* off the list.

As a final precaution, my wife and I nominated a 'danger-word'. I promised to call her every day if I could, and we decided that, if ever anything were to go wrong and I needed to discreetly let her know, either by telephone, email or letter, I would insert this word. She promised to stay optimistic while I was away, but her final words to me when I left the house that morning were, 'Just be careful. Please.'

My wife was right to be worried, and I knew that far better than I ever allowed her to believe. Arrests, interrogations, torture and executions have occurred in Tibet – and in China – with an unremitting consistence over the last sixty years. They are not of the overt kind, but are instead clandestine, and largely hidden from general knowledge. For many in Tibet, the twenty-first-century standard of life remains as dangerous and as compromised as it was during the Cultural Revolution. Three thousand Tibetans a year continue to flee from Tibet and seek refugee status in India, and a large number of the country's spiritual leaders have either joined them, or simply disappeared. For those monks and members of the laity who choose to stay, many continue to be imprisoned for offences as innocuous as flying a Tibetan flag or calling *'Bo Rangzen!'* ('Free Tibet!') in the streets, and once incarcerated they are often tortured in manners which contravene the Convention Against Torture – ratified by China itself in 1988 – including beatings with electric batons, submersion in sewage pits, being hanged upside down for inordinate lengths of time, and harassment by dogs. Death from such treatment is not uncommon.

Though it is the truth that only a handful of these instances have involved foreigners, many of those foreigners – the targets, if you like – have been writers, reporters or broadcasters: those with the means to reveal. Over the past eleven years, China as a whole has held the title for imprisoning the most journalists, surpassing Myanmar, Iran and Cuba. One filmmaker was arrested and detained after filming everyday scenes of Tibetan life within the autonomous region. Another had to endure the brutality of the Chinese Lhasa police before being deported for inadvertently catching a demonstration on camera. In 1999, an Australian and an American – both freelance researchers – were arrested and interrogated by the Public Security Bureau in Tibetan Amdo. The American was found some days later in hospital with serious injuries to his spine, liver and heels. His official paperwork claimed that he had incurred the injuries after jumping from a third-storey window of the hotel in which he was detained in an attempt to escape. Few believe this version of events. He was almost certainly pushed.

The examples go as far back as 1950, the year of Tibet's 'liberation' by China, when Robert Ford, an English radio operator who had worked for the independent Tibetan government for over a year, was captured by the invading Chinese army. Considered a spy, Ford was jailed for five years, enduring in that time countless interrogations, programmes of re-education, and the constant threat of execution. Clearly, the Chinese had no qualms about arresting Englishmen over the issue of words, and I knew then that all the conversations I was to have and all the notes I was to take would have to be quiet and encoded.

As the plane left Heathrow's runway and English soil with it, and as the flight map on the screen embedded in the headrest before me revealed a straight, dotted line – so unlike the one from *Seven Years in Tibet* – which marked out our journey around the globe from London to Beijing, I took out my Tibet guidebook and thumbed through its pages, stopping at a subheading entitled 'The Friendship Highway'. This was Tibet's main road – also known as the China-Nepal Highway – which crossed the 440 miles from the Tibetan capital, Lhasa, all the way down to Zhangmu, the border town across the river from Nepal. It was at the end of the Friendship Highway, in the deep south of Tibet, at Zhangmu itself, that I was to meet Lobsang: a man who, at the age of five, had fled with his family on 11 March 1989, after his brother Chogyal had become involved in the notorious Lhasa uprising of that year; a man who, at the age of five, had crossed the Himalayas on foot and on his father's back; a man who, at the age of five, had witnessed the execution of his brother Dorje (who had come to smuggle them into Nepal) by Chinese border guards; a man who, over the next twenty years, had lived a life more terrifying and hopeful and startling and courageous and enlivening than any man I have ever known.

On that plane, I had no idea where my own journey was to take me, nor to whom. I thought only about whether or not I would get into Tibet.

nyi

There was a wide and tumultuous river; there was a sloppy and burning meal which made Lobsang feel like his mouth was bleeding; there was a dark man who looked at Jamyang in a way Lobsang did not like and another who pushed his father in a way which Lobsang liked even less; there was a road so smooth it could be slept upon; there was a fat and hairless yak. And there was no Dorje. For all these reasons, Lobsang did not like Nepal.

He mentioned this in confidence to Chogyal, his voice low so that his mother would not hear him. She had not spoken since the mountains, had barely been able to walk, and it was Lobsang who woke her in the mornings. He did not mind the role-reversal, for it was only during the first few seconds of her eyes opening – when she would reach out to stroke his forehead – that he saw her smile anymore. But then her fingers would abruptly stop their tracing above his eyes, her lips would droop, and he would not see her smile again for another twenty-four hours.

'I want to go home,' he whispered to Chogyal.

'So do I,' Chogyal whispered back.

Lobsang liked it when his brother whispered to him.

There was a loud vehicle with three wheels; there was a naked old man doused from head to toe in grey ash whose eyes Lobsang could not meet; there was rain so fat and heavy that Lobsang could barely breathe, let alone stand.

Everything was upside down. While Lobsang's mother grew evermore distant and Chogyal grew evermore compassionate towards his little brother, Jamyang threw her jade amulet into a river and Lobsang's father, once so quiet, started to articulate everything. Each minute of the journey south was filled with his rambling descriptions of the stones beneath their feet and the sky above their heads, as if words had become his rosary beads to click through and mark off his place in the world and his path through it. And Lobsang stopped sleeping. What was the point? Without Dorje, why would he want to make the time pass any quicker?

There was a language he could not understand yet everybody around him could; there was something in his clothes, something which bit and drew forth soaring red welts which he scratched at in a maddening escalation of pleasure and pain; there was a night-time fire on a roadside which burnt not from dung but from wood, and which smelled delicious; there was heat throughout that night like he had never known, so intense he stripped off his clothes and lay naked beneath the stars, the tang of his own sweat both reassuring and unfamiliar.

And there was the journey. Such a long journey. Lobsang missed the Tibetan truck where his family had made a little nest, and where he had made a little den within that little nest, a den which stretched from the folds of his mother's skirts to the fraying lip of plastic sheeting which flapped down from the wobbling crates wedged against the wall, taller than him twice over. Lobsang had felt safe then, but he did not here in Nepal. He confessed this to Chogyal once as they sat on the edge of the road while their father begged passers-by for help on their journey south. Chogyal did not reply this time, but he picked Lobsang up and took him to see some chickens.

They returned to find that their father had been successful. A wonderful family, he explained in a thousand words too many, had shown them compassion and paid for them all to ride a bus to Kathmandu that afternoon. Lobsang met the family and agreed to dance for them in exchange for the soft and greasy sheets of folded, white *tsampa* which they pressed into his hands, and which he ate so many of that he had to run back to the safety of the chickens to be sick in private. When he returned, sheepish and quiet, it was not his mother who wiped his mouth clean, but Chogyal.

When the bus arrived, Lobsang decided that he was in love with it. Painted in a rainbow of haphazard and meandering colours, it shuddered and farted with such regularity that Lobsang laughed so hard he thought he might have to run off to the chickens to be sick again. Noting the two people sat cross-legged on the roof, Lobsang insisted that he was going to sit with them all the way to 'Cattandoo'. Chogyal took his arm and pulled him up the steps and inside to sit on a hard seat, where Lobsang decided he would have to cry if he was going to get his own way, but then the bus farted again and he was too convulsed with giggles to protest.

As the bus set off and careered along the road, Lobsang climbed over his brother and swayed down the aisle towards his mother, who had chosen a seat away from the rest of the family and had already fallen asleep. Climbing on to her lap, he wedged his head between her breasts and thought about Dorje until he, too, drifted off.

A shrill sound woke him, the sound of a mastiff at night, and Lobsang leapt to his feet, his face plunging into the bare belly of a middle-aged Nepali lady. She shrieked at him and, in a panic, he whirled about and became lost in the folds of her sari. His mother swept him into her arms as his anxiety peaked, carried him out of the bus and then passed him to Chogyal, who gently placed him on his feet beside a huge and shitting cow.

Lobsang gazed at the Kathmandu around him as his family began to dizzily walk through it: the horn-happy taxis and veering rickshaws; the thin, winding streets which splayed out in every direction; the bars and markets and travel agencies; the people so pale they were surely ghosts from those days his father talked about after he drank too much *chang*; the hawkers who grabbed Chogyal and Jamyang by the arms and whispered short but strange words Lobsang could not understand; the flashing pink neon lights above shop doorways which he would later learn advertised 'massage parlours' and 'novelty boutiques', and which promoted the sale of toys, lotions, lubricants, lingerie, fantasy, novelty and fetish, as if, in Kathmandu, everything was for sale, even the abstract and the incorporeal. He clamped his hand around Chogyal's and stuck to it, even when Chogyal became uncharacteristically ecstatic at a market stall which sold images of a kind-looking old man with glasses and a receding hairline and, next to them, small squares of canvas on which green and white beasts danced beneath a sunrise of bold red and blue.

Lobsang wondered if he had ever seen so many people gathered together before, and he was grateful for Chogyal's firm grip on his hand as they wandered from market to market while Lobsang's father repeated the fourteen Nepali words he had memorised to anybody who would listen. Nodding along to directions he did not understand, Lobsang's father marched his family along the paths of pointed fingers, chanting the same words again at each fresh junction.

It was dark and they had walked perhaps a hundred miles, or so Lobsang reckoned, by the time the family reached a red house squeezed into the middle of a line of fifteen others. Walking through the front room, where three men cut the hair of three other men, the family climbed a flight of stairs, and Lobsang's father knocked cautiously on the wooden door.

A young woman opened it, a woman so beautiful that Lobsang blushed to such an extent that he had to hide behind his brother's legs. He stayed there while he listened to the words exchanged between her and his father. Peering around Chogyal's right thigh, he watched as the beautiful woman crumpled to the floor and another woman – much, much older but still beautiful nonetheless – appeared from behind and wrapped her arms around her. Together, they cried in a synchronicity which astounded Lobsang. A man without a single hair on his head came to the door, looked at the two women, and beckoned Lobsang's family inside. One by one, they stepped over the weeping bundles on the floor, and entered what was to become their new home.

Lobsang was the last to cross the threshold. As he did, his eyes met the young woman's, and he felt a rush of adrenalin so fierce and engulfing that he tripped over his own feet and caught the side of his head on the door frame.

When he awoke, he found himself in a dark room, one soft sheet over him and three more between him and the floor. Chogyal was there. Lobsang could tell by the sound of his breathing.

'Lobsang,' Chogyal whispered. 'Are you awake?'

'Yes,' Lobsang murmured.

'I've got a secret,' Chogyal said. 'Do you want to hear it?'

'Tell me!' Lobsang said, ripping the sheet off him and hoisting himself to his knees. This was important. Chogyal was the most secretive of all the family and, for the first time, he was letting Lobsang in.

'I think I like Nepal,' Chogyal said.

Lobsang sighed. 'OK. Then I'll like it, too.'

Western Treasure

|

'You cannot go to Tibet,' the Chengdu travel agent said.

'So it's closed.'

'No. It is not closed. But Tibet travel permits are not available.'

Such a distinction was unclear to me. I later learned from a Tibetan that China never officially 'closes' Tibet, it just stops issuing permits, thereby denying any entry to foreigners. My Tibetan friend explained that this was as much a trick of semantics as it appeared, but one which served the Chinese authorities well if ever questioned by a human rights organisation.

'It is because of National Day,' the travel agent continued. 'This year it is the sixtieth anniversary, and we have an extra-long holiday for seven days. Tibet is closed from now until the eighth of October.'

'OK,' I said, assessing my options. 'I suppose I can wait. So can I book a ticket for the eighth of October?'

'No,' he replied.

'Why not?'

'I do not know if I can issue a travel permit for then.'

'So what's the earliest you can issue one for?'

'There is no earliest.'

It was semantics again. Tibet was not officially closed, nor was it officially closed indefinitely. But there was no way of knowing when permits would be issued again. It was a wait-and-see game, and the rationality was clear: if the Tibetans behaved themselves during the National Day celebrations, permits would become available. If they did not, if just one Tibetan flag or picture of the Dalai Lama appeared on Lhasa's streets over the whole seven days, there was no telling when foreigners could travel to Tibet again.

'Anyway!' the travel agent continued brightly. 'Xizang is a very boring place. You should go to Shanghai instead. *Very* fun.'

He had switched to the Mandarin name for Tibet: *Xizang*, which means 'Western Treasure'. It is no doubt innocuous, perhaps even flattering, but the connotations of the word 'treasure' have always disturbed me. Treasure is sought out and then taken, owned, used as ornament and trophy, or exploited for a bankroll. Treasure is a belonging, an object, and the implication of the signifier suggests the signified was once discarded, and that, if it has not been found already, it will be, and will be kept as a prize.

But perhaps Tibet is the kind of treasure which no longer holds such joy for its owner, a weighty and useless heirloom which the grandmother passes down to her granddaughter, and which the latter sees as cumbersome rather than precious. In modern colloquial Mandarin, all of today's west China is pejoratively known as *Xin-xi-lan*, a sort of mnemonic for Xinjiang, Xizang and Lanzhou (the capital city of Gansu

Province, which borders on the Tibetan plateau), which happens to translate literally as 'New Zealand'. To be sent to 'New Zealand' is to be sent to the Wild West, where opportunities are rich, but the civilisation is not – where, at its best, life is, as the travel agent explained, 'boring'. Another Mandarin slang-word for the Tibetans is *mantze*, which literally means 'untameable worm'.

I did not want to go to 'Western Treasure', nor to 'New Zealand'. I wanted to go to Tibet, though even that name comes from an Arabic translation – *Tibbat* – of the ancient Sino-Tibetan term for the country, *Tubo*. For Tibetans, and in Tibetan, Tibet is simply *Bo*. I liked that name. I also liked the country's nicknames, or perhaps we should call them subheadings: *The Roof of the World*; *The Land of Snows*. These were literal and almost scientific, but I found they made Tibet far more alluring than the fictional name *Shangri-La*, which brought to my mind thoughts of the fraudulent Lobsang Rampa, poorly named suburban bungalows, bad indie music, ersatz Indian restaurants in provincial English towns, and guidebook false promises.

Either way, I wanted in. Some thirteen thousand feet above this fetid and dirty city of Chengdu was a country of stone and ice, and, even though it was officially closed, there was still a way in. Tibet was not just on the horizon, it capped it.

2

All along the edge of the Tibetan Plateau, in the Chinese provinces of Yunnan, Sichuan, Gansu and Qinghai, there are a multitude of Tibetan prefectures outside of the Tibetan Autonomous Region, but which are considered by most Tibetans to be part of a theoretical 'Greater Tibet'. These are the regions of Kham and Amdo, non-autonomous provinces within the Chinese state which are, nevertheless, distinctly Tibetan. More ethnic Tibetans (2.9 million) live in these border-prefectures than in the TAR itself (2.5 million).

It is interesting to note that, before the Chinese invasion of 1950, when Tibet was truly and legally independent, its borders corresponded closely to those the Chinese have since carved out for the Tibetan Autonomous Region. The central Lhasan government had little power over the Khampas from Kham and Amdowas from Amdo, who were as fiercely independent to any form of unifying administration as the Tibetans are to Beijing today. One might even say that it was the Chinese themselves who, when they invaded, inadvertently encouraged the league of Kham, Amdo and U-Tsang (the current TAR) into one large and overarching Greater Tibet, an area of 965,000 square miles, twice the size Tibet had ever been during independence. There is nothing quite like the power of an external enemy to unite factions.

Today, when the exiled Dharamsala government speaks of Tibet, it speaks of this Greater Tibet; conversely, when Beijing does the same, it refers to only the TAR. This had one advantage for me: though the Tibetan Autonomous Region was closed, those parts of Greater Tibet in Chinese Yunnan, Sichuan, Gansu and Qinghai were not. And while I waited for the borders to reopen, I could begin my Tibetan odyssey by travelling through Kham and Amdo.

The train to Xining – the capital of Qinghai Province in Tibetan Amdo – was a green and black string of wobbling carriages. The flooring was dirty, the curtains along the corridors were stained with streaks of black mould, and everything smelled of meat. My cabin was cold, with a window which would not shut and a table stained with crusted rings. Wedging my backpack into the shallow compartment above the rattling doorway, I nominated myself a bed, rolled the duvet into a ball and propped it against the wall with my pillows, emptied my daypack on to the bed, sorted through the cups of dried noodles to find my map of China, and traced my finger over the railway line which would take me up into Kham and then through Amdo to Xining, skirting the foothills of the Tibetan plateau as it splintered into China.

The train started, and I wandered the corridors as we passed out of Sichuan Province. I seemed to be the only Westerner on the entire train, and I soon found myself in the dining carriage, passing hours by drinking green tea and reading my history of China as other passengers filtered in and out, cramming themselves into any available space so that they would not have to sit at my table. Dinnertime came, and an attendant placed a torn piece of A4 on my table. There was no English on this menu, no pinyin even, just a list of characters. I pointed at one, and was presented moments later with a plate of delicious fried beef and noodles, which I slurped greedily while the two children at the table opposite stared at me with open mouths.

Happy from a good meal, I strolled back to my cabin and settled into my bed. The wind rushed through the uncloseable window, refrigerating the compartment, but my sleeping bag tempered the lack of warmth and I turned the light off, content now with good food in my belly. No one else had joined me in my compartment, and out the window I fancied that I could see, beyond the occasional streetlights of the occasional railside village, the dark foothills of the plateau.

Back in the dining carriage the next morning, I ate breakfast and stared out the window. We were now in Amdo, just a few hours from Xining. We stopped in small stations plastered with posters advertising Tibetan Sheep Carpets, and those who sallied about the platforms and boarded the train gave a physical reminder that this was no longer Han China. The Tibetan, Tu, Hui and Salar ethnic groups seemed to dominate, and the faces of those who ate breakfast around me as we pulled into and out of each stop changed and merged. I cannot say that features softened or hardened – I've never been sure what that actually means – but the voices around me in the dining carriage lowered, and there seemed less inclination to shout. Out of the window, red crenulated mountains scored a new and different backdrop to that which I had become used to, and all the ramshackle huts perched on the side of the railway seemed to be covered in stacks of drying corn. The land itself was a bay of wet and seeping mud which formed strange patterns and shapes as interpretive as clouds. It was raining – a thin wash of drizzle which seeped from the low-hanging, sky-filling clouds – and all the land outside seemed to drip and form with the temporary consistency of the misty patterns on my window, like sloppy sand dunes.

The train arrived in Xining at midday, and I slipped into the chaos of the train station. Tibetans were everywhere:

Tibetan peasants entering or exiting the station with gigantic canvas sacks filled to bursting, which they carried in both arms; Tibetan monks strolling amongst them with young, excited apprentices trailing behind. A security gate at the exit – staffed by thirty or so Han policemen with hard-set faces, large guns and Kevlar jackets – funnelled three orderly queues out on to the streets, where they dispersed into the Tibetan market just outside the station. Most of the shops hung signs in Tibetan characters; most of the restaurants sold Tibetan food. Breathing in the cool Xining air, I joined a queue.

3

Outside of the floor-to-ceiling windows which segmented my guesthouse room from the sky, Xining had fallen to the night and incandescent high-rises lit the skyline with damasked neon. Hundreds of feet below, headlights cut lazy trails across the highway and, on one of the pavements, an old man crouched beside a sitting dog.

I showered and then, while I dried, switched on the television. It was tuned to one of the myriad CCTV channels: China's main television network. I flicked through them, through the military dramas and terrifying operas, until I came to CCTV9, an English Language channel. A programme called *Dialogue* was on, supposed to be a kind of debate talk show or 'question time' for authoritative and leading figures in the Chinese administration. In reality, there was no dialogue at all, but rather a series of one-sided and defensive lectures on China and its policies. The former president of

Hong Kong University was speaking, and I pulled out my journal to scribble down one of his sentences: *Many people of non-Chinese ethnicity, when they are told the correct history of the country, agree with the Chinese position in Tibet, and have no question about the sovereignty of China in Tibet.*

I turned the television off, got dressed and made my way to the hostel bar for a bottle of *Huang* beer. Another Westerner who sat nursing a cold cup of coffee smiled and invited me to sit with him.

'Charlie,' I said.

'Raul.' We shook hands.

Raul was Costa Rican. He had spent the last month in Xining in pursuit of a permit to visit the Tibetan Autonomous Region, but had been persistently refused. No one ever explained why to him. Each time he asked at his hostel or the local travel agents or even the train station why he was not allowed the permit, his interlocutor would either switch from English to a rapid and incomprehensible local dialect, or would begin to explain and then tail off and never finish the sentence. After four weeks of enduring this insurmountable wall, Raul's China visa was about to expire, and he was due to fly back to Costa Rica the following day.

'What a waste of time,' he sighed. 'I spent thousands of dollars on this holiday. For what? To sit in a Xining hotel room and masturbate.' He sighed again. 'You know, I have dreamed of going to Tibet since I was a boy.'

'Will you try again?' I asked.

He looked from my face to the window, and then back at me again. 'No,' he finally replied.

soom

One year and one month after his mother had woken him in the dead of the night and told him they were going on a pilgrimage to see Dorje, Lobsang began school in Kathmandu. Like all his first-grade classmates, he was six years old; though, unlike them, he had no friends from previous years at a nursery or late-afternoon street-long playtimes. From the moment they set foot in his sister-in-law's house, Lobsang was rarely allowed outside. Chogyal and Jamyang, already too old for school, had taken jobs. Lobsang's job, his father explained during the rare moments he was around, was to look after his mother, who had decided that she no longer had any need to talk, eat or, it seemed, walk, for she spent most of her days in bed.

When Lobsang took the job, it was with an air of pride and self-importance. Of course he would look after his mother, there was no one better suited for the position. He still did not quite understand what exactly had happened to Dorje (in dreams, he relived the scene on the border, but, instead of running away, he had stayed to watch his brother laugh at the six men, turn green as the yogi Milarepa had once done, float into the air above their heads and then whizz off into

50

the mountains), but he knew it was very unlikely he would ever see Dorje again, and this he accepted. He also knew his mother was ill because she likewise understood she would never see Dorje again, but this he could not accept. He would, he resolved, make her better.

As the days turned to weeks and the weeks turned to months, his task proved far more difficult than he had imagined. Sometimes his mother looked at her little son and cried as he coaxed tea into her mouth, but more often than not she remained cold and impassive, like the dead fish Chogyal sometimes brought home for dinner.

Once, Lobsang's father stormed into the room, ripped the sheets from her bed and slapped her twice across the face. 'Stop it, Dolkar!' he bellowed at her. 'Just stop it!'

Lobsang pitched himself at his father's knees with such force that his father fell to the floor. Lobsang climbed on to his father's chest and slapped him twice across the face. He may have slapped him more, but then his sister-in-law appeared, swept him up off his father's torso and carried him out into the street. Lobsang fell mute in her arms, bewitched as he always was by her beauty. *When I am old enough*, he wanted to tell her, *I will marry you so that you can have another Dorje.*

That evening, he heard his name murmured amongst the adults as he told his mother one of his made-up stories about a dog who thought he was human. His brother and sister entered the room.

'You are very lucky, old man,' Chogyal told him. 'You're going to start school in the new year.'

Lobsang's experience of school in Lhasa had been brief and he had not particularly liked it, but he did not want to offend his brother, who had lately started to call him 'old man', which Lobsang loved.

'Thank you, that is very kind of you,' he said. 'But I can't go to school because I've got a job.'

'And you're very good at it,' Jamyang said. 'But every boy your age will be starting school in the new year, and you must, too.'

'I don't know any other boys my age,' Lobsang replied.

'You should.' The words came from the bed, from Lobsang's mother. She had begun to talk more and more often over the past two months, but her utterances were nevertheless limited and carefully premeditated, as if she had chosen to only use her voice when it was important, and to never waste a word on unnecessary contrivances. 'You should know other boys your age.'

So it was settled. Chogyal took Lobsang to the nearest community school to enrol him as a first-grade student for the coming April. As Lobsang smiled at the adults who talked to him and his brother and walked in polite step behind them as they toured the small school, he was surprised to realise that he did not feel resentful for being torn from his mother's side and posited here in this cold and noisy building with its echoing corridors and concrete playgrounds. Beneath the smell of disinfectant and parping whistles of angry teachers, a strange vitality bubbled, one which suggested the hint of fun. He loved his mother, adored his sister and brother, and nurtured quite another emotion for his sister-in-law which was so close to those others and yet very, very different. But there was no fun to be had in that house. There was only endless duty. Lobsang was never one to complain about duty, especially when it served his family, who were everything to him, but here was an opportunity for some fun, and Lobsang understood then that he craved that more than anything except, perhaps, the return of Dorje.

When Lobsang arrived at the school for his first day – beaming in his white shirt, pressed grey trousers and new haircut – and joined the queue of other boys and girls who were being led towards their classroom, he suddenly realised with an epiphanic flash that a new obstacle lay between him and that promise of fun. Language. For, though Lobsang had been in Nepal for almost a year now, he did not know a word of Nepali. He had barely left his mother's room, let alone the house, in all that time, and the only language spoken there was Tibetan. Dorje's wife and family were themselves Tibetan – they had fled the homeland over a decade before, and Lobsang had heard the two fathers talk late at night about a time they called *thamzing* – and so Lobsang had never needed to acquire the new language of his new country.

As he sat on an uncomfortable wooden stool in the classroom and listened to the alien words flowing from his teacher's mouth, Lobsang wished he knew Nepali. Sat on the edge of her desk, the teacher held a sheet of paper aloft and announced meaningless syllables to which his classmates responded one by one, standing up from their stools and shyly gabbling back at the teacher and the rest of the class. Lobsang looked at these students, the ones he was supposed to have fun with, and fancied that the only way he could distinguish the boys from the girls was by their hair. His gaze fell on two boys close to the back of the room, their eyes and cheeks and mouths as familiar as sunrise. He was not the only Tibetan.

'Luw-sun.'

That sounded familiar, the first word he thought he recognised. He looked about the class to see who would stand up next and spout their own unfathomable sentences.

'Lud... *lub*-sun.'

Lobsang turned to look at the teacher, who was staring directly at him.

'Lub-sun,' she repeated, smiling at him.

It's me, Lobsang thought, leaping bolt upright from his stool and laughing nervously at his new audience. 'Good morning!' he announced in Tibetan, so loud it startled even him. The class exploded into a peal of laughter which ricocheted off the walls. He looked back to his teacher, suddenly afraid that he needed the toilet but did not know how to ask for it, and she smiled a beautiful smile at him and gestured with her delicate hand for him to sit down again. She said something else to the class – something which contained the word 'lub-sun' twice – and the boy next to him grinned and waved.

That day, Lobsang's first at school, they learned a song with unnatural intervals and key changes which required conscious thought to adapt to; they learned how to build a tower; and they learned what a clock did. The teacher, who never seemed to stop smiling, took Lobsang's hand at the first break-time and gently ushered him towards the two Tibetan boys who sat removed from all the others in their own corner. The boys introduced themselves as Garab and Tsering, pushing the palms of their hands into the carpet and moving to make space so that, when Lobsang sat down and crossed his legs in imitation of theirs, the three boys formed a rough triangle on the floor.

'Do you know the words?' Lobsang asked.

'All of them,' Tsering said proudly. He had been born in Kathmandu and raised to be bilingual.

Garab shook his head and scowled.

'Me neither,' Lobsang said. 'I want to learn.'

'I don't,' Garab replied.

'It's easy,' Tsering said.

'Are you from home, too?' Lobsang asked, and Garab nodded.

'Where? Lhasa?'

'Gyantse.'

'When did you leave?'

'One month ago.' This was untrue. Lobsang later learned that Garab had been in Kathmandu for three months before starting school – his family had walked across the Himalayas at the height of winter, where a guide had stolen their money and abandoned them – but, for the next few years, Garab continued to maintain that he had only arrived in Nepal one month ago. 'I don't like it here,' he said.

'I do,' Lobsang replied. 'My brother Chogyal likes it so I'm going to like it, as well.'

'Me, too,' Tsering chimed in. 'Are we friends now?'

They were, and their friendship was tight. After the first day, the teacher organised a fixed seating plan for the class, and Lobsang, Tsering and even Garab were delighted to discover that they had been placed next to each other. They spent their breaks and lunchtimes together, always in corners, and when group-work was offered in lessons, they chose each other instantly, and then retired to another corner. While Tsering and Garab developed strong feelings of attachment to the little group of three, and seemed to desire no other kind of interaction, Lobsang began to long for the company of more than just these two. He wanted everyone in the class to like him. He wanted to learn Nepali. Tsering could speak it but did not, even when Lobsang encouraged him, because it would make Garab sulky and disapproving. And so Lobsang began to listen to the others around him.

The first word he learned in Nepali was 'hello'; the second was 'refugee'. Then came other nouns, in a flow which Lobsang found remarkable, so that within minutes he had learned and imprinted on his mind forever how to say 'table', 'bag', 'teacher', 'lunch' and 'girl'. Tsering was right: Nepali was easy. More so – it was *natural*. Of course that was what a wall, a wood and a pen should be called, a dream was exactly how it should sound, and all those water words were unarguably fitting. His acquisition of Nepali reminded him of the time Jamyang took him to see the Kyi Chu River which, flooded with meltwater, had burst its banks and was seeping inexorably towards the city. Once the tide of Nepali had begun, there seemed to be no stopping it, and he wondered how long it would take before his head became so full of the language that it would start to drown the Tibetan words in there.

At home, he practised with Jamyang, who had also acquired the language with ease, but they had to do it while Chogyal was still at work, for he was struggling to learn the alien tongue, and it made him jealous to see his younger sister and brother so at ease within its grammar.

By the second grade, Lobsang was fluent; by the third he had a larger vocabulary than most of his Nepali classmates;

and by the fourth he had begun to excel in all his subjects to such an extent that his teacher once awarded him the coveted badge which said 'Top of the Class'. Lobsang showed it to his bedridden mother, who did not understand the strange characters painted across it until Lobsang translated for her. She then pinned it to her bed sheets and kept it there, only handing it back to her son when he managed to convince her, after two hours of gentle coaxing, that his teacher needed it back for the next round of awards, and that this did not mean he had been naughty, but that it was just somebody else's turn. Even then, when she unclipped it from the sheets and held it out to him with her face turned away, Lobsang was reminded of the tantrums he himself used to throw in Lhasa when he was told Dorje had gone away.

His circle of friends extended, too – or rather, he began to spend less time with Tsering and Garab and more time with the Nepali children in his class. Even by the fifth grade, with all of them now ten years old, the two Tibetan boys still did not like to integrate, and kept to their corners. But Lobsang did not approve of such childishness. There was far too much fun to be had with his new Nepali friends, who invited him to play out after school, where they transformed from angelic schoolboys into beasts of the evenings. Their favourite game was called 'Long Running', and it involved sprinting at high speed through the streets of Kathmandu. When a clear leader broke ahead of the pack, the rest then had to follow him wherever he went. The rules were simple, but the application of the game was not, for it was expected that the leader take them through the most difficult terrain he could discover, where market stalls, beggars, tourists and the general flotsam and jetsam of Kathmandu's streets formed dangerous and sometimes impassable obstacles, and where the cuffing palms of outraged adults slowed them as they ducked and weaved. You won the game if you kept up with the leader until he finally tired and stopped, and you lost if you dropped out or fell behind to such an extent that the group's twisting trajectory through the city became unknowable and impossible to rediscover, for it was always different. The losers would not show up again that evening, but they would be met the next day at school, and there they would be soundly admonished for their failure in the game.

Lobsang never had the speed to become a leader, but he made sure that he was never one of the losers. At the culmination of Long Running, the winners would collapse into a heaving, giggling heap upon whichever patch of ground the leader had stopped. Then there would be jokes, playful scuffles, and the long walk home.

When school ended for the Dussehra festival, Lobsang and his friends ran so far that evening that he wondered if they had left Kathmandu. The leader stopped at a small shrine in a dark and stinking courtyard. Three sadhus sat on rugs a few feet from the shrine and eyed the group of panting boys suspiciously.

Dipendra had been the leader that day. He was known as a leader who ran further than others, and some of the boys had groaned with the anticipation of exhaustion when they saw him take pole position. 'Hey, Suraj!' he called once they had stopped. 'Is that your uncle, man?'

'No,' Suraj replied. 'My uncle's in India.'

'But he's like these guys, right?' Dipendra said.

'He's not a sadhu. He's a monk.'

'What's the difference?' Dipendra laughed, and some of the others laughed with him. Teasing was customary at the end of a game, but it was always harmless. 'Lobsang, you're a monk, right?'

Lobsang laughed. It was his turn. He did not mind. 'Not a monk,' he said. 'I'm a *seer*!'

The boys around him snorted and playfully punched his arm. 'A *seer*!' they repeated.

'But aren't you a Buddhist, man?' Dipendra said, climbing on to the lower level of the shrine. The three sadhus shuffled closer.

'I'm a *Tibetan* Buddhist,' Lobsang said.

'What's the difference?'

Lobsang thought for a while. 'I don't know!' he said, and they all laughed.

'And you, Dipendra?' Ashok said. 'What are you?'

'Me, I'm a Hindu, man. So, you know, I believe in karma. Do you believe in karma, Lobsang?'

'Of course,' Lobsang replied.

'So, you know,' Dipendra jumped from the shrine and began to walk towards Lobsang. 'That's the reason, isn't it?'

'The reason for what?'

'The reason for *everything*, man. Why you're here, with us. Why you're not at home, in Tibet. You Tibetans, man, you did *bad* things to your own people. You made some bad karma for yourselves. And now you're paying for it.'

As he leapt forward, Lobsang felt merely surprise: surprise at his arm as it wrapped itself around Dipendra's neck; surprise at his free hand as it curled into a fist and began to punch the top of Dipendra's head with relentless fury; surprise that the other boys hadn't pulled him off yet and that he was still there, punching and punching at his friend's skull for what seemed a comically long stretch of time. A single touch on his arm – who was it? Suraj? – stopped him, and he let go of Dipendra, who dropped to the ground and held his face in his hands. Lobsang noticed blood seeping through Dipendra's splayed fingers.

Encircling Dipendra protectively in the centre of a makeshift phalanx, the boys took off out of the courtyard as one, leaving Lobsang alone. Still feeling little else but that all-pervading surprise, Lobsang shuffled towards the three sadhus, who stood up, rolled their rugs under their arms and disappeared into the fissures of the walls.

It took Lobsang three hours to find his way home, and all the while he wondered why he had done what he had done. Dipendra was his friend, and not even one of those bullies who you called a friend but secretly despised. No, he was good, even if he liked to call the other boys 'man' with an affectation which made Lobsang cringe. Dipendra had invited Lobsang round to his house for dinner, they had shared secrets, he had even suggested that Lobsang should get Tsering and Garab to play Long Running with them, and it was Lobsang who had refused.

So why had he done it? Was it because of what Dipendra had said about Tibet, about 'his people'? Lobsang loved Tibet, he always would, but for a long time he had stopped thinking of it as his home, and of Tibetans as his people. These days, a fifth-grader in Kathmandu, his people were his fellow Long Runners. But there was still a pride somewhere deep within him, and alongside it a shame, which connected him to Tibet and other Tibetans. The corner Tsering and Garab sat in at class, the other boys called it 'Refugee Corner', but Lobsang had never himself been able to utter the term. Once, in a lesson about the religions, each student had been asked to stand up and talk about the things they believed about life, about death, about gods and goddesses. Lobsang had proudly explained to the class that his god was alive and well in India, a man who could charm the world with a sentence and a wink of his eye, and four of the girls had tittered at his remarks. That night in bed, unsure why, Lobsang had grown so hot with fury that crying seemed to be the only way to release the overwhelming blaze inside him.

He found his house and stepped inside. This was later than he had ever come home before. He knew he was in trouble when he saw his mother out of her bed – something she only did on special occasions after hours of coaxing from various members of the family – and sitting in the front room with his father, his brother, his sister and his sister-in-law. They all stood as one when they saw him.

'Where have you been?' Jamyang lashed out at him.

'Long running,' Lobsang said in Nepali.

'*What?*' his father shouted.

'Playing,' Lobsang said in Tibetan. He looked over at his mother, who stared at the floor.

'You missed dinner,' Jamyang said.

'And he's not getting any!' his father interjected. 'Do you *understand* how worried we were? Do you? Do you even begin to *understand* anything?'

'Norbu, don't be hard on him,' his mother said, but his father silenced her with a swipe of his hand through the air which came too close to his mother's face for Lobsang's liking.

'I want to know what you were doing,' his father said, approaching Lobsang with such ferocity that Lobsang found himself involuntarily backing towards the door. 'I want to know why you're late. I want to know why your friends are more important to you than your family.'

'They're not!' Lobsang suddenly cried out, surprised once again by his reactions when he seemed to view them so emotionlessly from a place somewhere else. 'I hate my friends! They don't get it! They think we *deserve* this!'

His father backed away, his face transformed from rage to blank curiosity.

'What did they say to you, old man?' Chogyal asked.

Lobsang told his story, repeating the words Dipendra had uttered and describing the aftermath. 'I hit him really hard,' Lobsang concluded. 'He shouldn't have said that.'

'Go to bed, Lobsang.' It was his mother, who stood up and, without looking at him, took herself off to her own bed. His father left the house through the front door. Jamyang went to the kitchen and his sister-in-law stared at him, her eyes wet and even more beautiful with it.

'Come on, old man,' Chogyal said, taking his brother by the hand and leading him to his bed. 'Stay there.' Moments later, Chogyal returned with a bowl of rice and a jar of tea. Lobsang consumed them greedily.

'I'm sorry I was late home,' he said when he had finished. 'I'm sorry I made you worry.'

'Mother was scared for you,' Chogyal said. 'And so was father.'

'I thought they would understand when I told them what happened. Why aren't they proud of me?'

Chogyal thought for a while. 'They were proud that you defended Tibet. So am I, old man. But there are right ways and wrong ways to defend it.'

'Was my way the wrong way?'

'Yes. You should never use violence. You told those boys you were a Tibetan Buddhist. Well, part of being a Tibetan Buddhist means you cannot be violent. Ever. If you are violent, you are not a true Buddhist.'

'Am I going to hell now?'

'No!' Chogyal laughed. 'Definitely not. You're one of the good ones, old man, trust me. But you must not fight again, no matter what anyone says to you.'

Lobsang raised the jar to his lips, knowing it was empty, but hoping the action would encourage his brother to refill it. He did not. 'So what's the right way?' he asked, and then tried out a word he had not heard or used for a long time. 'Protest?'

'I don't know,' Chogyal replied. 'That's a question I think about every day. And I still don't have the answer.'

Ancient Tibet

|

Much of Tibet's appeal to the Western world – its perceived pacifism and tolerance, its quiet isolationism and focus on the spiritual rather than the material, embodied by the prototypical monk meditating alone atop his mountain – disregards a history as varied and sometimes bloodied as any other country across the world. Tibet has in recent times been subject to atrocities on a par with those perpetrated in countries such as Rwanda and Cambodia, but it cannot be ignored that Tibet once itself instigated war and promoted aggressive expansionism, that it was once a major Asian power.

When Songsten Gampo came to the throne at the age of thirteen in AD 630 and united Tibet as one nation, his fierce armies spread out into Asia. Despite his place in Tibetan history as a hero, Songsten Gampo became so because he was at heart a ruthless warrior. He once arranged the marriage of his sister to the king of Zhangzhung: when she led the king into an ambush, Songsten Gampo killed him and conquered his land.

Over the next century, Tibet pushed outwards, so that, when Trisong Detsen – Songsten Gampo's great-great-great grandson – ascended to the throne in AD 755, his Tibet extended out into areas of Xinjiang, Nepal, India, Pakistan, Afghanistan and China, and controlled the Central Asian trade routes. It was an empire. Those Tibetans who today live along the foothills of the plateau in provinces such as Yunnan, Sichuan and Gansu – those outside of the Tibetan Autonomous Region, but part of Greater Tibet – are descendants of the first Tibetan settlers from this propitious time. Tibet's armies pushed out so far east that some historians have suggested they may have reached the Yellow Sea and thereby encircled China, whose dynasty – the Tang – was briefly endangered when Trisong Detsen's armies took the capital of Changan (the modern-day Xian) and deposed the emperor.

China felt the threat, and immediately began drawing up a peace treaty with Tibet, which the latter reneged upon when they kidnapped a number of Chinese officials. The bloody border-war, dominated along most sectors by the superior Tibetan forces, finally culminated in AD 821, when an accord between the two countries was reached. The terms of the treaty were inscribed on three stone tablets, one of which still stands – like a patronising reference to a childhood fist-fight – outside Lhasa's Jokhang Temple:

Tibet and China shall abide by the frontiers of which they are now in occupation. All to the east is the country of Great China; and all to the west is, without question, the country of Great Tibet. Henceforth on neither side shall there be waging of war nor seizing of territory. All shall live in peace and share the blessing of happiness for ten thousand years.

Not long after this treaty, like all great empires ultimately do, Tibet's soon began to recede. The fallout began in AD 842, when a monk killed Trisong Detsen's successor with an arrow through the heart. (Legend has it that the monk escaped by fleeing on a horse coloured with charcoal. The horse ran through a river, washing itself of its fake black tint, the monk reversed his cloak, and the two were never seen again.) Over the next four hundred years, Tibet dissolved into warring factions, and the previously deposed Tang Dynasty took advantage and won back all that Tibet had stolen from China.

In many ways, it was Genghis Khan himself who saved Tibet in the thirteenth century. His Mongol Empire spread out across Asia, becoming the greatest superpower the world had seen since the Romans, and more so. Though they never reached Lhasa, the Mongols came close, and they saw within Tibet something they had not within the other countries they had conquered: a spiritual way. Under Genghis Khan's grandson, Godan, the Tibetan form of Buddhism was given its world stage, and the Mongols converted to it, offering Tibet in the process a prestigious seat in the Mongol Empire. Though far from independent, such recognition gave Tibet the chance to regroup and rebuild and, though it never regained its empire status again, it hunkered down and formed a fierce resistance against any outside influences. It is said that, from the time of the fifth Dalai Lama in the 1600s to that of the thirteenth in the 1900s, little changed in Tibet. Visitors to the country over the last hundred years or so have remarked upon Tibet's similarity to medieval Europe: where people rode on horseback and bartered for their goods, and where religion ruled the state. Tibet had become not so much a place, but an anachronism.

Yet a *country* it still firmly was, by the reckoning of most nations. At its strategic location in Central Asia, Tibet fell into and out of the hands of China and Britain throughout the 1800s in documentation only. Despite frontier battles and delegations of ambassadors, Tibet had been its own for a long time, and knew it. In 1913, the Chinese tried to prove their sovereignty over Tibet to the British, and within six months were laughed off by both the Tibetans and the British. Thrashing against the evidence provided by the Tibetan government, China admitted Tibet was but its protectorate, and claimed 'suzerainty' over the country.

What is remarkable is that Tibet actually agreed to such a status within China's foreign policy, as did the British. Perhaps what is more remarkable is that, when it came for the three nations to sign on the proclamation, the Chinese government was the only one of the three to not sign the accord. Tibet, by all legal rights, became truly independent.

Tibet's reluctance to act upon this recognised independence was the beginning of its fall. Though offered a seat at the League of Nations, Tibet refused, choosing instead to withdraw even further from all global affairs. Tibet's self-imposed isolation from the rest of the world was in part aided by its inaccessible location, but the Tibetans themselves encouraged their 'otherness', resisting the freedom of movement which many other powers of the time were embracing and thriving on. In his book, *Seven Years in Tibet*, Heinrich Harrer recounts the hostility of some Tibetans towards foreigners, documenting the laws which proscribed strict penalties upon those who engaged in commerce with a foreigner.

It was perhaps the fourteenth, and current, Dalai Lama himself who instigated a change in the four-hundred-year-old Tibetan thought patterns. Many accounts and interviews with the man confirm his desire to push Tibet forward, to modernise, and to give Tibet its rightful place on the world stage. It is unknown whether those monks and lamas who forged their pilgrimage to find him, the next incarnation of their god-king, ever anticipated that this man would be one of their most progressive Dalai Lamas, and one of their most loved.

Following the signs laid out by the thirteenth Dalai Lama – Thubten Gyatso, who died in 1933 at the age of fifty-seven – they found the new heir to the Tibetan throne in Chinese-ruled Amdo, in the small mountain-village of Takster. His name was Lhamo Dondrub, and he was a two-year-old boy.

Takster was not far from Xining and a cheap taxi-ride if you shared. It holds no religious significance for Tibetan Buddhists – it is not their Bodhi Tree – but it seemed to me an appropriate place to begin.

2

Shen was Chinese and on a year-long tour of his own country. With his finger, he traced the outline of his journey across the map on the hostel bar's wall: a zigzagging trajectory which plummeted north to south, performed a hairpin turn, soared back up north and then continued in the same fashion as it slowly wended westwards. Xining was his base for month eight as he toured Qinghai Province. From there, he had only Tibet and Xinjiang remaining, and four months within which to travel them.

'Have you ever travelled your own country, Charlie?'

I told him I had.

'It is the best thing.'

We agreed to visit Takster together and caught the first bus to Pingan, arriving at sunrise as the town came to life: streetsellers set up on the pavements, stretching their produce of fruits, bags or slippers over canvas sheets which spilled out on to the roads; men in shabby suits stared out at us from restaurant windows while slurping noodle breakfasts; a monk crossed the road before us with a mobile phone pressed to his ear.

A taxi driver – a local of Pingan and of Tibetan ethnicity – agreed to take us on the round trip to Takster for a fixed price. He and Shen chatted to each other in Mandarin, and Shen occasionally turned around to translate into English for me. Now in his late thirties, the driver had never left Amdo, and he smiled with friendly assurance as he drove and talked, punctuating most of his sentences with joyful and amiable laughter. Pingan deteriorated around us as urban turned to rural, high-rises to huts.

If China is red and Tibet orange, Amdo lies somewhere in the middle: the earthy tones of Uluru or Utah; the deep auburn of a late sunset, or of mud. Mud encapsulated this place. It crumbled in chunks from the mountains, burst and streaked down the hills, flooded the roads in thick, miry streams, and then coloured the silty rivers a chocolate brown. Mud constituted the walls of houses and sheds; mud set around steps and pathways; mud caked the boots and trousers of pedestrians, the wheels and bumpers of cars.

Our road knifed its way through the mud and then, with a single lurch, it rose up, so that soon we were winding through the mountains as they pierced the low-hanging clouds. Pingan disappeared, and with it any evidence of human settlement, save for this rough road and its occasional six-shack village or uneven farm. It was through these cold and desolate mountains that a party of Tibetan officials marched in 1937, led by Lama Kewtsang Rinpoche of the powerful Sera Monastery, searching for the new incarnation of the recently deceased thirteenth Dalai Lama.

Back then, Takster – which means 'Roaring Tiger' – was similar to how it is today. The Dalai Lama, in his autobiography *Freedom in Exile*, recalls it as small and poor with unpredictable weather, and that its pastures had only been settled for a brief time. Before that, it had been used on occasion by passing nomads, but never for long. The Dalai Lama's family, one of only twenty in Takster, lived from farming: growing barley, buckwheat and potatoes, though often hailstorms or droughts destroyed their crops. It is miraculous perhaps that this two-year-old boy was ever discovered in such a remote and far-flung region of Tibet, thousands of miles away from Lhasa.

For Tibetans, his discovery had nothing to do with luck. It was inevitable.

The concept of 'Dalai-Lamaism' depends upon reincarnation. Each Dalai Lama is a reincarnation of his predecessor, and therefore a reincarnation of all of them, as the same spirit passes from body to body through the ages. According to some schools of thought, such thinking is a convenient way to marry the oxymoronic ideals of royal lineage and monastic celibacy; according to others, it is simply truth, and therefore each new Dalai Lama *will* be found, for there is only one at a time – the single recurring soul of all who have preceded him, and ultimately the living incarnation of Chenresig, revered in Tibetan Buddhism as the four-armed Bodhisattva of Compassion, and the patron of Tibet. Thus, the Dalai Lamas are more than just the kings of their land – in many ways, they are perceived as living gods.

The first recognised Dalai Lama was Sonam Gyatso, abbot of Sera Monastery, who in the late sixteenth century was given the title by the Mongol king, Altan Khan: 'Dalai Lama' being a Mongol phrase meaning 'Ocean of Wisdom'. Though Sonam Gyatso was the first to be given the title, he was, paradoxically, the third Dalai Lama, as it had already been established that he was a reincarnation of earlier leaders of the Gelugpa (or 'Yellow Hat') sect of Buddhism. Thus the title of first Dalai Lama was bestowed posthumously on Genden Drup, disciple of the legendary Tsongkhapa and founder of the Tashilhunpo monastery in Shigatse – Tibet's second city – and his next incarnation, Gedun Gyatso, was nominated the second, and his name Gyatso was passed to all future Dalai Lamas.

So close was the priest-patron relationship between the third Dalai Lama and Altan Khan that when the former died his spirit passed to the latter's great-grandson: Yonten Gyatso, the only non-Tibetan Dalai Lama, who died at the age of twenty-seven and passed the torch on to another Tibetan, Lobsang Gyatso.

This fifth Dalai Lama is revered as one the greatest of all the Dalai Lamas, challenged in superiority only by the current (who, one Tibetan once told me, 'we believe is the reincarnation of Sakyamuni himself' – Sakyamuni is the Tibetan name for Siddharta Gautama, the founder of Buddhism). Enthroned as the spiritual and political leader of Tibet in 1642, he ordered the construction of the Potala Palace in Lhasa, installed the first Panchen Lama (meaning 'Great Scholar') in the Tashilhunpo monastery as his second-in-command, and introduced the lines of Tibetan society which existed until China's twentieth-century invasion. So revered was the fifth Dalai Lama that, when he died in 1682, it was kept secret from the Tibetan public for fifteen years, so that the building of the Potala could be completed and the next Dalai Lama could be found.

Finally, in 1697, the sixth Dalai Lama, a young Epicurean by the name of Tsangyang Gyatso, was enthroned. It is a testament to the absolute faith of Tibetans in their religion that this poetic aesthete, who differed from all other Dalai Lamas, was and continues to be so revered. A lover of women and wine, he was said to have frequently sneaked out from his solitary confines in the Potala Palace to indulge himself in the brothels and bars of Lhasa. Never much of a ruler, he is now remembered instead for his poetry: songs which fluctuated between bittersweet love and carnal desire. The struggle between his teachings and his corporeal weaknesses are encapsulated perfectly in the following three verses:

I incline myself
To the teachings of my lama
But my heart secretly escapes
To the thoughts of my sweetheart.

Even if meditated upon,
The face of my lama comes not to me,
But again and again comes to me
The smiling face of my beloved.

If I could meditate upon the dharma
As intensely as I muse on my beloved
I would certainly attain enlightenment
Surely, in this one lifetime.

It was not long before Tsangyang Gyatso began to renounce his duties as Dalai Lama, fleeing from the Potala to live alone in a tent in a nearby park. He died soon after on a journey to China, and many have it that his death was in fact murder.

The Dalai Lama line has continued over the ensuing three hundred years plus. Often, when one died, it was years before the next was found, for Tibetan Buddhism states that reincarnation need not occur at the moment of death.Hence, two years passed between the death of the thirteenth Dalai Lama and the birth of the fourteenth.

That Tenzin Gyatso – the current Dalai Lama – was found in his birthplace of Takster was due to a number of auspicious signs. When the thirteenth died, his embalmed body was placed in the Potala in the sitting Buddha posture and facing south, as was traditional. One morning, the head was discovered to have turned, seemingly of its own accord, and now instead of facing south it faced north-east towards Amdo. Not long after, a senior lama in the Tibetan administration had a vision of the Kumbum monastery – only a few miles away from Takster – and of a small house on a mountain with odd guttering.

Following these signs, the search party set off, walking from Lhasa to Amdo's Kumbum Monastery. Here, they perused the local villages and interviewed a list of young boys, but none fitted their criteria. Finally, they came to Takster, finding there a house the same as all the others in the village save for one peculiarity: its gutters were made from gnarled juniper wood. The party entered in disguise as servants, and were immediately greeted by a two-year-old boy who rushed out to them, pointed at Kewtsang Rinpoche, the lama from the Sera monastery who was also attired in servant garb, and called out, 'Sera aga! Sera aga!' – dialect for 'lama from Sera'.

The search party took their time, keeping their true identities hidden while they conducted ritual tests upon the small boy. They presented him with possessions of the thirteenth Dalai Lama – rosary beads, a walking stick, a drum – alongside other identical items, and asked him which ones he preferred. The boy chose each correct article without hesitation. Finally, they looked him over for all the physical signs which denoted the Dalai Lama: large ears, tiger-stripes on the legs, sad eyes, and the moles on the body which signified Chenresig's other pair of arms. The boy had them all.

Before revealing themselves and their true purpose to the boy and his family, the delegation approached the governor of the province – Ma Bufang, a Chinese warlord who controlled the north-western region of Amdo – and stated that the boy was a possible contender for the title of Dalai Lama. Though they already knew he was the one, it would have done them no favours to admit it to the Chinese, who would have exploited such a discovery. Indeed, Ma Bufang exploited the delegation anyway, effectively selling the boy to them for 100,000 Chinese dollars. When Kewtsang Rinpoche paid without question or hesitation, Ma Bufang demanded another 300,000. This was likewise paid, and the new, two-year-old Dalai Lama and his family were packed up and transported to Lhasa.

Of course, beneath the auspices and signs and spiritualisms, the discovery of Lhamo Dondrub as the fourteenth Dalai Lama was not perhaps so splendidly miraculous. His family were already well known by the Lhasa-based Tibetan administration. Both his elder brother and his great-uncle had been nominated as important reincarnate Lamas, and his uncle enjoyed a prestigious position at the Kumbum monastery as the controller of finance. They were by no means a rich family, but neither were they poor, and though they lived on the very outskirts of Tibet, it is likely Kewtsang Rinpoche knew of Lhamo Dondrub's existence before leaving Lhasa, and likely the boy's family knew the search for the new Dalai Lama might come their way, and thus could have prepared the boy accordingly. Even Ma Bufang himself was actually a friend of the family.

Nevertheless, such cynicism aside, there were doubtless thousands of young boys across Lhasa who could have fit the administration's rules had they chosen to illicitly bend a few, but they did not. Instead, they struck out across unforgiving terrain on a fierce pilgrimage to get to this child, and – whether their intuitions were grounded or not – they found the boy who would become an international figure on a par with Nelson Mandela and Mahatma Gandhi.

In our taxi, Takster was simple enough to reach. But we would not have tried if it weren't for an agenda, and it seemed to me that one had to *want* to get here, for it was far too easy to turn back. We three in the taxi fell silent as we approached the village, staring out upon the green and wet mountains, shrouded in the dank mist, as if we were the fourteenth Dalai Lama's physical forbears themselves, looking out upon a land ready for cultivation; a place to, with a hardy resignation, call home.

The taxi stopped on a small path overlooking a terraced field and Shen and I got out. The farmer working in the field dropped his hoe and climbed up on to the path, followed by three small children who appeared from nowhere, two women with dirty faces, and a man stepping down from his single-cylinder tractor. The children stared vacantly at me, but I noticed the attention of the adults was fixed firmly on Shen. There was a large wooden gate in the wall behind me, with white *kata* scarves (traditional ceremonial scarves which signify goodwill and compassion) hanging from its iron rings.

'Shen,' I said, 'ask the driver if this is the house.'

'He doesn't know,' Shen replied after dipping his head inside the taxi. 'He has never been here before.'

Four more children arrived and clustered around the women.

I had been learning Tibetan for the past month, and decided to try it out. 'Is this the house of Tenzin Gyatso?' I asked the crowd, who stared back at me without answering. 'Tenzin Gyatso,' I repeated, and then, in English: 'The Dalai Lama.'

The villagers still refused to speak to me, but I noticed one of the boys break into a brief and nervous smile at my final words. Suddenly, as one, they moved in front of the gate and remained there. An old woman opened it and stepped out, and I caught a brief glimpse of the house – like a temple, and fronted by a concrete but tree-lined garden – before the gate was slammed shut again. I searched the faces of the villagers for signs of hostility, but could find none. As our taxi driver went over to talk to them, they began to smile, and some looked over to me and nodded amiably. Nevertheless, there was a clear imperative in their collective posture: we could not pass.

Shen spoke with the driver as we climbed back into the taxi and set off down the mountain. After a few minutes, he turned in his seat and spoke to me in English.

'A very few tourists used to come here and were allowed inside. But last year the villagers decided they would not let foreigners in anymore. It is not the law, but they are worried that, if they do let foreigners in, they will get into trouble.'

'So it was my fault we couldn't enter,' I said.

'No,' Shen replied, 'I was not allowed in either. The driver said I confused them. They are used to turning away people who look like you. White people. It has been a long time since any Chinese ever came here.'

shi

After his fight with Dipendra, Lobsang stopped Long Running and devoted his evenings instead to his family and to private study. He graduated into lower secondary and then secondary school with ease where, recognising his talents, his teachers placed him alongside other high-achieving students. By the time he was sixteen, Lobsang rarely saw his former classmates, with the exception of Garab, whose brother worked with Chogyal. The two families would often join forces to celebrate the Tibetan festivals such as Losar and Monlam Chenmo. As the years passed, both Lobsang and Garab found these meetings increasingly uncomfortable. They had less and less in common. While Lobsang adored school, Garab dropped out at thirteen to work on his father's market stall; while Garab still claimed he had only left Tibet a month ago, Lobsang found it more and more difficult to even mention his homeland; while Lobsang spent his evenings on homework or engrossed in the English novels his teacher loaned him, Garab could still only speak a handful of Nepali words.

'What are you bothering with English for?' Garab asked shortly after his own sixteenth birthday.

'I like languages,' Lobsang replied. 'And Nepali's too easy now. I know it all. English is hard, but I like that. I'm good at it.'

'Don't you know what the English did to us in Gyantse?'

'What did they do?'

'Only gunned down about three thousand people.'

'*What*?' Lobsang was stunned. How had he not heard of this atrocity? 'When did this happen?'

'1904,' Garab replied.

Lobsang laughed, and then stopped himself when he saw the irritation on Garab's face. 'But that's eighty years before you were born, Garab,' he said. 'Why do you care about that?'

'So what? The Chinese invaded Tibet thirty-five years before I was born. The Dalai Lama was chased out twenty-five years before I was born. Just because all these things happened a long time ago, it doesn't mean I shouldn't care about them. I love my country, even if you don't.'

Lobsang looked at the floor, unsure how to reply.

'You actually don't, do you?' Garab said, stunned by his revelation. 'Do you care about Tibet? Do you care about China? About what it's doing to us? Do you care that, you and me, we can't ever go *home*?'

Lobsang remained silent and, feeling this was answer enough, Garab left the house and the two boys did not speak again.

The truth was, Garab had highlighted and vocalised questions Lobsang had been grappling with for a while. As he had grown into a young man, his position within the family had changed. After his homework and the evening meal, Lobsang now sat with the two fathers and Chogyal, while Jamyang, his sister-in-law and her mother formed their own clique on the other side of the room. The men drank *chang* and smoked, talking first about work and money, then giggling over dirty jokes, and finally ranting about Tibet as the *chang* did its work.

Though they accepted him as one of them now, Lobsang himself felt a vague sense of displacement amongst the men. He did not like *chang* and he did not smoke and, while the others harangued imaginary PLA (People's Liberation Army) officers over their offences on the plateau, he found himself curiously indifferent. He knew all about Tibet's twentieth-century history – every Tibetan boy did – and he had tried to stand up for it once, but that had only ended in violence and recriminations. These days, he was more interested in a book he was reading called *Gulliver's Travels* or the life cycle of a star or the shifting of the tectonic plates beneath his feet. Could it really be, as Garab had accused, that he simply did not *care* about Tibet anymore?

Whatever the answer to that question – and Lobsang did not know what it was – he was certainly not about to admit his possible indifference to his father, whose growing pride in him was as startling as it was welcome. The day Lobsang got himself a part-time job so that he could pay his own fees for the higher secondary school was his father's proudest.

'My son!' he exclaimed to his best drinking companion, Dorje's father-in-law. 'My son is already more clever than all of us in this house put together, *and* he will grow even more clever, *and* he will do it all himself! Brains, strength and willpower, what a combination!'

Lobsang felt his cheeks flush red.

'Good work, old man,' Chogyal winked at him, and Lobsang laughed for – on the brink of thirty and as stuck in his ways and routines as their father – it was Chogyal who was fast turning into the old man.

Even Lobsang's mother, who spent so much time in bed now that her legs had withered and she could no longer walk, asked to see him that day and gave him a dry kiss on his cheek.

Lobsang did not admit to his family that, in fact, he had received a great deal of help finding his job. His English teacher, a broad-shouldered giant of a man from the Himalayas who claimed he was half-Yeti and who had attended university in Southampton (a name which Lobsang loved, though he could not explain why), had grown outraged when Lobsang revealed that he would be leaving school at the end of the tenth grade with his School Leaving Certificate because his family could not afford to put him through the final two years.

His teacher had threatened to march directly to his house and accost his parents for their selfishness until Lobsang managed to convince him that it was not selfishness at all, but genuine poverty. And so his teacher offered him an alternative. His brother was a duty manager at a hotel in the tourist district. He knew the hotel currently had vacancies for extra security staff on the weekends. If Lobsang was prepared to work every weekend and use half of his wages for his fees, then his teacher would promise to get him the job.

Years later, sat at a computer on the campus of an Indian university, Lobsang remembered the deal he had made with that teacher and, after some quick research into the average cost of fees for Grades 11 and 12 in Nepal, came to the conclusion that his payments – his weekly instalment of half his wages – would barely have scratched the surface. Whatever his teacher had done to get him into and then keep him at the school – whether it was the twisting of arms, the negotiation of a scholarship, or even the payment of the rest of the fees from his own meagre teacher's salary – Lobsang realised that, not for the first time in his life, he was where he was thanks to the sacrifice of others.

Lobsang's first shift at his new job was much like his first day at school: he arrived beaming in his fresh uniform of peaked officer's hat and navy jacket with shining golden buttons. However, unlike school, Lobsang soon grew to hate his job. The reason for this was his immediate superior: a short and fat security guard called Jyoti who took an instant dislike to Lobsang and, for some reason Lobsang could not fathom, liked to call him 'Little Panda'. When Lobsang asked Jyoti why he had been awarded such a nickname, Jyoti snapped at him.

'I am a Brahmin, a high-caste. You speak to me only when I speak to you first.'

Jyoti was from Janakpur on the border with India. He was a proud Nepali who despised Indians and, as Lobsang soon learned, Tibetans.

'These Tibetans are a problem,' Jyoti said to the other guard on duty, Thakur, when a group of Tibetan men walked past the hotel's gated entrance. Jyoti spoke loudly: perhaps not loud enough for the Tibetans to hear, but certainly loud enough for Lobsang to hear.

'They don't bother me,' Thakur replied. He was casual and lazy at his work, he was less officious and more sympathetic, and Lobsang liked him for that.

'They're a *very* big problem,' Jyoti continued. 'I have a lot of respect for Buddhists, they're good, peaceful people, not like Muslims or Christians. But the Tibetans who come here just come here to beg. We've already got enough Nepali beggars.'

'Lobsang's not begging.'

'Little Panda begged for this job. Why should he have it when there's so many unemployed Nepalis in the city?'

'I don't know,' Thakur remonstrated. 'I think we should help Tibetans. The Chinese are doing some awful things to them.'

Jyoti dismissed the sentiment with a wave of his hand. 'China is a good country. They are helping the Tibetan people. The Chinese government is a good government.'

Thakur fell silent at this and looked awkwardly at Lobsang who, frightened of speaking to Jyoti, reciprocated the silence.

'I know that they *were* bad,' Jyoti capitulated. 'Mao Zedong was a very bad man. But Jiang Zemin is a good man. See what he has done for unemployment in China. Everybody there has a job.'

'No they don't!' Thakur exploded into laughter. 'There's still plenty of poverty in China, and especially in Tibet.'

Lobsang found himself unable to remain silent any longer. 'It's not that, it's not that at all!' he burst out.

Jyoti turned to look at Lobsang, his face incredulous but curious with it. 'So then, Little Panda,' he said. 'What is it?'

'It's much simpler,' Lobsang replied, straining to keep emotion from his voice, for he felt angry and sad and brave and frustrated. This was the same conversation which floated in circles around his house each evening, and Lobsang was bored of it there. But here, posited in the mouths of two Nepali men, one of whom he disliked, the conversation suddenly and inexplicably demanded Lobsang's opinion. 'Tibet doesn't want to be a part of China. It's as simple as that. Tibet wants to be its *own* country, and wants to maintain its *own* culture.'

'Little Panda, culture is not the most important thing in life.' Jyoti's voice was thick with syrupy condescension. 'The most important thing in life is survival. The most important thing is being able to take care of your family. And you can't do this without a job. Work *must* come first. Without it there is no culture, only starvation.'

'Oh, yes?' Lobsang threw out his ace card. 'And how would you feel if China colonised Nepal?'

Jyoti trumped him, without hesitation, and in four words. 'I would welcome them.'

There was nothing else left to say after that.

From then on, whenever Jyoti launched into his condemnations of Tibet and Tibetans, never directly to Lobsang but always loud enough so that he could hear, Lobsang refused to involve himself. Soon, Thakur began to employ the same tactics, so that after a while Jyoti's rants became monologues to which no one but he listened, and Lobsang and Thakur signalled his madness to each other with quiet sign language and stifled chuckles.

As two years passed, as Lobsang turned eighteen, as his time at school neared its end and as he began to consider the possibility of university, as he worked more and more hours at the hotel and full-time during the holidays, as Thakur left and a boy younger than Lobsang started, as he gained seniority at the gate and enhanced standing among the staff while he started to drink with some of the younger men and started to sleep with some of the younger women, Lobsang found himself growing even in Jyoti's estimation. The two men never became friends, but Jyoti's contempt for the Tibetan diminished with time, as did his routine monologues which lambasted the beggars and refugees who had spilled over the Himalayas to pollute his beautiful country. He did not, however, desist in calling Lobsang 'Little Panda' and, one day, after two years of enduring the nickname, Lobsang built up the courage to ask his superior why for a second time.

For a moment, Jyoti had to think, to remember how it had all started and where it had come from. The nickname had become second nature to him now, and it no longer signified what it once had – to him, it was simply another way of saying 'Lobsang'. 'Pandas...' He slowly grasped meaning from the recesses of his memory. 'The pandas... that theory about them... did you ever hear it?'

Lobsang said that he had not.

Jyoti smiled. He remembered now, and he remembered well. 'Pandas are an endangered species. They are endangered because of humans, but they would be extinct now *without* humans. Do you follow me?'

'Conservation,' Lobsang nodded. He had once undertaken a school project on the pandas of Sichuan Province, and had briefly resolved to move to Chengdu and work with the animals when he was older. He gave up on the idea when Chogyal explained that none of his family would ever come to visit him if he moved to China.

'Exactly!' Jyoti grinned. '*Conservation*! Keeping the pandas, breeding them, putting them back in the wild. But this is what I think. I think our conservation is actually wrong. Pandas *should* be extinct! They have had their time. They became too remote from everything, and their life became too difficult for them to continue. Do you know that they have to eat for twenty hours a day because their bamboo has so little nutrition? That they don't like sex? They have pushed themselves to the edge of life and they haven't adapted to the modern world. It is right, it is *life*, that they should die. The rest of the world has evolved, and they have not.'

Lobsang stared long at Jyoti, for his words seemed too brutal, too clinical, for the smiling mouth which accompanied everything he said.

'I think you disagree with me,' Jyoti said, that same smile playing across his lips.

'I do,' Lobsang replied. 'Pandas would continue to survive if it weren't for the human act of deforestation in Sichuan.'

'But this is what humans *do*! We're just responding to our nature. That is the evolution of the world. Animals must die for other animals to live. Are you understanding me yet?'

'I understand that you don't like pandas.'

'I don't dislike them, I just think what is happening is natural. But my point is your name. Little Panda. You Tibetans, you're like the pandas. You became too remote, too different, and you can't survive in the modern world. Evolution affects culture just like it affects nature, and you Tibetans are not equipped to contend with modern culture. What is happening in Tibet is natural. What is happening is just the evolution of culture.'

Jyoti's common disavowals of Tibet and the Tibetans often made Lobsang want to punch him in the mouth. This time, however, he did not. Instead, he felt a shiver of fear deep beneath his skin and he wandered away for a routine check of the hotel's grounds. Along the way, he replayed the conversation through in his head a score of times, and that shiver of fear persisted, nagged and then transformed into a dull ache somewhere in the bones as he ruminated on Jyoti's words, increasingly terrified that, perhaps, he was right.

When he returned to the gate, it was to find Chogyal, who stood beside a sheepish-looking Jyoti. Lobsang felt a moment of elation: Jyoti had attempted his ridiculous theories on Chogyal, and his brother had knocked them down with his own superior knowledge of Tibet. Nobody knew about Tibet like Chogyal did. Lobsang straightened his back and marched towards the two men, ready to rejoin the fray and defend his homeland alongside his brother. But, as he neared, as he saw the expression on Chogyal's face, as he felt the pressure from Chogyal's hands on his shoulders, and as he listened to Chogyal's words, he understood the true purpose of his brother's visit.

Their mother had died.

Amdo Days

|

I wandered Xining: very much a Chinese city, with the Chinese predilections for skyscrapers, neon-lit signs, and speakers outside shop doors with the bass turned to maximum. But its people were a melting pot of minorities, and I had never before seen in a Chinese city so few Han. In turn, I was stared at relentlessly, for there were few Westerners here, and each group gazed in a different way. The Han were the most unabashed, stopping midstride and gaping, sometimes calling *Helloooo* and laughing, albeit in a friendly way; the Tibetan Buddhists stared, too, though quietly, and passing monks tilted their heads inquisitively, nodding if I nodded first; and the Salar Muslims – of Turkic origin, and with white, exquisitely embroidered hats – looked, but quickly turned away if I met their eyes, as if they had been impolite.

I bought skewers of meat from a food stall for lunch. Once, in the main square, a beggar sat on the uneven paving slabs, propping his back against a wall. His legs were thin and twisted and, as I drew closer to him, he shifted the waistline of his fraying trousers down to his knees and wiped the backs of his legs with a saturated tissue. A brown and watery stream coursed from his seat down to the kerb. He had shit this pale river without moving, and passing pedestrians hopped lightly over his excrement without a pause in their conversations. I knelt next to him and held out one of my skewers. He mumbled something and stared ahead of him, and I realised he was also blind. I pushed the skewer closer to his face. He took it with a limp hand and then held it at his side. I walked on and then looked back. The skewer, meat intact, was still in his hand.

2

If Xining had been Sinicised, the small town of Repkong just a hundred miles away had retained its Amdowan identity. To get there I had climbed aboard the bus and settled into the wrong seat, for which ignorance a teenage Tibetan girl shouted at me, grabbed my ticket from my hand, pointed at the numbers on it and then held it high above her shoulder, as if about to swing her hand down and strike me across the face with my own ticket. An ageing Salar gestured me towards the correct seat with his thumb and then giggled at the girl, who threw my ticket at me and then sat elsewhere.

The Repkong bus soon filled with life and colour. One young couple had brought their blind kitten along for the ride. The driver's extraordinarily happy dog took the seat next to its owner. The array of headwear was tremendous: white Muslim skullcaps; a cowboy hat with a red feather poking from its band; a beret; a thick, woollen beanie, brown and black; purple and orange headscarves; a fluorescent, striped forehead-sweatband; cloth tied into plaits or hanging from ears; my own flappy Soviet hat.

A twenty-year-old Tibetan took the seat next to me, smiled, pulled all the food out of his bag and on to the strip of cloth he had laid across his lap, and motioned for me to help myself. I took out my own supplies, laid them with his, and offered that he do the same. As the bus coasted out of Xining and followed the river east, we picked at our combined meal – a feast of spearmint chewing gum, Oreo cookies, Lay's crisps, chicken-feet and fizzy Orange Mirinda – exchanging not one word, but plenty of nods and smiles. After two hours of sporadic munching, he fell asleep, his head slowly dropping on to my shoulder. I fixed my gaze on Amdo as it passed outside the window.

It was a wet and mud-filled landscape: green lakes and brown rivers, vast, fiery red mountains with patches of grassy skin spat upon them like impetigo, where wild and woolly goats grazed at their bases and streams of prayer flags webbed over the lower peaks, on the higher ones nothing at all. Large sections of our road had crumbled into the rivers and were cordoned off with the same flimsy strings of flags. These mountains seemed soft and impressionable, easily riven by the water which coursed down them and along their feet. The road had been cut in a similar fashion, navigating passes where brightly painted pictures of deities and divinities gazed at us from the cliffside rocky walls, juxtaposed by the huge slogans daubed in blue, white, red, yellow – some pro-Party, others advertising a thirty-per-cent discount for the China Mobile phone network. Passengers got off the bus along the way: some at stops by tiny collections of mud huts with smoke rising from their chimneys; others at, it seemed, nowhere at all, stepping off the bus and then disappearing over the lip of the road.

This was Amdo, Greater Tibet, and I was taking my first few tentative steps up and on to the plateau, although in Chinese parlance I was still in Qinghai Province. After the Communist Party takeover, Qinghai – China's largest non-autonomous province, bigger than France, but populated with just five and a half million people – became notorious as China's Siberia, when Chairman Mao set up a string of gulag-esque labour camps in the region. The treatment of prisoners at these camps – many Tibetan, but most Han from the political purges of the fifties and sixties – comes straight from the pages of a Solzhenitsyn novel. Prisoners got up at 4 a.m., ate little more than a small bread roll for breakfast, and then worked fourteen- or fifteen-hour shifts, feeding on a supper of thin porridge and then having to endure lectures in Marxism before collapsing into exhaustion.

The labour was hard: working in mines, building bridges, or even just farming, which was an intensive pursuit in this frozen landscape. Survivors of the camps recall collapsing during the day and then being beaten until they regained consciousness, or of the weather being so cold that their flesh would stick to the shovels and tear from their hands. If the indoctrination of the lectures did not work, officers resorted to hanging the prisoners upside down and beating them until they repented. Since the food was so scarce, the prisoners ate anything they could – leather from bags or shoes, rope, rats and frogs, even the worms they would find in their own faeces. The Dalai Lama's physician, Dr Tenzin Choedrak, remembers a teenage boy who killed his mother for the stock of barley she had hidden, and a man who killed and ate an eight-year-old child.

Many of the labour camps became the farms which now pepper Qinghai Province, often worked by ex-prisoners now granted their freedom but, their entire families dead from the Cultural Revolution, with nowhere else to go. I wondered, as our bus passed this or that farm, at the history of each, and whether, in a previous incarnation, it had ever been the home, and the cause, of so much suffering.

3

Repkong was a small village by all accounts, and I understood quickly that I was the only Westerner around. Nobody spoke a word of English, but neither did they seem to speak Mandarin: all here were, if not of the majority Tibetan populace, then Salar, Hui or Tu. It is sometimes easy to forget that sixty per cent of all China is made up of provinces dominated by non-Han ethnicities – in particular, Tibet, Xinjiang, Inner Mongolia and Manchuria – and, in places like Repkong, the striking absence of Han is immediate. These minorities (there are fifty-six ethnic groups in total, including, along with those aforementioned, Zhuang, Yi, Buoyi, Dong, Tujia and Hani) constitute only eight per cent of the entire Chinese population and, though there have always been struggles for power between them and the Han – with, sometimes, the minorities coming out on top: the last

Chinese dynasty, the Qing, was Manchu – Han supremacy in China was clearly denoted by the Chinese Communist Party's Propaganda Office following the 1949 birth of the People's Republic.

Here, amongst these minorities, it was impossible for me to be alone. People appeared from nowhere to sit or walk or stand with me. Often, they did not even talk, just stared, smiled, and nodded comfortably. On the way to the Longwu monastery, passing the marketplace lined with sheep's heads and trinkets and yak-butter stalls, I felt like a rolling snowball, gathering children and teenagers as they followed so close they stepped on the heels of my boots. I turned and looked down on one scampering beneath my elbow, said *'Tashi delek'* (the traditional Tibetan greeting) to him, and he sprinted off to spin a prayer wheel beside the temple entrance before hurrying away to gleefully chase a scrawny chicken.

I stopped in the Regong Culture Square outside the monastery at the three-faced, 30-foot-high Dumu Icon, and my followers danced back to the village, giggling. I pulled my journal from my pack to note down the inscription on the statue's plaque:

The Dumu Ikon, who is determined to help people all over the world to be safe and to live a happy life.

As I wrote, an old monk circumambulating the statue stopped beside me, stared uncomprehendingly at my journal, grinned, and then delivered a sound thwack to my shoulder before continuing his circle.

I entered the Longwu monastery, swept into the whirlpool *koras* of the villagers who sped in circles around the various temples and statues and then spurted out on to the thin and twisting dirt-tracks which ringed the rooms and halls. Atop the main hall, now empty but soon to be filled with novice monks, hung a giant portrait of the tenth Panchen Lama, the second most venerated figure in Tibet after the Dalai Lama. I stopped and sketched the Mona Lisa smile which played about his lips, so unlike Mao's stern gaze from his place on the Forbidden City's Gate of Heavenly Peace.

A young monk approached me and smiled.

'*Tashi delek*,' I said.

'*Tashi delek*,' he replied and then, in English: 'Where are you from?'

Eager for my first conversation in Tibetan, I replied in his language: 'I am English. Where are you from?'

He didn't understand. The dialect here was too far removed from the phrasebook I had ripped my stock sentences from. I tried again in English.

He nodded. 'I am Tibetan. From here. I am Buddhist. Like Dalai Lama.'

I looked about me at his last words. I had not been in the People's Republic of China for long, but I had already become attuned to the danger which surrounded his final two words. Just mentioning the Dalai Lama could lead to arrest. The monk, mistaking my caution for ignorance, reached deep inside the folds of his robe and pulled out a tiny photograph, cut from a magazine and no larger than a fingernail.

'Dalai Lama,' he said again, pushing the photo up towards my nose.

I delved inside my daypack for my history of China, removing it and thumbing to the correct page. 'Dalai Lama,' I said, showing him my own photograph.

He burst into a laughter so deep and throbbing it resonated throughout my body. Taking me by the arm, he guided me into the hall and through a maze of corridors and chambers, finally stopping in one, a hidden backroom lit by a single yak-butter candle, where a fifteen-foot *thangka* (a large wall-hanging painted or embroidered with images from the Tibetan Buddhist canon) depicting a monkey and an ogress coated the wall. Tiptoeing to the dark end of the room, the monk lifted a corner of the *thangka*, revealing on a small ledge an A4 framed photograph of Tenzin Gyatso, the fourteenth Dalai Lama, at the age of perhaps forty – long after he had left Tibet – with his trademark glasses and receding hairline. He was smiling, and when I looked back to the monk, his own smile was as wide as the Dalai Lama's.

'Dalai Lama!' he said again, and we both gazed at the picture in silence for the next few minutes. My silence came from the acknowledged tenacity of this monk, who had revealed a picture of the Dalai Lama to a stranger. In China today, such pictures are illegal, and any person caught with one can face prosecution. To carry my own around China had been dangerous enough, but to hold one here, in a Buddhist monastery in a Tibetan village, was highly dangerous, and its very presence put the abbot and most of the monastery's monks at risk should the Chinese police ever find it.

I wanted to discuss this with the monk, but my lack of Amdowa Tibetan and his lack of English negated the possibility. And anyway, it was preferable to ask no questions at this serene moment of intimacy, to not talk at all, but just be thankful for a welcome I felt in the twitches of my smile.

4

It was mid afternoon when I left the Longwu monastery, the weather still cold but clear and with no wind, so I walked towards some nearby hills to enjoy the scant rays of the nearby sun before it set behind them. One rose several hundred feet above the rest, and I climbed its gentle gradient to the web of prayer flags strung pyramidically at its peak. In the glory of solitude, I bellowed an impromptu song into the air, revelling in the lack of echo as my melodies sucked into the sky. Turning towards the network of flags, in full flow now in complete and tuneless abandon, I stopped in shock as I suddenly noticed that which I had not before. A tiny, shaved head, that of a novice monk no older than ten, poked out from the mesh of prayer flags. He grinned cheekily at me, gave a quick and mocking impression of my vocal disaster, laughed once, and then disappeared back inside his nest.

I took dinner – a bowl of oily noodle-soup laced with corn and cubes of yak-meat – in a small restaurant on Repkong's main street. A senior monk walked in with his four novices, who appeared to be between eleven and fourteen. As the monk chose their table in one of the restaurant's booths, his apprentices surrounded me and gabbled to each other. I tried speaking Tibetan to them, but they looked at me blankly each time. To ford the language barrier, they pointed at my journal, reading a word – 'do!'; 'just!' – and then smiling happily when I nodded at their pronunciation. I told them my name, and then the monk snapped at them and they all fled to his booth. As the curtain was drawn, I heard the varied interpretations of my name, sung happily over the pelmet: *'Carly!'*, *'Charry!'*, *'Sally!'*.

The routine of my first day replicated across each new one in Repkong – a Longwu morning; an afternoon walk; the evening meal. I had no desire to return to Xining, and thus bided my time in Repkong. My hotel was a dingy affair: home to young Chinese soldiers on their way back from a Tibet posting who ran up and down the corridors each night shrieking hysterically because there was no one there to tell them off; and with toilets so stinking and shit-smeared that I remembered better in a Romanian bus station. But the days were slow and wonderful, filled with perambulations and circumambulations, a festival of footsteps leading to and around, the synchronicity of pilgrims circling a prayer wheel, my head poking up above the rest.

nga

An earth burial was too expensive, a water burial not allowed and a sky burial out of the question, and so Lobsang's mother was cremated atop a funeral ghat on the banks of the Bagmati River. Only Lobsang, Jamyang, Chogyal, their father, their sister-in-law and her family attended. Lobsang's mother had barely left her bedroom, let alone the house, in the thirteen years since they had fled Tibet, since Dorje had died, and she had made friends with no one.

'If my Dolkar had died in her real home,' Lobsang's father muttered to himself, 'all of Lhasa would have come.'

'This is Hindu,' Chogyal said to his sister. 'It's not right.'

Jamyang gestured at the lama officiating: a Nepali, but a Buddhist nonetheless.

'It's not right,' Chogyal repeated.

'All of Lhasa would have come,' their father echoed.

Lobsang said nothing as the two utterances melded into a chorus and drifted along the river with the smoke from his mother's burning corpse. He felt little except a profound and seismic sense of loss: the loss of his mother, but also a reawakening of the loss of Dorje, which he was only now, perhaps for the first time, truly beginning to understand. A puerile notion had persisted in his mind since childhood, refusing to mature while the rest of him had: that perhaps Dorje would one day return. Now, he finally knew that he never would, and neither would his mother. His family was shrinking, and he could not risk losing anything more by leaving what remained of them and moving to India for university.

When he announced his decision that night to stay, Jamyang was furious.

'If you turn this opportunity down, if you throw away everything you've worked for and everything we've worked for, if you turn your back on all the kindnesses everyone has done for you over the past year, then I swear, Lobsang, I swear I will never talk to you again, and neither will Chogyal or father. *Then* you will lose your family!'

Lobsang looked at his father and at Chogyal, both of whom said nothing and sipped tea with blank looks of tired resignation.

'It's my decision whether or not I go to university,' Lobsang told his sister. 'It's got nothing to do with you.'

'Nothing to do with *me*?' Jamyang launched herself at Lobsang, grabbed him by the collar of his shirt and dragged him towards the old chest of drawers which filled one corner of the room. Lobsang, shocked that his older but considerably smaller sister had so much strength, allowed her to bully him along. Jamyang wrenched open one of the drawers and pulled out a bundle of copied letters and forms which she dropped at Lobsang's feet. With a final imprecation, Jamyang instructed Lobsang to read through the papers and change his mind, warning him with a protracted silence what would happen if he did not, and then she left the house.

Lobsang sat next to his mute father, poured himself a cup of tea and began to leaf through the documents. Until then, it had not occurred to him how he had really secured his place at the University of Delhi or secured his scholarship so that he could afford to attend. It had not even crossed his mind how he was going to get to India. He had merely been asked where and what he would like to study. *Delhi*, he said. *Physics*, he said.

Now, poring over the papers, he came across myriad letters from Jamyang petitioning the Tibet-in-exile government in Dharamsala to consider Lobsang as a candidate for the Central Tibetan Administration's Scholarship Program; he came across dozens of references from each of his teachers from first to twelfth grade which gushed with praise for him – even one, and Lobsang could not quite believe this, written by Jyoti, which called him a 'worthy and intelligent man'; he came across the application forms for the scholarship and the degree course, all bearing his signature yet not written in his hand; he came across the correspondence from Dharamsala, congratulating him on being one of the fortunate 200 out of a thousand to be awarded the full scholarship and offering aid with visa applications, all of it stamped with the seal of His Holiness The Dalai Lama; he came across letters from the University of Delhi offering him a place to study a degree in Physics and a single room in the 'Men's Hostel 2' hall of residence; he came across an airplane ticket with his name on it. Finally, he came across the copy of a letter from his mother to the Central Tibetan Administration, thanking them for their generosity in more words than Lobsang had heard her say aloud in the past five years.

'Why didn't you tell me about all this?' Lobsang asked Jamyang when she returned.

'You were busy with your studies.'

'I could have helped. I had no idea.'

'You were busy. And we were happy to do it for you.'

'I'll go to university.'

'There's no question.'

The same people who attended his mother's funeral attended Lobsang's departure at the airport. There were not so many tears, but still a substantial amount, and Lobsang had never been kissed so much in his life. Jamyang and Chogyal escorted him through the door and towards the check-in desk while the rest remained outside.

'An aeroplane, eh, old man?' Chogyal whistled. 'Hope it doesn't fall out the sky!'

'Don't be mean, Chogyal!' Jamyang admonished him, nudging Chogyal in the ribs with her elbow. 'You'll scare him.'

The truth was, Lobsang was too overwhelmed by everything to feel one single emotion like fear. The separation from his family, the recent loss and subsequent revelations, the prospect of the journey which lay ahead, to another country, across a border, which in itself brought up shadows of recollections of his one prior border crossing – all of it gathered and entwined, leaving his fingers numb and his thoughts incoherent.

That muddled emotional disorder, that swampy sense of everything at once and yet nothing at all, persisted through his farewells to his brother and sister, through the flight and landing, the bus ride to his halls, his first glimpse of Delhi, his induction at the university, his first lectures, his classmates, his teachers. It endured, in fact, for such a length of time that later Lobsang could barely remember his whole first month in India.

When Lobsang finally popped up from his fog, he discovered that he was happy. He enjoyed his course and respected his lecturers, his room was spartan but comfortable enough, Delhi was new and loud and malodorous and exciting, there were pretty girls everywhere, and he had quickly found himself ensconced within a pack of close friends.

They were all first-year international students, and none of them was more surprised than Lobsang when he became closest to a Chinese boy called Ji. Ji was from Xian and studied Art. 'Xian has the best art colleges in the world,' he would say, 'which is why I'm in India.'

At first, Lobsang and Ji's friendship was mocked by the others in the group. 'A Chinese and a Tibetan, and they're best friends. Hey, Ahmed! We need to find you a Jew buddy!'

But it soon died down, in large part due to Ji's transparent bewilderment at each round of mockery. 'Why can't we be friends?' he would ask Lobsang. 'We're virtually brothers.'

It became clear to Lobsang that, when Ji said this, he meant it. To him, Tibet was indisputably a part of China, and therefore Lobsang, a Tibetan, was by extension Chinese. Lobsang took no issue with Ji's presumptions because he could see they came devoid of malice. For Ji, it was simple geography, and his Sino-centric perspective fascinated Lobsang.

'So, tell me, Ji,' Lobsang once asked. 'For how long has Tibet been a part of China?'

Ji whistled through the gap in his front teeth. 'Like forever.'

'Now, come on. China hasn't been China forever. Everything starts somewhere. What did they teach you in school?'

Ji thought about it. 'It was maybe one and a half thousand years ago.'

'One and a half thousand years!' Lobsang guffawed. 'That long!'

'Why not? Yes, it was one and a half thousand years. Your Qizonglongzan, he agreed that Tibet should be a part of China, that it would be for the best.'

'I've never heard of him.'

'Not possible. Everyone has heard of Qizonglongzan. Especially in Tibet. He is a very famous historical figure there. He married a Chinese princess and she became Queen of Tibet. Together, they brought peace to Tibet by bringing it into the Empire.'

Something clicked in Lobsang's mind. 'Do you mean Songsten Gampo?' he asked.

'I don't recognise that name.'

'Songsten Gampo. He married Princess Wencheng.'

'*Yes*!' Ji's face lit up with joy at the name. 'The Queen of Tibet. Supposedly, a very beautiful woman.'

Lobsang laughed. 'But that's not what happened at all! Songsten Gampo was the first true king of Tibet. All he wanted was to unite his own country and bring peace to it, so he married Princess Wencheng to create a peaceful alliance with China. He also married a Nepali princess called Bhrikuti

Devi for the same reasons – but that doesn't mean Tibet became a part of Nepal, does it?'

The joy had left Ji's face, replaced by confusion and a vague undercurrent of sorrow. 'But why did they tell me a different version in school?'

'Maybe if they teach all their young people that Tibet has always been a part of China, it makes it easier to justify their invasion in 1950.'

'You mean the liberation of Tibet.'

'No,' Lobsang said. 'I mean the invasion. You said Tibet has been a part of China for one and a half thousand years. The truth is that it has only been a part of China for fifty.'

Ji became quiet. His hands fidgeted about his knees and his eyebrows arched and drooped. 'The truth…' he muttered to himself. Finally, he looked back up at Lobsang. 'Perhaps my teachers did lie to me. But have you considered that maybe *your* teachers lied to *you*.'

Lobsang was about to remonstrate when Ji stopped him.

'I am not calling you a liar. I'm saying it's possible, that's all. And I'm saying that we should find out for ourselves.'

Ji's idea appealed to Lobsang, and together the two boys began an extracurricular and autodidactic course of Chinese and Tibetan history. They started light, renting VHS cassettes of *Seven Years in Tibet* and *Kundun* and watching them in the hall's common room. Both left Ji unsettled and queasy. 'I had no idea,' he murmured. 'Let's watch them again.'

Moving from the video store to the university's well-endowed library, they devoured histories and textbooks and travelogues and guidebooks and narrative accounts of the two countries, and then shared their findings with each other late into the night. During spare moments between lectures, they separately scoured the Internet and then emailed each other links to a variety of websites and pages. Together, they debated the veracity of every source and examined each fragment of information they had corroborated, constructing between them a tower of Sino-Tibetan knowledge which was as steadfast and unshakeable as they could possibly make it. And, as that tower grew, curious things happened to the two boys.

Ji, who had always been thin, began to lose even more weight. He took less care with his appearance, often going a whole week without washing his hair or changing his socks, and he began to drink less beer and smoke more cigarettes. His works-in-progress, which lined the walls of his room, had started to take on the forms and expressions of Hindu imagery, something he had consciously tried to avoid during his first few months in India. He liked to joke to anyone who would listen: 'Turns out I'm the villain!'

Lobsang, on the other hand, drew strength from their combined research. He discovered that he had also been fed a lie or two throughout his own education – and Garab had once told him about the Chinese Red Guards and the violence they had wreaked in Tibet, but had neglected to mention that many of the Red Guards were Tibetan – but overall their findings made him feel vindicated and assured.

More importantly, however, Lobsang discovered something else, not within the leaves of books or the scenes of films or the pages of websites, but within himself, something he thought he had lost years ago, perhaps with that fight beside the Kathmandu shrine. It was a passion. A passion that was sometimes angry and sometimes righteous, but always deep and inherent, as if it had in fact never left him, but merely been locked away. A passion for Tibet.

The Highest Railway in the World

|

National Day had passed without incident and Tibet's borders had reopened while I was in Repkong. The travel agent greeted me with a beautiful smile as I rushed in to buy tickets, passes and permits. Though travel was allowed, access was still restricted, and I would have to join a group and adhere to their fixed itinerary. A group of three, the travel agent informed me, were already on the train from Chengdu: I could join them when it stopped at Xining on its way to Lhasa. I was reluctant – the thought of a fixed itinerary stung especially – but the travel agent cajoled me into it. The borders could close again, she said, at any time.

The train was due to pass through Xining after dark, so I spent the afternoon in my hostel's Reading Room. There, I relinquished the history of China I had travelled with thus far to its shelves: with a picture of the Dalai Lama contained within, the gamble of taking it into the Tibetan Autonomous Region was too severe. To replace it, I found a slim text printed by New Star Publishers called *China's Tibet: Facts and Figures 2005.* If anything, it would make interesting reading on the train.

The station was quiet at night, quiet and cold. A guard sat beside me, the only company I had while I waited, and perhaps the only company he had, too. He checked my passport, visa and Tibet travel permit four separate times – eyes wandering from face to photographic facsimile to face again – as if he were killing time. I did not mind his presence nor his scrutiny, but I did wish he would put away his rifle.

The Lhasa train arrived, gliding silently into the station, a smooth and white flagship of Chinese rail travel; the shining symbol of China's determination to integrate Tibet into the motherland's twenty-first-century superpower status. No expense had been spared, whether Tibet liked it or not. I boarded and walked the length of the train, through the seat carriages – where passengers sat upright for forty-eight hours straight – to the sleeper carriages. My group, I knew, had booked out a four-berth cabin, and I hunted for it and them.

When I found it, only two were present: Joe and Tanya, a young and happy couple from Switzerland immersed in their epic world adventure. I asked after our missing companion and thought I saw Joe roll his eyes while Tanya shrugged. 'We've barely seen Gavril since Chengdu,' she said.

Gavril appeared in the cabin doorway as the train slid from the station. He was from Bulgaria, on a journey whose focus seemed to be the Himalayas, though he did not clarify why until much later. He wore a skintight Lycra vest and combat trousers, and his thick, tousled hair poked out from under the rim of his woolly hat. Holding one hand out for me to shake, he sipped from a jam-jar of green tea in the other.

'I see you have also chosen the *soft-sleeper* option,' he said, laying heavy stress on the hyphenated words.

'It's a long journey,' I replied. 'I thought it was worth the extra.'

'Gavril's not staying with us,' Tanya said. 'He's got a hard seat.'

Gavril nodded sagely.

'Sounds uncomfortable,' I said.

'Not for me,' Gavril replied. 'I like to be with the people, travel the local way.'

Again, I fancied that I saw Joe roll his eyes.

'Have you spoken to many of your neighbours?' I asked.

'No.'

'What will you do to pass the time?'

'I have my laptop. Or my digital dictaphone. And I take a lot of photographs.' He pulled out a digital camera worth perhaps five hundred pounds.

'Very local of you,' I said.

2

The following morning, revelling in the indolence of the long-haul railway passenger, I settled back against my pillow and read the book I had found in Xining: *China's Tibet*. Published by the New Star Publishers – a Party-approved company based in Beijing which publishes English-language books – it was a pocket-sized text with a picture of the sacred

Tibetan lake, Nam-Tso, on its jacket, sliced through by the bold, capitalised and red title. Its 194 pages documented the 'facts and figures' of China's Tibet.

The first chapter began with the line: 'Tibetan is one of the ancient ethnic groups of China'; and the second, entitled 'Religious Beliefs', ran for nine pages without mentioning the Dalai Lama once. Scores of photographs supplemented the text: one featuring, as its caption informed me, three Tibetan farmers driving 'tractors to mark the 100th birthday of Deng Xiaoping'; and another depicted a Tibetan woman gazing at the picture of a young Mao on her mantelpiece – 'This old Tibetan lady was a serf before the Democratic Reform in 1959. She has been paying respect to the late Chairman Mao Zedong for decades'.

Chapter Eight ('Education, Science and Technology') began with the words: 'In old Tibet, there were no schools in modern sense', Chapter Ten ('People's Livelihood and Social Security') opened with the sentence: 'Tibetans have ridden the reform tide to a better life', and hundreds of sentences throughout the book started with the words: 'Since the peaceful liberation of Tibet.' The 'History Appendix' informed me that Tibet had been a part of China since the thirteenth century, the 'Republic of China Appendix' affirmed that Tibet had never been legally independent in the early twentieth century, and I finally had to put the book down at page 176, which gave the following description of Tibet's 1950 'liberation':

The military forces of the PLA in Tibet entered Lhasa smoothly and they were greeted by a grand welcoming ceremony consisting of more than 20,000 people

*including officials from the local government of Tibet
and the monks and the lay people. Wherever the troops
arrived, they were welcomed by the Tibetan people. By
this time, Tibet was truly liberated and the unity of the
Chinese mainland was achieved.*

I ruminated on these Facts and Figures from my bed as we
moved inexorably towards the Tibetan Autonomous Region.
It was all a far cry from the literature I had read at home,
which documented the 1950 'liberation' as a time of shellings
and uprisings.

Out the window, the landscape changed from the Amdo I
knew: mud morphed into hard stone, the rivers and streams
filtered from brown to white, and the air grew crisper and
cleaner. High-altitude clouds streaked the sky like thinning
hair, and the first traces of snow dusted the mountains.
Civilisation disappeared within minutes as we climbed, but
the wilderness still held long indications of Han tenacity:
from the barbed-wire fences running alongside the railway
line to the huge-scale construction projects where further
roads, railways, bridges and flyovers rose from the ground.
As we travelled, the tarmac stopped, in its place only the stilts
of future map-lines: large, totemic plinths which seemed as
if they were left behind by an ancient civilisation. Labourers
scurried about their bases, but I could not see their faces.

We rose higher quickly. Inside the cabin, crisp packets
burst with sudden claps, and my tube of antihistamine bite-
relief cream popped its cap and oozed out into my daypack.
Skirting the northern border of glassy Qinghai Lake, where
the foothills of snow mountains changed to conical sand

dunes, we continued up to elevations higher than any railway has crossed before.

3

For all its controversy, the Qinghai-Tibet railway is a remarkable feat of engineering, long thought impossible, but now, in the twenty-first century, an actuality. The first train to Lhasa forged its maiden voyage in 2006. Before that, the only routes to Tibet were roads, and even these were built by the Chinese, since the Tibetans, in their self-imposed splendid isolation, had no need for such connections to the outside world. The Sichuan-Tibet Highway, opened in 1954 after a four-year construction project, was the first proper road to Tibet, crossing 1,560 miles and fourteen mountain ranges to join Chinese Chengdu with Tibetan Lhasa. Following that came roads linking Tibet to Qinghai, Yunnan, Nepal, and – the highest road in the world – the Xinjiang-Tibet Highway, built mostly by political prisoners, and completed fundamentally as a means to allow the traffic of the Chinese army into Tibet.

But roads were never going to be enough. When Mao Zedong came to power, railway lines became his symbolic means of unifying China under the Communist flag. In 1875, eighteen years before Mao was born, the first track had been laid in China, only to be destroyed by the local officials who distrusted machinery. More lines were built over the next seventy-four years, but they went underused, and so it was that the Party inherited 13,000 miles of railway, and sought to not only use it, but to modernise and extend it.

One such project culminated in the railway to Lhasa. It took five years, 100,000 workers (few of them Tibetan) and 4.1 billion US dollars to build the line from Golmud to Lhasa. With eighty-six per cent of the railway above 13,000 feet, its crescendo comes at the 16,640-feet Tangula Pass, and it even has a tunnel at 16,092 feet above sea level. Perhaps the most incredible aspect of the design comes from the railway's ability to deal with the permafrost across which most of it lies. Such ground flits between solidity and malleable mud, depending on the season, but the engineers have countered this by building the lines on to elevated platforms. These platforms rest atop hollow concrete pipes which burrow deep into the earth and keep the lines at a below-freezing temperature so that, no matter what the season, the railway will not buckle from constant expansion and contraction.

The controversy of the railway comes from the Tibetans, who never asked for this railway to be built to their capital, and who remain increasingly sceptical at the plans for it to be extended all the way to Tibet's Zhangmu border with Nepal. According to many Tibetans, the railway has engendered no increase in employment (most of the workers continue to be Han), and is in fact little more than a means to lasso Tibet to its coloniser, and make the Han relocation which is relentlessly diluting Tibet's culture even easier. As one Tibetan once told me: 'It's only there to ship the Chinese in. Most of them are soldiers. And they're still building. When they reach the Himalayas, they'll reach Nepal. That's what they want. Tibet will just be a filling station.'

4

'Have you heard of sky burial?' Tanya asked.

I nodded. Sky burial is the traditional Tibetan practice for disposing of the dead.

'I saw one.'

I sat forward, intrigued. Few outsiders were ever allowed to observe a sky burial.

'You can do it in Chengdu. You get on a bus with a bunch of other tourists and they take you to a funeral in one of the Tibetan areas nearby.' She paused for a moment, and then continued. 'It was barbaric.'

For a sky burial, the body is washed and shaved of all its hair, then wrapped in a shroud and taken to the nearest sky burial altar. Lamas will attend to chant the incantations which help assist the soul in escaping the body, but the main work is done by the sky burial masters who, despite their title, are the 'untouchables' of the Tibetan caste system, considered as low in the human order of things as blacksmiths and butchers. It is up to the sky burial masters to carry the corpse to the site and then dismember it, carving it into pieces, beating the chunks of flesh into a pulp and mashing the bones up with yak butter. All of this is then fed to vultures, who are summoned with a fire of juniper and mulberry. Thus, the dead body is disposed of, gorged on by the vultures until nothing remains, and the soul is released into the heavens.

Communist China took a particularly dim view of sky burial, perceiving it as an example of Tibetan savagery, and another reason for instigating the country's liberation from itself. But, in fact, sky burial is at once practically, spiritually, and ecologically sound. Upon the Tibetan plateau, where just one per cent of the land is arable and the earth is frozen over for most of the year, to dig a grave is nigh on impossible, and the absence of readily available firewood makes cremation an expensive luxury. Similarly, by feeding their corpses to the birds, Tibetans are leaving behind no waste nor pollution, but are instead perpetuating the cyclicism of their tough ecosystem.

There are exceptions to sky burial: ground burial is allowed for those who have been murdered; water burial for those who are too poor to afford the costs of the traditional funeral, where bodies are thrown into the river and the fish perform the vultures' duties; or cremation – fire burial – which is reserved for high-ranking lamas alone. But, for those families who can afford it, sky burial is an important part of their religion and culture. Death is immaterial for Tibetan Buddhists, just a brief transitory point on the great wheel of reincarnation, and it is said that the juniper and mulberry fire not only calls down the vultures, but also opens up a five-coloured road which the spirit can traverse on its way to the next life.

The vultures are seen not as scavengers, but as spirits, angels even: there is a Tibetan legend that no one has ever seen a vulture's corpse, and this is because a vulture only touches the ground to feed. When they defecate, it is done so high that it disintegrates before reaching soil; when they near death, they fly as high as they can until the wind tears them to pieces. Thus, the soul is carried skyward with the bird, and will not touch the ground again – where it might become bound to purgatory – until it is ready to find its new incarnation.

As a deeply religious and intimate practice, sky burial is a closely guarded facet of Tibetan culture, and it is rare for any non-Tibetans to have ever witnessed a sky burial. Even close family members of the dead are not invited to the ceremony. But it seemed that some Chinese tour companies based in Chengdu had capitalised on the lure exclusivity promises to travellers eager to see something new – *come and watch the savages and their ancient burial rites!* – and had begun bussing tourists out to a nearby sky burial site, for a reasonable fee, on the auspicious days when a ceremony was guaranteed.

'Just barbaric,' she explained. 'I could barely watch.'

Rummaging through her bag, she produced her camera, switched it on and navigated through the photographs on the display screen.

'Here,' she said, holding the camera out to me. 'See for yourself.'

The miniature slideshow revealed Tibetan men in robes brandishing smoking twigs from a small fire; a pack of thirty-five vultures grounded but blurry with movement; a close-up of the clear outline of a body beneath a white sheet, bent double so that the head touched the discernible toes; a sweeping panorama of the forty-strong tour group gathered on the hill some fifty yards from the site. Everyone had a camera. I saw expressions of gleeful shock, sunburned boys laughingly chiding their gawping and sunburned girls, smiles everywhere.

'They've made a funeral a tourist attraction,' I said.

'That's what I mean,' Tanya replied, 'by barbaric.'

5

Night encroached. The altimeter in the cabin read 3,500 metres, and a sneezing fit left me breathless and exhausted. By 9 p.m., I retreated to my bed, lethargic and listless. An attendant entered the cabin to hand out coils of thin, transparent tubing. I plugged mine into the small nozzle above my bed marked 'Oxygen Supply', inserted the other end into my nose and breathed in the flow of pure oxygen, suddenly giddy, air-drunk.

At an average height of around 13,000 feet, the air in Tibet has close to thirty per cent less oxygen than the air at sea level. For all but the Tibetans themselves, altitude sickness is common on the plateau and can strike anyone, no matter what their age, health or number of previous visits to high-altitude areas. It occurs during the first few days of exposure to the high altitude, when the body undergoes a period of acclimatisation to the lack of oxygen: heart rates and breathing patterns are slowly modified to increase the blood's oxygen-carrying capacity. The best way to aid acclimatisation is to ascend from a low to a high altitude area slowly, as I was doing on this train. Those who fly to Lhasa are at much greater risk of altitude sickness as the switch in atmospheric pressures is too sudden, and altitude sickness has been known to cause severe headaches, breathlessness, irritability, nausea, and even death.

That night, as the train rose to 16,400 feet, I slept and woke and drifted and woke again, often disoriented and confused. Consciousness brought with it a desperate panting for breath, and twice I dreamt someone was sitting on my chest, dreamt I was close to suffocation. All dreams that night were strange and stressful – turning up for an exam without revising, on stage for a play and not remembering the lines, stuck in an argument which was impossible to win.

At breakfast, I had no appetite, and eschewed food for two capsules of *hong jing tian*, said to lower the blood pressure and ease the altitude sickness. It made me feel better, though perhaps it was only psychosomatic. In the cabin, the effervescent excitement which had permeated the atmosphere over the previous twenty-four hours had disappeared, replaced by an ethereal and dreamy wonder as we gazed from the window in silence.

The sun rose over a brown and white desert criss-crossed by thin, frozen streams. I saw the animal tracks first, and then the animals themselves: large herds of yak whose coats swung gently beneath their bellies as they walked; sparser gatherings of antelope who stood rigid, staring in fright at the train as it passed; marmots and pikas which would scramble and dash away from us with frenetic rodent-panic when we drew close; and the occasional eagle, always sat far off, watching this metal bullet which was so alien up here.

Human activity was fleeting but not uncommon. The railway follows much the same path as the Qinghai-Tibet Highway, and we passed the odd lonely motorcyclist trundling along the road. Off it, low-walled enclosures dotted the desert. The occasional black nomad tent with a smouldering outdoor fire had been pitched about the strange frozen lakes which were dappled with shimmering ovals of green and red algae. Sometimes, I caught sight of shepherds wandering far away from these homes, visible momentarily amongst their flocks of yak. Most common were the long convoys of army trucks which raised clouds of dust along the highway and stretched in slow-moving lines for minutes at a time. Apart from these, there was nothing up here – a web of prayer flags spidering out from an electric pylon, perhaps – but, other than that, little except horizon-wide stone and ice.

By midday, a shiver of activity ran down the length of the train and, from our open door, we saw our fellow passengers as they spilled from their cabins and marched up and down the corridors. Within the chatter of dialects, we heard the same clear word punctuating the sentences of a score of voices, *Lhasa*, and rose from our beds, donning our cotton slippers, and walking out into the corridor.

When entered by train, most cities (and, especially, capital cities) seem to begin miles before you expect them, gradually building from the soil of the countryside to an exponential density. Cities begin when you pass back gardens. But Lhasa is swift, appearing suddenly and wholly as the railway rounds a mountain. To my left, a young Chinese girl pointed out the window, and I followed her tiny finger to see the Potala Palace, a small chunk of red on a hill above the glimmering rooftops. Within minutes we were at the station. We stepped off the train. And into Lhasa.

doog

The train began to pull out of the station, the early-morning Delhi air already stifling in the crammed and claustrophobic carriage. Lobsang had been neither early enough to secure a seat nor rich enough to 'buy' one off a fellow passenger, and so he remained on his feet for each of the tortuous eight hours to Amritsar. There, he spent the night in a cheap guesthouse, sharing a dormitory with eight backpackers from France and England who stayed out late drinking, bundled noisily back in at 2 a.m., and fell into drunken stupors with the lights still on. The following morning, he rose early, shaved in the filthy shared bathroom, drank tea for breakfast while he read a book by Tsering Shakya, and then strolled to the bus station. Seven hours later, he alighted in Dharamsala.

He was not supposed to be there. He was supposed to be at home with his family in Kathmandu. Jamyang's letters – which appeared regularly at the beginning of each month and which sprawled on for pages and pages without saying much at all – had betrayed her growing excitement at his imminent return. They were planning a party for him, the Educated One, and Jamyang had listed out all the food they were going to buy for it and which of his friends were coming and all their plans for him over his summer holidays so that it seemed his entire two months were already filled with engagements and activities. When he wrote back to explain that he would be a few weeks late, that there were obligations he needed to meet first, that it was probably better to postpone the party or perhaps cancel it altogether, that they shouldn't be spending so much money on him anyway, when he wrote all this down, he felt like he was kicking his sister in the stomach. He knew she would be upset, as would Chogyal and some of his friends, but when he got back after a few weeks in Dharamsala and explained where he had been and why, he hoped they would all forgive him.

It had been Ji's idea.

'You should go on a pilgrimage.'

'Where? I can't go back to Tibet. I left illegally. They won't let me back in.'

'I know that. I mean to Dharamsala. It's where I would go if I were you.'

'Why don't you come with me?'

'Me?' Ji laughed. 'Have you forgotten? I'm the villain.'

'I wish you'd stop saying that.'

'It's only a joke.'

'It's not a very funny one.' Lobsang remembered something Chogyal had once said to him, remembered how much it had comforted him, and decided to try it out on Ji. 'You're one of the good ones, old man.'

Ji spluttered on his food. 'Who are you calling old man?'

'Just an expression. You shouldn't be blamed for something your grandfathers did.'

'You know as well as I do that my generation is still doing it, just in a different way.'

'And you know as well as I do that some of your generation are doing it, but others aren't. Others who are like you, righting wrongs and learning the truth and speaking out.'

Ji did not argue against this, and Lobsang thought he detected the slightest hint of a blush rise to his cheeks. 'Still,' Ji said, 'I can't go. My brother's got a job in Shanghai and he's invited me to work with him for the summer. I need to make some money so that my parents don't have to keep sending it to me while I'm here. Plus, my brother says the girls in Shanghai are unbelievable.'

Lobsang laughed and nudged his friend with his shoulder. 'I should have known it would be girls.'

This was in February, and for the next two months Lobsang could not shake the idea of a Dharamsala pilgrimage. If he could never return to Tibet, surely this was the next best thing: the seat of the Tibet-in-exile government, the home of the fourteenth Dalai Lama himself, a tiny replica of his homeland displaced and relocated in the hills of Himachal Pradesh. When Lobsang discovered that the Dalai Lama liked to personally meet every Tibetan who came to the small village of McLeod Ganj within Dharamsala, his resolve was set. He would leave Delhi on the last day of term, travel north by train and bus, spend a week in Dharamsala, meet the Dalai Lama, and then make his way home. Jamyang could wait; this pilgrimage could not.

As he stepped off the bus, the view of Dharamsala, and McLeod Ganj above it, seemed to somehow collapse together the topography of Lobsang's whole life. The hillside apartment blocks were definitively Indian; but the smell, monkeys and stone *chortens* reminded him of Nepal; and the ring of mountains and, of course, the people, cast him hazily back to Lhasa, the city he could barely remember anymore.

He booked into another guesthouse for the night, and this time was woken hours before dawn by backpackers who rose early to greet the sun with yoga on the balcony. He walked Temple Road from end to end, enquiring along the way about how to arrange a meeting with the Dalai Lama, and was told by all that their spiritual leader had just left the hill, that he was on a tour of India, or Switzerland, or Russia, or New Zealand, but that he would return soon.

Lobsang decided to wait. He had a full two months before he had to return to Delhi. If he had to wait the whole two months here, on this hill, then so be it. He would see his family and Kathmandu at the end of the year anyway, but he might not have this chance again. His guesthouse was too expensive and his dormitory fellows, for all their talk of peace, too noisy, so he decided to rent a room above a shop in McLeod Ganj. It was miniscule, more like a closet with a bed, a sink and no window, but it was cheap and it was furnished and there were three shelves which he began to fill with books.

The days passed swiftly. Lobsang met new people every day – Tibetans, Indians, Nepalese, Americans, British, Germans, Swiss, Australians, French – and found that, however much he liked and enjoyed the company of each individual or group he fell into conversational step with at cafes and bars and shops and temples, he rarely returned to them the next day, but instead sought out new companions. He loved the fact that each day he would have to move from Tibetan to Nepali to English, sometimes within the confines of a single conversation, and that he was able to practise his newest language, Hindi, and even begin to learn some German. The very spirit of McLeod Ganj welcomed this kind of social promiscuity, and he spent his days gregarious and happy with it, wandering from person to person and learning not just about Tibet, as he had anticipated, but about the world.

Finally, at the end of June, the news spread through Dharamsala like rain. The fourteenth Dalai Lama, Tenzin Gyatso, His Holiness, was to return for his ritual public meetings at Gangchen Kyishong the following week. McLeod Ganj was thrown into a flurry of activity, and this both enlivened and impeded Lobsang's own preparations. He knew that, as a refugee from Tibet, he was entitled to a meeting with the Dalai Lama, but he still had no idea how to go about arranging it. It seemed like everybody in Dharamsala had met the Dalai Lama at least once, but none of them could remember exactly how it came about and anyway, they told him, the rules changed every year and would certainly be different now.

Lobsang thanked his fortune when, the day before the Dalai Lama arrived, he met Pasang. Like him, Pasang had crossed the Himalayas on foot at a young age and then grown up in Nepal; unlike him, he was informed and had arrived in Dharamsala just two days before, cognisant of the Dalai Lama's timetable and movements. For his eighteenth birthday, he had asked everyone he knew to gift him money, no matter how small the sum, so that he could pay for his pilgrimage to India and meet the Dalai Lama. That was over three months ago. Tracking his leader online from the safety of a Nepali Internet cafe, Pasang had collated all the information he could find, judging from it that the most auspicious time (and the time he was most likely to meet the Dalai Lama) would be at the beginning of July in the hills of Himachal Pradesh. He kept the money secured in a tin in his house and did not touch it – though he counted it every day to make sure his brother had not stolen from it – as two months passed. As the third month began, he started to walk.

'You *walked* here?' Lobsang asked in amazement.

'It wasn't so far,' Pasang said. 'And walking isn't even proper pilgrimage. I should have prostrated.'

'Sounds tough to me.'

'You walked over the Himalayas!' Pasang reminded him.

It was Pasang who sorted everything out for the two of them. The Dalai Lama's office, he discovered, had earmarked a day for the Dalai Lama to receive all new refugees. Together, they visited the office to register for an appointment. As evidence of his identity, Lobsang took with him his copy of the letter from the Central Tibetan Administration's Scholarship Program.

'His Holiness will be pleased to see you,' the official said to Lobsang when he saw the letter. 'He takes a great interest in our scholars.'

The day arrived and Lobsang met Pasang at a cafe in the heart of McLeod Ganj. He was offered tea but was too nervous to stomach it. The two left together and walked down the street: Pasang filled with effervescent energy; Lobsang on the verge of vomiting.

'You need to relax a little,' Pasang told him.

'I can't.'

They were ushered through the front door where they sat in a bright room with thirty other Tibetans of all ages. A baby began to scream piercing shrieks which bounced off the walls, resonated with the metal ornaments, and clogged up Lobsang's brain. He was tired, his lungs ached, this had been a terrible idea, his eyes throbbed, he craved darkness and solitude, sweat poured from his forehead, he should have gone back to Kathmandu. He didn't want to be here, didn't want to meet the Dalai Lama anymore, not if it made him feel like *this*.

A door opened. He kept his focus on the floor. The door closed. He heard a rustle of clothes and looked up, directly into the eyes of the Dalai Lama. He smiled.

Lhasa - I

Outside the station, two short men stood back from the surging crowd and held up a flimsy sheet of yellow paper with our names handwritten across it. These were Tashi and Dawa, our guide and driver respectively, who – along with Dawa's Landcruiser – we had been obliged to hire for our journey through Tibet in order to get our travel permits granted. Tashi was young, in his early twenties, and dressed like a Western biker, with a leather jacket covered in sewn-on badges. Dawa was twice his age, a weathered and relentless smoker who sparked up his first cigarette the moment we left the station and held it outside the wound-down window. There was a noticeable difference between the two: while Tashi was tight-lipped and serious, Dawa smiled broadly each time he caught my eye in the rear-view mirror.

We crossed the Kyi Chu River and navigated through the recently built Chinese areas which now dominate Lhasa. They were as characterless as a business district. For every Tibetan face on the streets, there seemed to be two or three

Han, and it felt incredible that we were so far from Beijing when it all looked so similar.

A hostel had been booked for us in the Tibetan Quarter and we checked in to our shared room. While the rest unpacked, showered, settled, I bought a bottle of cola and took it and my journal up to the rooftop – only four storeys up, but enough of a climb at this altitude to leave me out of breath at the top. Walking out over the flat roof, my eyes latched on to the centrepiece of this city, the Potala Palace, which stood in majestic profile above everything else. I gazed at it in silence, this sacred building which, for me, had existed until this point only in photographs and upon book jackets. Its tangibility was a symbol of my arrival, of my being finally and truly in Tibet, and I felt happy. The Potala was just as I had imagined it to be.

The rest of Lhasa, sadly, was not. From up here, I could see how squashed and diminished the Tibetan Quarter had become in the wake of the Chinese Communist invasion. The name itself said everything – as conceptually ridiculous as having an Indonesian Quarter in Jakarta or a Greek Quarter in Athens. The Tibetans had not so much been marginalised within their own capital city – this was still very much the centre of things – but they had instead been compacted, tinned almost. Stretching out to the mountains were grids of blockish, Soviet-style high-rises, their concrete grey an overwhelming suck on the red and white of the few remaining traditional Tibetan buildings. The old West Gate entrance to Lhasa had been cut through by a busy four-lane highway; the Chagpori hill, once the site of Lhasa's esteemed Medical College, is now topped by a telecommunications mast; and just a few feet away from me on top of a neighbouring building, I noticed two soldiers partially hidden beneath parasols, their guns pointing downwards at the crowds in front of the Jokhang Temple.

Sixty years before, when Mao Zedong gave his victory speech from the Gate of Heavenly Peace in Beijing, Lhasa was a very different place. One-twentieth of its current size, it existed as Tibet's genuine capital, not just the seat of a local government within China. Tenzin Gyatso had not yet been proclaimed the fourteenth Dalai Lama – he was still a fourteen-year-old boy in training for his future leadership role – but he had been in Lhasa for over a decade, and Tibetans were, in most respects, enjoying their isolation from the rest of the world in much the same way as their forebears had centuries before.

Nevertheless, they were not so naive as to ignore what was happening with their neighbour. Some accounts have it that China's invasion of Tibet was successful because the latter was unaware of the former's intentions: but, on the contrary, when Beijing announced its plans to liberate Tibet and reintegrate it into the motherland, the Tibetan government was already mobilising its scant army. The old pasture lands around Lhasa – lands now plotted with concrete developments – were turned into training areas for the Tibetan soldiers, and the National Assembly called for the subscription of fresh troops from each district. By the end of 1949, the Tibetans informed the visiting Indian Political Officer that the army now stood at 13,000-strong, though other sources contest this figure, some stating that the Tibetan army had no more than four thousand soldiers. India supplied Tibet with a number of Bren guns and Sten guns, mortars and ammunition, but it was soon clear that such equipment would last six months at best, and that the army would stand no chance against the well-equipped and numerous PLA forces who were said to be entering Tibetan terrain soon, many of them war-wise and vainglorious after decades of fighting, and then beating, the Kuomintang.

Realising a military defence against the Communists was untenable, Lhasa sought to negotiate with Beijing. The Sino-Tibetan relationship, they claimed, had always been one of priest and patron, never one of imperial ownership. But the Party's responses remained fixed, as the Chinese ambassador told a Tibetan delegation in Delhi: 'Tibet must be regarded as part of China.'

On 7 October 1950, around forty thousand PLA troops entered Tibet from the north-east, encircling and defeating the scant border guards and then moving forward. Twelve days later, the Tibetan army in that area surrendered. Rather than march on to Lhasa, the Chinese army stayed where it was, sending delegations to the capital to boast of the PLA's might and convince the Tibetan government to acquiesce to their own liberation peacefully.

Unsure what to do next, the Tibetan government consulted the two State Oracles, who said: 'If the All-knowing and All-seeing Guru assumes responsibility for the religious and political system, then the Dharma, Tibet and all beings would benefit.' And so, though he was only sixteen – two years younger than the traditional age – Tenzin Gyatso was enthroned as the fourteenth Dalai Lama. The Dalai Lama has often recounted how reticent and fearful he felt at taking power at such a volatile time, but almost immediately – beginning the reputation which would ultimately lead to him winning the Nobel Peace Prize in 1989 – he laid out his resolve to seek a peaceable resolution to the conflict.

A Tibetan delegation was despatched to Beijing with the knowledge that, as a last resort, Tibet would accept Chinese sovereignty, but only with the conditions that Tibet must retain internal independence, no Chinese troops would be stationed in Tibet, and the Tibetan army would be responsible for the region's own defence. The delegation soon discovered there was to be no real negotiation. The Chinese presented the delegation with their 17-Point Agreement – which opened with the sentence:

The Tibetan nationality is one of the nationalities with a long history living within the boundaries of China and, like many other nationalities, it has performed its glorious duty in the course of the creation and development of the great motherland.

There was no question, it stated, that Tibet was and always had been a part of China, that the Tibetan government was little more than a local government within China's political confines, that the central authorities would not impeach upon the local culture, religion, language and agriculture, but that, in effect, the Central People's Government would have the last say in all affairs. The Chinese took the view that these seventeen points were generous enough, and explained that they were non-negotiable. The Tibetan delegation, seeing that they had no room for manoeuvre, gave in and signed the accord, at which point Beijing hastened to publicly declare that Tibet had been liberated, and there was much celebration – though it is interesting to note that the Tibetan delegation had never been granted the authority to officially sign such an agreement.

The PLA moved down through Tibet, soon inundating Lhasa and Shigatse with around twenty thousand Chinese soldiers. For the first few years, accounts have it that their occupation of Central Tibet was tolerable. Rather than commandeering houses, they camped on the outskirts of the cities in fields and woodlands, refusing to cut down any of the trees for firewood and instead waiting for the Tibetans to bring them whatever fuel they could supply. They were disciplined and orderly and, instead of seeking reform through force, they chose instead the power of propaganda, projecting pro-Communist films on to gigantic screens for evening entertainment, and even opening a dispensary in Lhasa to give free medical treatment to any Tibetans who came along. Though their focus remained on Lhasa and Shigatse, they often sent squadrons out to nearby villages, yet even these were not militant troops with guns, but drama troupes with scripts and silly costumes. The monk Palden Gyatso describes in his book *Fire Under the Snow* – an account of his time as a prisoner in Tibet – the Chinese who used to come to his small village, Panam, in 1952. They would set up huge tents and perform elaborate and impressively energetic dances which depicted the PLA helping peasants with their harvest or rescuing pretty maidens from their despicable landlords. Sometimes they would show films on huge white screens, and confused villagers would jump behind the screens to try to catch out the actors who must have been hiding behind them. These films showed the PLA fighting either the Kuomintang or the Japanese, and the PLA always won. When they left, the soldiers-cum-actors would hand out silver coins to anyone who had helped them.

In 1954, the Dalai Lama and an entourage of around four hundred travelled to Beijing to meet Mao Zedong (Mao never once in his life went to Tibet). Their meetings were said to be, overall, cordial, and it was during the visit that the foundations for the Tibetan Autonomous Region as it exists today were established. In February 1955, Mao and some of his senior leaders held a lavish banquet for the Dalai Lama to mark the Tibetan New Year, and the Chinese press claimed that the Dalai Lama had given a speech in which he proclaimed the 'greatness and splendour of our Motherland'.

Though the 'liberation' of Tibet had clearly been very much enforced, it seemed at the time to those in Central Tibet that it was in fact as peaceful as the Communists were attesting. Such had not, however, been the case in the eastern and northern regions of ethnic Tibet: Kham and Amdo. Both provinces, which straddle the Sino-Tibetan border, have always been dubious of both Chinese and Tibetan control, and it is possible that, were Tibet ever to gain independence, both areas might secede from the secession. Kham, in particular, is historically notorious as a Central Asian bandit territory, and no power before the Chinese Communist Party had ever held much sway over the local Khampas who, though officially considered to lie under Tibetan rule, had always largely disregarded any but their own governance.

The Khampas are mostly nomadic, fiercely resistant to any outsiders, and even in Marco Polo's time they were well known across Asia as violent and indefatigable bandits. When Heinrich Harrer struck out across the Himalayas and away from his prisoner-of-war camp in British India, the only Tibetans he feared along the way were Khampas (whose name, he decided, was synonymous with 'robbers'), when a family of them kidnapped his dog in the hope of luring him back to their tent. He left the dog to its uncertain fate and walked away, certain they would butcher him for his possessions should he enter the tent.

Khampas are known in Tibet for being fierce warriors, both tough and ferocious, usually much taller than their Western cousins, and part of their traditional dress is a sword or dagger. To say that the word Khampa is synonymous with robber is perhaps an unfair assumption on Harrer's part: the region of Kham is stark and unforgiving, and the battledress attire of the traditional Khampa comes not so much from a need to rob others, but from a need to protect themselves in these lawless landscapes where, before the Chinese annexation, there had never been a police force.

While the Chinese sought to quell the Tibetans in and around Lhasa by discussion, they did not use such tactics in Kham and Amdo, most of which spread into Sichuan and Qinghai, and therefore was already under Chinese rule. There was no need for any 17-Point Agreement here, and thus no need for any soft approaches to bring this region, infamous for its dissidence, under the one-party rule. In 1954, the Chinese, worried at the fact that every Khampa seemed to have a sword or gun woven into the fabric of his dress, called for an amnesty on weaponry, demanding that all Khampas relinquish their arms. The Khampas revolted, and the Chinese cracked down.

The horrors which the Red Guards were to splash upon Tibet during the Cultural Revolution in the sixties and seventies was foreshadowed in Kham and Amdo throughout the late 1950s by the People's Liberation Army. After the weapons amnesty, local skirmishes broke out between the Khampas and the PLA. Few lives were lost on either side, but the PLA saw their chance to prove their military might. In Changtreng, they dropped bombs from a single aeroplane on to the monastery, which held three thousand monks and thousands of villagers taking refuge from the fighting. In Lithang, similar tactics were employed: the PLA bombed the local monastery while six thousand people were inside it, killing four thousand of them.

While the inhabitants of Lhasa merely complained that the Chinese soldiers were consuming their food and fuel resources, the atrocities in Kham and Amdo continued. The surviving monks of Changtreng and Lithang were publicly tortured to strike fear into the rebels: some were doused with boiling water, others clubbed to death with an axe, immolated, disembowelled or buried alive. One particularly horrifying account from a monk in Chamdo tells of how he watched as his friend's nose and ears were torn from his head, and one Chinese soldier stuck his fingers into the monk's eyes and shouted: 'Now, where is your God? If he exists, call him!'

The Khampas reacted in kind, forming horseback vigilante groups to terrorise the PLA intruders, but they never managed to overcome the sheer tenacity and bloody-mindedness of their enemies. News of such atrocities spread to Lhasa with the Khampa and Amdowa refugees who escaped the turmoil for the capital city (one of the first was the Dalai Lama's eldest brother, Takster Rinpoche, who revealed that the Chinese had kept him imprisoned in his monastery and attempted to 're-educate' him, offering him his freedom if he would travel to Lhasa and persuade his younger brother to bow down to the Chinese and, if the Dalai Lama would not, then to kill him), but such news was mostly brushed under the carpet. The Dalai Lama and his government were increasingly perturbed by each fresh account of what the Chinese were perpetrating in the border-regions, but things were dubious and uneasy enough in Central Tibet, and, with every move of theirs carefully watched by the Chinese, they had no means by which to help their beleaguered brothers. That is, until 1959, an entire decade after the founding of the People's Republic of China, when Tibet united against its oppressors.

2

The sky was still light, but the small alleys I walked down in search of dinner were already dark and cold in the shadows of the close buildings. A young man appeared from a doorway, pushing back a hung black sarong to reveal a room filled with low tables and cushions, upon which sat Tibetan boys and girls not long out of their teens, who smoked cigarettes and flicked their ash into empty cans of Coca-Cola.

A waitress appeared as I sat down, and I tried out my Tibetan by ordering *tsampa*, yak soup and yak-butter tea.

She smirked, stared for a while at my ski-jacket, then giggled and disappeared into the kitchen. I looked about me at the other customers. They were gazing back at me, bemused, over bowls of rice and bottles of Lhasa beer.

The yak-butter tea arrived first, in a large flask with a small cup. Yak-butter tea is the traditional drink of Tibetans, consumed in great quantities by the older generations and nomads, though rather unfashionable amongst the more cosmopolitan youth of the cities. Made from a tiny sliver of tea mixed with large lumps of yak butter and fistfuls of salt, it has the consistency of soup and tastes like a spoonful of lard dipped in seawater.

The *tsampa* and yak soup were not much better, but I knew I had to grow accustomed to them, as they would be my staples on the road. These three foodstuffs – yak-butter tea, *tsampa* and yak meat – are an important part of Tibetan culture, as ingrained into the traditional psyche as Buddhism, pilgrimage, or any other aspect which has survived the impositions of the Chinese. Aside from its taste, yak-butter tea is perhaps the perfect drink for high-altitude existence: the fatty butter helps the body protect itself against searing cold; the salt works against the onset of dehydration by restoring electrolyte balance; and the filmy liquid creates an effective balm for the lips. *Tsampa* – nuggets of dough made from barley flour and yak butter – is likewise widely consumed across all Tibet, and has taken on a kind of unifying and almost nationalistic quality, as encompassing as a flag, encapsulated by the Tibetan saying: 'The Chinese eat rice; we Tibetans eat *tsampa*.' The Tibetan historian Tsering Shakya once presented the theory that, of all the ethnic Tibetans who stretch across Asia and indeed the world, there is only one common element applicable to all – they eat *tsampa*.

Finishing up and leaving behind what I hoped would be enough money, for the waitress had disappeared and nobody could tell me how much I owed, I meandered back along the streets towards Jokhang Square. The hawkers and stall-owners had packed up and gone home, but the streets still teemed with life: strolling monks, cavorting teenagers, pilgrims and Chinese police. I looked up to the rooftops to see peaked caps and gun barrels poking over the residential ramparts.

Such barefaced military presence in the Tibetan Quarter was a result of scores of riots and demonstrations which had peppered Lhasa's history over the last fifty years. The first was in 1959, when these same streets had filled with Tibetans unifying against their oppressors in the wake of the atrocities perpetrated in Kham and Amdo. Indeed, it was in this very year that a call to revolt was published in Tibet's only newspaper, *The Mirror*, addressed to 'All *tsampa* eaters'.

By 1958, over fifteen thousand families from Kham and Amdo had arrived as refugees in Lhasa. What the Dalai Lama's government had known for some years could no longer be withheld from the masses: the Chinese were at war with the Khampas, and the refugees' stories of their mistreatment at the hands of PLA soldiers finally united the Tibetans as one against their colonisers.

The spark for the uprising came on 9 March 1959, when word spread through the streets that the Dalai Lama would be attending a show in the Chinese military headquarters the following day. Aware of the PLA's war with Kham, the Tibetans interpreted this as a Chinese ploy to abduct the Dalai

Lama and take him out of Tibet, using him as a hostage to quell the Khampas' rebellion. Rumours spread that a large number of Chinese planes had landed at Lhasa's recently constructed airport, and that convoys of trucks were filtering along the new roads towards the military camp.

Monks from both the Drepung and Sera monasteries went to the Dalai Lama's summer palace, the Norbulingka, to persuade him to stay where he was and not travel to the military headquarters, but the Dalai Lama refused to listen to them. As a result, they sent out junior officials to encourage the public and the Drapchi regiment of the Tibetan army to flock to the Norbulingka the next day, not so much to protect the Dalai Lama, but to stop him leaving.

By the morning of 10 March, several thousand people had camped outside the Norbulingka palace, armed with kitchen knives, sticks and bottles, and chanting 'Chinese go home', 'Tibet for the Tibetans' and 'Do not sell the Dalai Lama for silver'. In one act of mob madness, they set upon a Tibetan monk known to be a collaborator with the Communists, who had arrived alone and on a bicycle, and clad in Chinese attire. When a rumour spread that he could be here to assassinate the Dalai Lama, he was stoned to death by the crowd.

Whether or not the Chinese actually wanted to abduct the Dalai Lama – and most evidence suggests that they did not – this was inconsequential to the Tibetans, who had already decided to fight to their deaths in defence of their spiritual leader. The Dalai Lama himself never attended the Chinese show, primarily because he could not leave the Norbulingka. As opposed as he was to the demonstrations for fear that they might incur the wrath of the PLA, he had lost any control over the crowds, and watched in dismay as they built barricades along the roads which led to his palace.

Ironically, at the same time, the Chinese authorities suspected that the Dalai Lama was being held against his will in the Norbulingka, and considered how to react. The stand-off lasted for the next seven days until, on the morning of 17 March, a hundred Chinese army trucks entered the city. Not long after, two shells landed in the palace gardens. The Dalai Lama consulted the State Oracles and was told that his life was in danger. Dressed as laymen, the Dalai Lama, his family and a host of monks, bodyguards and officials slipped out of the Norbulingka and made their escape from Lhasa, and ultimately from Tibet. To this day, he has never returned.

While the Dalai Lama made his clandestine escape across the Kyi Chu River and south towards Lhuntse Dzong – where he intended to set up a temporary government within Tibet's borders and continue negotiations with the Chinese – little happened in Lhasa for the next two days. Both the Tibetan mob and the Chinese army remained unaware of the Dalai Lama's departure, and the former remained fixed in position outside the Norbulingka while the latter ruminated on what to do. The PLA's actions, when they resolved them, were swift and heartbreaking. First, they shelled the palace, killing hundreds of Tibetans and driving many of the dazed survivors towards the river where they were drowned. Next, they bombed the Potala, the Sera Monastery, the Medical College on Chagpori hill, and scores of buildings about Lhasa.

The Tibetans reacted in a number of ways: some took to the streets to fight back with stones and petrol-bombs, and were shot dead by PLA snipers already in position on the rooftops; others barricaded themselves in their homes; and ten thousand Lhasans sought refuge within the confines of the Jokhang Temple. On the morning of 22 March, three tanks trundled towards the temple and shelled it with relentless abandon, while individual soldiers fired their machine guns at anyone who fled from its burning walls. This action – a precedent to how China would deal with future revolutions in this troublesome western region – marked the end of the 1959 Lhasa uprising, and over ten thousand Tibetans had died in the conflict. For the first time, the Red Flag was hoisted above the Potala Palace, symbolically marking the end of peaceful co-existence between Communist China and Buddhist Tibet. With the Dalai Lama gone – he crossed into India and his freedom in exile on 30 March 1959 – the 17-Point Agreement was effectively torn up, and China cracked down upon Tibet, the newest 'region of China', with radical assimilationism.

Between 1959 and 1964, China discarded its policy of dialogue and negotiation with Central Tibet and set about instead to bring the region up to speed with its Marxist ideology. The renminbi (the official name for the yuan, Chinese currency) was introduced as the legal tender of Tibet, and the Tibetan government was effectively disestablished. All of the monks and leaders thought to be involved with the uprising, and most of the Tibetan army, were arrested and sent to labour camps, where hundreds died from the insufferable conditions.

Next came a period of land redistribution. Many Tibetan peasants were pleased when the aristocrats were stripped of their properties, though felt violated when the same happened to the monasteries. Now owned by the state, such land was used to supplement the disastrous effects of Mao's Great Leap Forward (when the Great Helmsman whipped China into a program of agricultural reform so ill-conceived that millions starved to death as a consequence), and many of the farmlands which had been used to grow barley (the fundament of *tsampa*) for centuries were turned over to the production of wheat and rice, which could not grow at such high altitudes. A famine broke out across Tibet, lasting until 1963, during which time it is said that seventy thousand Tibetans died of starvation.

Many of the ex-landlords and monks were subjected to the same struggle-sessions perpetrated across much of China at the time – publicly beaten and humiliated for their lives of Rightist tyranny. A swathe of monasteries were forced to close over these years as monks were despatched to prisons and families were encouraged not to send their sons to the monasteries to replace them. This did not just happen in and around Lhasa, but throughout most of Tibet's towns and villages, and the struggle-sessions in particular – which went from focusing on those involved in the uprising to anyone thought to have counter-revolutionary sentiments – demoralised the Tibetans by pitting family members and friends against each other. Thousands died from the sessions: some from the beatings, others from exhaustion, while yet others committed suicide, and there are even reports of children who were forced to shoot their mother and father as punishment for their parents' reactionary ways.

By 1965, the society and administration of traditional Tibet had been changed significantly. There was just one step left: on 1 September 1965, Tibet was formally changed to the

Tibetan Autonomous Region, and any of the standards of cultural independence laid out in the 17-Point Agreement were dissolved. Tibet was finally inseparable from China, and completely controlled by it.

3

It was too early to go to bed, and so I found a small bar where I could sit in a corner and drink a high-altitude beer. The bar was dim and quiet, with nothing on the walls and wooden boards over the windows. The seats were low and inflexible, and I banged my knees on the table each time I jostled for comfort. A score of middle-aged men sat about the room in packs of four or five: most were dressed in dark and nondescript clothes and wore tatty cowboy hats on their heads. Some looked around at me to nod or smile, but most stayed largely immobile save for the movements of their arms as they raised their cups to their lips. They talked to each other with slow and measured phrases, and I noticed that their dialogues seemed to be free of overlaps and interruptions. None looked drunk.

In China, whenever I had been around a group of men this age, the same creeping questions nagged at the back of my mind. Had they been Red Guards during the Cultural Revolution? What atrocities had they committed in the name of Mao, the Great Helmsman? But here in Lhasa the semantics of such questions differed somewhat, and I found myself thinking: what had these men suffered during the Cultural Revolution? What atrocities had been committed upon them and their families? Though perhaps this was naive of me. Many Tibetans had themselves been Red Guards, and many others had been 'Students of the Revolution' – like assistants to the Guards – and had conducted struggle-sessions and beaten and killed each other with or without the goading of the Chinese.

When Mao kick-started the Great Proletarian Cultural Revolution, it did not take long for the terror to reach Tibet – the first Red Guards entered Lhasa in July 1966 – and Tibet was to suffer from the decade-long chaos perhaps more than any other Chinese province. After staging a rally in Lhasa in August, the Chinese Red Guards unleashed their new Tibetan disciples from the Lhasa Middle School upon their first act of mayhem – to destroy the Jokhang Temple: the cathedral of Lhasa, and one of the holiest and most sacred sites in the world of Tibetan Buddhism. Ancient scriptures and paintings were burnt, statues were decapitated, walls were torn down and, after days of orgiastic rampaging, the Jokhang was but a shell, renamed Guesthouse Number Five: the monk's lodgings turned into Red Guard headquarters; and the rest used as a pigsty and slaughterhouse.

With this precedent, the Red Guards – both Chinese and Tibetan – washed through the country, destroying anything else of religious significance which had not already been taken apart by PLA troops. Before the Chinese invasion, there were over six thousand monasteries and temples in Tibet. By the end of the Cultural Revolution, just a handful remained.

It was not just the buildings which were attacked, but anything connected to religion, which was itself the epitome of Mao's hated 'four olds' (old thoughts, old culture, old customs and old habits), and the detested influence which was preventing Tibet from actualising its own freedom. Tibetans were instructed to remove any shrines or prayer flags or monuments or even prayer beads from their homes, and told never to talk of Buddhism or anything connected to it, for fear of brutality should they not comply. All homes and workplaces which once had a picture of the Dalai Lama on some mantel or other now replaced them with a Mao portrait; Mao's *Little Red Book* became a mandatory text for every individual; and the core Tibetan Buddhist mantra *Om mani padme hum* was officially changed to *Mao Zedong wan sui* ('May Mao Zedong live for ten thousand years').

What was perhaps most terrifying of all to the Tibetans, however, were the constant threat of arrest and – the greatest of all terrors – the struggle-sessions, or *thamzing* as they came to be known in Tibetan. By 1970, *thamzing* had replaced periods of worship as the daily ritual. Tibetans call this harrowing period the time 'the sky fell to the earth'.

There is some irony (or perhaps justice) in the fact that the first victims of the public struggle-sessions were the same lamas and aristocrats who had originally cooperated with the Chinese and helped establish the TAR. According to the Red Guards, they needed to be punished for their class backgrounds and previous oppression of serfs and peasants before the liberation; according to others, they were perfect examples by which to engender support for *thamzing* from the local populace, many of whom themselves got involved with the beatings, encouraged to take out their anger on these turncoats.

Monks and nuns were the second targets of *thamzing*, paraded through the streets wearing dunces' caps and whipped as they walked by Red Guards. Many of these celibate men and women were forced to marry each other, and some even to have sex in public. Those who did not eat meat were given jobs in slaughterhouses; those who did not drink were force-fed alcohol. Anyone trying to help a monk or nun was afforded the same *thamzing* punishment and, before long, struggle-sessions became commonplace for anyone, no matter at what level of society they existed, often for the most arbitrary 'offences', such as wearing traditional Tibetan dress, or even keeping one's hair in plaits.

Many died from the struggle-sessions, and many of those who did not were sent to prisons, where the conditions were as brutal and inhumane as any throughout the People's Republic of China during those dark days. One monk has reported his fifty-eight-day introduction to a Tibetan prison, where he was kept with his hands manacled above him with ice-blocks on top of them, where he was fed once every five days, where he was beaten twice daily, and where he even considered himself lucky – his floor had a crack through which he could shit and piss; his neighbour's cell had no such luxury, and his watery defecate would freeze over the floor, which the prisoner would lick thirstily when the guards forgot to bring him water. Prisoners were not allowed to talk to one another and, if they did, they were accused of treasonous plotting. A common sanction for such a crime was a knife in the testicles: an often fatal punishment.

When Mao died in 1976, the Cultural Revolution ended across the People's Republic and, if China had changed, Tibet was never to be the same again. What the Party had tried to achieve in their 'Western Treasure' over the previous seventeen years had been accomplished in the first four of the Cultural Revolution.

4

A single beer turned me queasy and light-headed, and I left the bar to walk back to the hostel. The streets, lit by faint orange lights, were all but lifeless in their comparison to the afternoon. A few packs of pilgrims still walked their clockwise circumambulations (known as *koras*) around the Barkhor (the half-a-mile of streets which circle the sacred Jokhang Temple) and, though the guards had left their posts for the night, soldiers in formations of six with rifles, helmets and heavy military jackets patrolled the streets, walking in the opposite direction to the pilgrims.

I made my way back up to the hostel roof. The two soldiers were still atop the adjacent building, though they sat back in deckchairs and waved the bright tips of their cigarettes at each other, their guns resting beside them on the floor. The Potala, lit in a dim yellowy-orange, was beautiful, but the weight of all I knew of this country's past sixty years had begun to bear down upon me and, though I had first seen the Potala just a few hours before with a kind of triumph, now I felt suddenly emotional, and very sad. Perhaps I had hoped that all those books I had read before coming here had exaggerated or even lied about the domineering Han presence in Tibet, and, if not that, then maybe I had hoped that the twenty-first century – which none of the books mentioned – had in fact been favourable to Tibet, and that it had been able to reassert itself as a region with genuine autonomy. But, as I looked out at the city, I could not ignore that still, in 2009, Lhasa was irrevocably Chinese.

Following Mao's death, the major policy the Party adopted to ensure that Tibet remained integrated with the People's Republic – a policy which continues to this day – was that of societal dilution. The fundamental core of Tibetan culture had been battered and raped by the Red Guards, but it had somehow survived, and the Party recognised that one resource had still not been used to its potential effect: the sheer number of the Chinese themselves. Thus, a policy of encouraged Han relocation to Tibet was put into place in the hope that such immigration to the plateau might serve to homogenise the TAR and make it what the Party had always wanted: just another province of China, run by the Chinese, and inhabited by the Chinese. Such tactics had already proved effective in Xinjiang: between 1949 and 1983, the Han numbers in Xinjiang rose from 200,000 to seven million, more than half of the province's total population. Looking out across dark Lhasa from my rooftop vantage point, I could see the effects of this policy far more than any hangovers of the Cultural Revolution or Great Leap Forward. This one had, without a doubt, worked.

Also following Mao's death, however, the new Chairman of the CCP (Chinese Communist Party), Hua Guofeng, relaxed China's political control over Tibet. The Red Guards were stripped of their title, study- and struggle-sessions were done away with, and many of those imprisoned during the Cultural Revolution were released. Traditional clothes and institutions and even the religion began to be somewhat tolerated again and, in 1980, Tibet's borders were opened for the first time in decades, allowing in those Western writers – such as Paul Theroux, Vikram Seth, Alec Le Sueur, and even Heinrich Harrer on a clandestine two-week tour which he recounted in his sequel, *Return to Tibet* – whose books gave us the first non-Chinese and non-Tibetan accounts of the country since the 1950s. Important religious festivals, which had been banned since 1967, were celebrated again in 1986, and Tibetans – funded mostly by local whip-rounds – began to restore the destroyed temples and monasteries.

There were still, of course, riots and demonstrations, usually on the streets of Lhasa, as there continue to be to this day. 1989 – the year of the Tiananmen Square massacre, the year the Dalai Lama won the Nobel Peace Prize, the year of the thirtieth anniversary of the 1959 Lhasa uprising, the year Lobsang and his family escaped Tibet – was especially eventful. What started as a peaceful protest against one-party rule soon escalated into a three-day-long riot after Chinese police began shooting at the unarmed demonstrators. In much the same way as their parents had when they heard the Dalai Lama was to be abducted in 1959, the Tibetans took to the streets with whatever weaponry and ammunition they could muster. And, as their colleagues were to react to the protestors in Tiananmen Square, the Chinese soldiers cracked down with massive and indiscriminately used firepower until the protest was quelled. Martial law was installed, hundreds of Tibetans were arrested and possibly tortured, CCTV cameras were placed around the Tibetan Quarter, photographs or pictures of the Dalai Lama were outlawed, and the borders were closed again.

Such impositions, along with reintroduced study-sessions and public denouncements and ration-cuts, never achieved the severity of those put in place during the Cultural Revolution, but what many of them *did* achieve was a semblance of longevity, and today it is easy to see that Tibet still exists under a kind of martial law, that arrests and the torture of those considered to be anti-Party (today, the terminology is 'splittist') are still going on, that the study-sessions have in a way filtered down to Tibet's Chinese-dictated educational system, that there are more CCTV cameras in Lhasa than ever before, and that pictures of the Dalai Lama are still very much illegal.

Likewise, the success of the Han relocation to Tibet is inescapable. In the early 1980s, Tibet was still considered a backwater by most Han living in China: it was the *Xin-xi-lan* of Mandarin phraseology. But, understanding that in order to engender the influx they would have to tie some attractive perks to the prospect, the Party proclaimed that anyone assisting in the vital unification of the motherland and the liberation of Tibet would benefit from it. The Chinese writer Sun Shuyun recounts how, in 1986 after graduating from Beijing University, for eight years' service in Tibet she was offered double pay, housing priority, a place on the fast-track scheme to promotion and guaranteed Party membership: far more than she could ever have got in Beijing. Other perks included interest-free loans, some freedom from the one-child policy, generous periods of paid leave and subsidised housing. Needing such stability after the chaos of the Cultural Revolution, in the single year of 1984, over 100,000 Han moved to Tibet, adding to those already there to, according to some sources, raise the Chinese inhabitants to one-third of the entire population of Central Tibet.

Though their official purpose was to raise the living standards of the Barbary that was Tibet, the influx of Han Chinese into the area actually caused the opposite. Large areas of forest (an essential commodity on the frozen plateau) were cleared for the building of Chinese tenements. The skilled Chinese graduates who had been targeted for the immigration policy soon took over Tibetan jobs and, in Lhasa alone, during the 1980s nearly thirty thousand Tibetans lost their jobs to Han immigrants, causing many of them to turn to begging at a time when food and fuel prices in the city had never been so high.

While the Great Leap Forward and the Cultural Revolution, for all their atrocities, actually ended, this policy of Han relocation continues to this day, and those Chinese who have accepted the call to Tibet and all the monetary and social perks that come with it now very much dominate the TAR. They have the highest-paid jobs and the best standards of living and, as a result, they have created a rich-poor divide in New Tibet which surpasses even that which Mao detested and attempted to turn on its head when planning his 'liberation' of this feudal country.

We must also factor into this Han relocation the number of Tibetans who died as a result of Chinese actions in Tibet. The official, and widely used, statistic is that out of six million Tibetans living inside the TAR and the Tibetan areas of Chinese provinces since 1950, 1.2 million have died as a consequence of the sixty-year 'liberation': a genocide by any account. The critically acclaimed writer Patrick French, however, after much personal research into the subject, has since come to the conclusion that such a high number of deaths is an impossibility, and that in fact 500,000 Tibetans probably died due to the Chinese impositions on Tibet.

Nevertheless, such a figure – though only half what the Tibet-in-exile government in Dharamsala claims – accounts for one-twelfth of the Tibetan population, and, even if it does not qualify for the term genocide, it is still distressing enough. Above all, it consolidates why the influx of Han Chinese into Tibet has been so successful. Whether the number of Tibetans who died was a million or half a million, it is still a tragedy, and one which the Chinese have capitalised on by filling the vacancies left by the dead with their own bodies and ideologies. For today, in the twenty-first century, China has finally achieved, and exceeded, the goal laid out in its 1950 17-Point Agreement. Tibet is a part of China, *is* Chinese, simply because so many Chinese live there.

dün

Lobsang spent three days trying to describe his meeting with the Dalai Lama to his family, but struggled to articulate the event. Each time he began, he came to the phrase, 'It was the most significant moment of my life', repeated it, and then could go no farther. His family, grateful that he had salvaged one week at the end of his holiday to spend with them in Kathmandu, and proud that he had met and spoken with the fourteenth Dalai Lama, continued to persist with their questions. Lobsang's father was particularly garrulous in his queries. He had seen the Dalai Lama twice at public addresses in Lhasa as a young boy – his own father had taken him – and he had been thirteen when he heard the news that the Dalai Lama had fled Tibet and may not return. The idea that he might not see the man as a man – for the Dalai Lama had been young in those years, too – saddened Lobsang's father, and now he was eager to find out as much about him as he could from his son.

'How tall is he? Did he sit or stand when you met him? Does he still shave his head or is he just bald? What did he wear on his feet? Anything? Did he speak to you in Tibetan? Did he use a dialect? Did you recognise it? How deep is his voice? Did he touch you at any point? Did he seem tired? Does he look old? What are his eyes like?'

This last question was one Lobsang felt he might be able to answer. 'His eyes,' he said, 'his eyes were... they were... *arresting*. Once I looked into them, I couldn't look away. Maybe that's why I remember so little else. He didn't say that much to me personally, but the way he looked at me was enough. It made me feel welcome, it made me feel at peace.'

'Honestly, Lobsang,' Chogyal, exasperated, sighed. 'Is that really all you can remember? What did he say to you?'

'He asked me about my studies,' Lobsang said. 'He wanted to know where I had taken my scholarship and if I was enjoying it.'

'And what did you tell him?'

'I said I was at the University of Delhi and I began describing it, but then I started babbling and I got embarrassed.'

'Useless,' Chogyal said.

Jamyang laughed. 'Come on, little brother, what else did he say to you?'

Lobsang thought for a while. 'He told me to be a good Buddhist,' he said.

'Of course,' his father clucked. '*Very* important.'

'And he told me,' Lobsang said, 'he told me that, once I finished my course, that I should go back, back to Tibet.'

Aside from the mesmerising eyes, this was the part of the meeting Lobsang remembered best. It was the last thing the Dalai Lama said to him, to all of them in the room, and it came with a signal from one of the officials standing nearby which indicated that their time was up. Lobsang had back-stepped away, awkwardly bowing and carving strange gestures in the air with his hands which were supposed to be respectful or supplicating or adoring but were probably inexplicable, and the closing words of the Dalai Lama had echoed in his head.

The words stayed there for a long time, nagged at him throughout his last days in Dharamsala, followed him as he journeyed to Kathmandu and poked at him while he spent time with his family, then snapped at his heels all the way back to Delhi.

'Maybe he's right,' Ji said to him on their first day back. 'Have you thought about what you're going to do after you graduate?'

'I was hoping to travel,' Lobsang replied.

'Isn't going to Tibet travelling?'

There was less historical research for Lobsang and Ji in their second year, and this was for a number of reasons. Ji became enthralled with a local street-artist and began to spend most of his time badgering the poor man into becoming his mentor, Lobsang discovered that his course had grown substantially more difficult since the previous year and required substantially more effort, Delhi seemed hotter than ever that year, sapping energy and encouraging afternoon siestas, and Lobsang, much to his surprise, fell in love.

Her name was Drolma. She had long, straight and sleek black hair which fell to her waist, she wore jeans everywhere, she was tall with large feet, and Lobsang found her exquisitely beautiful. He first saw her at a bar – though she did not see him – and pointed her out to Ji.

'I don't know,' Ji said. 'I'm not really into Tibetan women.'

'Racist,' Lobsang laughed.

'I don't like Han women, either,' Ji protested.

'So who do you like?'

'Germans,' Ji replied with a satisfied grin, and Lobsang decided it best to end this line of investigation.

The second time he saw her, at the same bar (he had never been there before, and had returned in the hope of seeing her again), she caught him staring at her and marched over to him. Lobsang, panicked, considered darting out the door.

'Are you Lobsang?' she shouted over the blaring music.

Lobsang contemplated lying, and did not know why. He nodded, a silly grin frozen across his face.

'I'm Drolma,' she said, holding out her hand, which he took. He noticed that she shook hands in the same way the Americans in Dharamsala would: a firm grip, a single pump of the arm, a slight bend of the elbow which pulled you in closer. 'I thought I knew all the Tibetans on campus. There's not many of us. I was told there was a guy called Lobsang who hangs around with the Chinese. That must be you.' She looked at Ji distastefully.

Ji held up his drink to her and smiled, as if to say: *Don't mind me, I know I'm the villain.*

'We should get to know each other,' Lobsang offered, then immediately regretted his semantics. It was far too forward, too blatant a betrayal of his attraction to her.

'OK,' she smiled. 'But it's too noisy here. There's a cafe I know not far from here. It's better for talking. Will your friend be coming?'

Lobsang looked imploringly at Ji, who understood, necked the remainder of his drink, made his excuses and left.

'He's a good person,' Lobsang said.

'I doubt that,' Drolma replied, and they walked out into the warm night-time air.

Years later, when people asked how they met, Drolma would say how Lobsang had charmed her that night, but all Lobsang could remember was his own awkwardness in Drolma's presence: his poor attempts at jokes, his ridiculously dull anecdotes, his inability to sound or look or act even remotely interesting. When she ended up in his bed that night, he had no idea how he had managed to get her there.

Drolma soon became the centre of Lobsang's world. He would have missed lectures to be with her, but she let him know that if he ever did that she would break up with him; he spent less and less time with Ji, in part because Drolma could not get past Ji's heritage and never warmed to him; he spent most nights and all weekends with her so that, by the time their third and final year rolled around, it made sense for them to move into a small apartment off-campus together. Twice, she travelled to Kathmandu with Lobsang to meet his family and, as he expected, they loved her as much as he did. Jamyang clung to her like a child, his father talked to her for hours about Lhasa, and Chogyal admitted to his little brother that he had 'done very well'.

Lobsang, however, was unable to visit Drolma's home and family, for they still lived in Tibet and, unlike every other Tibetan Lobsang knew, had not fled into exile. Drolma was the first to admit that her parents were very wealthy and members of the Communist Party and that, with both those things, there came certain privileges – such as the ability to send one's daughter to a prestigious university in India without recourse to a scholarship. They owned and ran a karaoke bar in central Lhasa, and they regularly sent Drolma more money than she needed.

Drolma rarely spoke to Lobsang about her parents, for she was still trying to reconcile the deep love she had for them with the deep hatred she had for everything they stood for. They were distinctly pro-Chinese and not afraid to admit it. They believed in communism passionately. Drolma had no brothers and sisters since they adhered to the CCP's one-child policy, even if it was barely enforced in Tibet. They had initially encouraged Drolma to study in Beijing, but she had rallied against the suggestion with such vehemence that they had acquiesced and allowed her to choose Delhi instead.

'Are they Buddhist?' Lobsang once asked.

'Yes,' Drolma replied. 'They believe Buddhism is compatible with communism – they're both godless, they're both for the good of all rather than a few. The thing you have to understand about my parents is that it's worked for them. They really believe Tibet is a better place because of the Chinese. They both grew up in this tiny village far out in the west – I don't even know its name! – and the Cultural Revolution completely passed them by. They hadn't even heard of it until they moved to Lhasa. Their village was so remote – I think they must have been cousins, but they won't admit it to me – and they had nothing. All they remember of it is being hungry all the time, of being dirty and ill. Out of all four of their parents, only one lived beyond the age of forty. But when they moved to Lhasa, everything was different – they seemed to find jobs immediately and they suddenly had money, enough money to live in a decent place and afford good food every day. And they decided that it was all thanks to the Chinese. They had lived a purely Tibetan life back in their village, and they had hated it. But they loved life in Lhasa. So they joined the Party, they moved into a Chinese area, they publicly argued with anybody who dared to imply that Tibet should be free and they publicly praised China to anyone who would listen and, what a surprise, my father began to make a few quite influential friends. He became one of the ones the Party would wheel out whenever foreign journalists visited Lhasa so that he could spout on about how his poor and simple Tibetan life had improved immeasurably since the Chinese liberation. And I suppose they treated him well for it – that karaoke bar is a goldmine, and they practically gave it to him. Both my parents never quite managed to get to grips with Mandarin, but they try to speak it instead of Tibetan whenever they can. They even called their daughter Ling.'

It was not until Ling was fifteen that – partly through the teenage need for rebellion, and partly through the contrasts she noticed between what her Chinese and Tibetan school-friends would tell her – she started to question the blind faith her parents had in the Chinese Communist Party. Three years later, maturing quickly, she knew enough about recent Tibetan history to feel a deep suspicion towards her parents, one that she was not comfortable harbouring. Deciding to get away from it all for a while, she opted for an international university, found Delhi and moved there, studying Political Science and changing her name to Drolma.

During her first year, Drolma had revelled in the company of the Tibetans she met in Delhi who came to the university from all across the subcontinent. Some had fled Tibet as young children, but most had been born outside the country, particularly in Nepal or in India. They all wanted a free Tibet, but most had no idea how to achieve it, nor any inclination to involve themselves in the struggle. They talked of Mao Zedong as if he was still alive and enemy number one, of struggle-sessions and public denunciations, all the things, Drolma realised, their parents would have experienced and told them. But they knew nothing about twenty-first-century Tibet, about the country it had become since they had left, about the Han mass-immigration policies and the CCTV cameras and the environmental degradation and the railway line running across the plateau which was due to open any day now.

And then Drolma met Lobsang, who had a passion for their homeland which matched hers and who seemed to know more about it than even she did. Together, they debated the Dalai Lama's 5-Point Peace Plan for realistic Tibetan autonomy, the efficacy of the Chinese leader Hu Jintao, whether Jawaharlal Nehru had helped or hindered the Tibetan cause, the 1989 riots in Lhasa and Beijing, and whether or not the CIA financed the Khampas. Drolma found herself falling deeply in love with Lobsang, so much so that, when they moved in together in their third year, she confidently told him that it was the best decision she had ever made.

Though it lingered around the peripheries of many of their conversations, it took a long time for Lobsang and Drolma to address a problem which grew closer with each passing day.

They avoided it consciously, for they already knew what the likely outcome was to be. One day, not long after graduation, one of them was going to want to return to Tibet; and so was the other, even though he would not be able to.

Lhasa - II

|

Lhasa.

It is not said. It is sighed.

The name is an aggregation of the Tibetan words *lha*, meaning 'the gods', and *sa*, meaning 'earth' – Lhasa is figuratively the land of the gods, and the seat of the god-king, the Dalai Lama.

Pre-1950, Lhasa did not extend much further than the small village of Shol at the foot of the Potala and the buildings which surrounded the Jokhang, today's Tibetan Quarter. This latter site grew around three expanding pilgrimage circuits, or *koras*: routes by which Buddhists walk around sacred sites or objects to show their devotion. The circularity of such *koras* matches the spinning of the prayer wheels outside temples and the cyclical nature of reincarnation and Buddhism itself. One must always follow a *kora* in a clockwise direction – to walk anticlockwise is sacrilegious – and the three *koras* of the Tibetan quarter (the Nangkhor, which circumnavigates the Jokhang's interior; the Barkhor, the streets around the Jokhang's exterior; and the Lingkhor, the pathway around the whole Tibetan Quarter) are flooded with windmills of pilgrims from sunrise to sunset. It can seem that all Lhasa moves in this same clockwise fashion, and even those whose houses lie ahead of their place of work on the Linghkor must backtrack through alleyways or even take the long route so as to avoid walking in the wrong direction.

I became addicted to the Barkhor from my first morning. The market stalls which lined the *kora* were already at business, selling everything from jewellery to headphones to torches to prayer wheels to 'yakkety-yak' T-shirts to food to belts to radios and cassette-players to raincoats. Hawkers called out 'Helloooo! Lookee lookee!' as I passed, and I stopped to buy a string of prayer flags for my mother, a jade necklace for my wife, some socks for me.

I walked the Barkhor whenever I had a free moment and must have circled the Jokhang close to a hundred times, not because of any desire for spiritual merit, but because it was only there that I felt I could experience twenty-first-century Lhasa in genuine. Sometimes, I would purposefully lose my way down back-alleys where stray but well-fed dogs congregated about the open gutters and the occasional parked car; other times, I would stroll out towards the eastern Chinese areas where air-conditioned shops stood next to high-walled enclosures and where the roads were well paved and busy. But the appeal of the rest of Lhasa dulled in comparison to the Barkhor which, though far removed from how it must have been sixty years before, still teemed with prostrating pilgrims and Mexican waves of prayer: a human tide which sucked me in with the unending relentlessness of a rip tide or roundabout.

Movement was perpetual on the Barkhor. Nobody stood still. To do so, one had to move to the sides of the streets, which were flanked by shops and stalls, and once you took a moment next to them you were immediately drawn into haggling for something you neither wanted nor needed by men and women with Tibetan faces but characters more suited to a Turkish bazaar. I was content to follow the pilgrims, who moved at that point between a walk and a run, their clothes and accessories a melding rainbow of colour. During the Cultural Revolution, the standard and dreary Mao-suit had been imported by the Chinese and forced on to the Tibetans, who wore it with resignation. Over the last thirty years, however, traditional Tibetan dress had returned with aplomb. Though many of the hawkers and younger Tibetans wore the globally nondescript uniform of T-shirt and jeans, the *chuba* – a sheepskin-lined cloak with long sleeves, one of which is often wrapped around the waist during warm weather – was still the favourite. Women wore their hair in long and sumptuous plaits, adorned with red coral and jade, and many of the men's hair was just as long, though free and untied, kept in place only by the non-leather cowboy hats which have become a staple in China's Wild West over the past decades. Blue and black dominated, but on closer observation everyone seemed to be trimmed with subtle flashes of turquoise or yellow, mauve or dusty green. Across each dress or *chuba* was something unique, and the only uniform element came from the scores of monks – some young and giggly; most old and contemplative – with their fading red robes, bare heads and bare shoulders.

And there was, of course, the police: stood individually on sentry podiums, sat on camping chairs beneath canvas gazebos, marching in synchronised formations, and peeping out over the rooftops. They were the only ones who walked anticlockwise around the *koras*: even the Chinese tourists conformed to the simple etiquette. All held guns: huge and heavy rifles or sparkling Kalashnikovs or quick pistols. 'Don't take a picture,' Tashi told Joe when he aimed his camera at an officer stood on duty in Jokhang Square. 'They will take your camera.' Their uniforms denoted their differences to each other – whether Lhasa Police, Public Security Bureau or People's Liberation Army – but all were as one to the Tibetans: a collective Chinese fist, there to keep the Tibetans secure from themselves.

2

The Jokhang was dark and quiet despite the hordes of pilgrims I joined as they marched around the temple's Nangkhor *kora*. Lit only by yak-butter candles, the smell of burning incense made from dried azaleas and juniper twigs clung to the walls and *thangkas*. My stroll from chamber to chamber synchronised with a monk who was dressed in all the regalia of a Tibetan Buddhist but did not look Tibetan. My suspicions were confirmed when he announced that he was Laotian, here on pilgrimage.

'This image of Sakyamuni is natural!' he said, grinning and pointing at a blob on the wall which had the rough dimensions of a face. After our introductions, he had taken it upon himself to be my unofficial guide to the temple. 'It appeared from the wall as the temple was built. Yes! It did! And this, this is a fox which also appeared naturally. It is very sacred.' He gestured at a weird stump on the floor in a corner which looked like it had risen from the drippings of yak-butter candles. We came to a pillar. 'Look inside that hole,' he said, pointing at a nook in the concrete. Inside was a human tooth. 'That is the tooth of Sakyamuni.'

'How did it get there?' I asked.

He looked at me disparagingly. 'It is natural. It appeared.'

A line had begun to form, and we joined it to slowly approach a large statue. 'This,' the monk whispered when we reached it, 'is the most sacred object in all Tibet, and in all Buddhism. It is Jowo Sakyamuni, and was given to Songsten Gampo by the Chinese Princess Wencheng. My pilgrimage was for this. I have come to it every day for six weeks.' He bowed his head, placed his palms together, and then fell silent and motionless. I left him in peace.

Nobody joined me at the Norbulingka – the summer palace of the Dalai Lamas – and I was left to stroll through the well-tended gardens and rooms alone. It is said that the fourteenth Dalai Lama yearned for the Norbulingka each winter as he was cooped up inside the cold and echoing Potala Palace: he loved the colour which washed through the gardens and the humble activity here which, though still far removed from everyday life, was as close as he could get – it was far brighter than the overwhelming administrative and political character of the Potala. I entered his old bedroom and peeked out of the same window which he used to stare from to watch the Tibetan operas performed in the gardens for his amusement.

'Look,' I heard someone ahead of me proclaim as they entered the en suite bathroom. 'Western toilet.'

I went into the old and miserable zoo that sat at the rear of the Norbulingka. It was customary for official visitors to old Tibet to bring a gift to the Dalai Lama, and this was often in the form of an exotic animal. These animals were kept in an enclosure behind the summer palace and tended to by the Norbulingka's servants. Today, it is run by a Chinese business (there is an entry fee for the zoo on top of the entry fee for the palace), but it can make little profit, for few people come here anymore to observe the maddened bears pacing their tiny cages, or the sight of the warden kicking the fence of the resident tiger cub's cage to make it hiss and snarl in anger for your pleasure.

I caught a bus back to the Tibetan Quarter. Five minutes along the road it was stopped by two policemen, who climbed on and walked along the aisle checking for identification. I produced my passport and the photocopy of my Tibet permit as they came to me, which they studied intensely. Seeming satisfied, though not making eye contact, they passed my documents back to me and moved on down the bus. Two Tibetans behind me had no ID on them. They were escorted from the bus and quietly led away.

3

Tashi had bookmarked a day for us to visit the Potala Palace. We could only go as a group, led by our guide.

I had gazed at photographs of the Potala for accumulated hours at home while planning my journey: lost in aesthetic rapture at its sheer size and presence; the way it spills down the Marpori hillside like terraced rice-paddies; the smaller, lighter windows of its lower storeys receding under the larger ones above, giving the impression of a shimmering water-reflection. For me, this was the pinnacle of sightseeing in Tibet, the single place which could not be missed, like perhaps the Angkor Wat in Cambodia, the Acropolis in Greece, the Louvre in France, Uluru in Australia. Go to Kenya and you safari; go to Tibet and you visit the Potala.

Yet to do so, a ticket must be bought in advance, often the day before. At the entrance is a security checkpoint similar to an airport's and all liquids – even sunscreen – must be relinquished. Once inside, you have one hour before you have to leave, and if you go over that hour you may be fined. The entire governmental section of the building is closed off (in Tibet, the administrative sections of buildings are painted red, while those allocated for religious observance are painted white): in effect, most of the Potala. The official claim behind all these strictures is that they ensure that the Potala will not become clogged with visitors, thus making one's experience of the place more pleasurable; though in reality it is more the case that the Party want to rush tourists through so that they only get a fleeting glimpse of this ultimate symbol of Tibetan sovereignty. When Heinrich Harrer revisited Tibet in the early 1980s, he predicted that the Potala Palace would soon devolve into the soulless tourist trap that Beijing's Forbidden City had already become by that point. As I handed over my bottle of water and factor-50 sunscreen to the Chinese guard at the security checkpoint, I understood the prescience of his words.

We climbed the slippery, polished stairs up the thirteen storeys to the white, religious centre of the palace. Around us, families of Tibetan pilgrims who had paid the same entry fee as us laboured up the steps brandishing their holographic tickets, making the most of their one hour's allowance into the corridors of their birthright. I stopped to pause for breath after seven storeys and watched as a woman in her seventies continued on up, grinning at me through her silver plaits as she passed.

'Where are all these people from?' I asked Tashi as he came up beside me and lit a cigarette.

'They are pilgrims,' he replied.

'From Lhasa?'

'Some. Some from Shigatse, some from Gyantse. But most from Kham and Amdo.'

'Where do you think she's from?' I asked, pointing up at the still-grinning grandmother as she stoically rose up the stairs without pause.

'She is a Khampa. She will have come here by bus. Probably a five-day journey. She will spend a month in Lhasa on pilgrimage, and then take the same bus home.'

'Is this her only chance to see the Potala?'

'No. She has been here before.'

'How can you tell?'

'Look at him,' he said, pointing at the three-year-old boy who scampered up and down the steps and giggled at the ankles of the old lady and the men and women of all ages who surrounded her. 'This is his first time here.'

'How do you know?'

'Because he is young. All Tibetans make a pilgrimage to Lhasa as many times as they can afford. Except for him, everyone here has been here many times before. It is what we do. He will return many times in his life. This is not the woman's first time. And I do not think it will be her last. Do you save money?'

'I try,' I said.

'What for? A house? A car? Computer?'

'No,' I said after thinking. 'Usually it's to travel.'

'Ah, so you see, Charlie,' a rare smile played about his lips, 'you are just like these people. Many of them are nomads, Khampas. They live in the same tent as their grandfathers. They use their horses or their yaks to travel. They do not need computers. So, when they save any money they earn, they use it to travel here, or to other important sites for pilgrimage. But mostly here.'

Our hour passed on a whirlwind *kora* about the inner sanctums of the Potala. Tashi, aware of the restricted time, pushed us on mercilessly through the rooms of the successive Dalai Lamas, who had each built a new chamber as their own private quarters after being enthroned.

'Does that mean,' I asked Tashi as we stood in the tenth Dalai Lama's chamber, 'that, if there ever is a fifteenth Dalai Lama, he will also build a new section?'

Tashi looked about and laughed nervously. 'This I cannot answer.'

Everywhere lay money, as it had in the Jokhang, the Norbulingka, and all the temples and monasteries I was to visit throughout Tibet. Left by the visiting Tibetans as fiscal homage and sacrifice to the gods and the Dalai Lama himself, they were in miniscule denominations, but paper nevertheless, and floated about the stairways and corridors: one yuan, ten yuan, twenty yuan. These hundreds of thousands of notes all depicted the face of Mao: his image had become the most common in these holy places.

The hour was up, and we descended back down towards the West Gate where Tashi insisted we visit the souvenir shop at the base of the Potala. 'It is included in your ticket.'

Leaving the others to it, I walked across the busy highway and on to Potala Square. Much of the old Tibetan village of Shol was razed to make way for this square in 1995, built like a mini Tiananmen to commemorate the thirtieth anniversary of the founding of the TAR. Its design is typically Chinese Communist. This is the ritual base for Chinese army parades, flanked by flagpoles and huge speakers, and all but empty on this sunny afternoon. I crossed the square and walked towards the Liberation Monument at its base, where a guard stood on duty and stared at me. Knowing it would be illegal to take his photograph, I instead pulled my journal from my daypack and scribbled some notes. He watched me, confused.

Large plinth statue. One guard stood in the middle, perfectly framed. Two statues either side him of joyful Tibetan workers being liberated, playing instruments and proudly brandishing swords.

I walked back across the square towards the Potala. Along the way, I made eye contact with a Tibetan man in his forties, one of the few people in this lonely square, who laughed at me as we passed. He pointed at my journal.

'You make a picture. And he cannot stop you,' the man said, not missing a step.

4

I left Tashi and my group to continue my perambulations of the city alone. Three teenagers invited me over to play pool with them on a table outside of a Barkhor cafe. Each time I passed them the cue, they would stroke my exposed, blonding arm-hair and coo and laugh. That latter device became common. The Tibetans, it seemed, loved to laugh, and it appeared to me that they did so almost like the English: the nervous laugh, used to cover embarrassment or non-understanding, or as a punctuation mark in sentences. No matter, it made them smile a lot, and I found this endearing.

Such smiles were never rare, though they might have been more frequent were it not for the surgical face masks worn by most of the Chinese tourists, and many of the locals. This was the time of the swine-flu epidemic, and during the National Day holiday two children had died in Lhasa after contracting the H1N1 virus. In comparison to most Asian cities at that time, riding on the back of the paranoia wave that had spread from SARS-infested Hong Kong to much of the Far East in the early twenty-first century, face masks in Lhasa had not quite become the fashion accessory they had in other Asian cities, but they were close to becoming commonplace.

I took frequent stops to drink yak-butter tea and snack on *momo*: delicious doughy parcels of yak-meat deep-fried and presented with thimbles of chilli sauce, which I devoured happily as a substitute to the tasteless and ever-present *tsampa* on offer. It was in one of these cafes that I met Tenzin, a man in his mid twenties who saw me sat at a corner table and politely asked if he could join me.

'Of course,' I said, gesturing towards the free seat opposite mine.

'Thank you,' he said, sitting down and placing his milky tea on the table. He looked at my yak-butter tea. 'You like that?'

'No,' I admitted. 'But I'm trying.'

He laughed. 'I hate it. My parents drink it all the time. But I prefer this.'

I put my Dickens book back in my daypack and we introduced ourselves.

'My name is Tenzin,' he said. 'Like Tenzin Gyatso, the Dalai Lama.'

I must have winced at this, for he laughed at me. 'It's OK,' he said.

'I'm sorry, I just thought people didn't say his name in public.'

'You are right, we do not. But here is OK. The owner is my uncle. And we are sat in a good place. If you had been in the middle of the room, I would not have sat with you.'

'Why not?'

'You never know who is a spy.'

'Even here?' I looked about me. The cafe was filled with Tibetans, and there was not one Chinese face in sight.

'Oh, yes, even here,' he said, catching my drift. 'This is the first mistake of the foreigner. You think it is only the Chinese. But there are many Tibetan spies.'

'Really?'

'Of course! Why not? There is money.'

I took a sip of my yak-butter tea and contemplated Tenzin's words. His tone seemed flippant, but I knew from the literature I had read that he was speaking the truth. There are many Tibetan informants throughout the country. Some work for money, but most proffer information to the Public Security Bureau as compensation for any transgressions they may have made, or are fearful of making. A friend in the PSB is a friend indeed. Such 'spies', as Tenzin labelled them, were the ones to be afraid of, for while the Chinese police and military patrolled the streets and cafes and hotels in uniform, such spies, in their *chubas* and cowboy hats, were impossible to spot. And they could be anyone, from ageing peasants to young tour guides.

I told Tenzin about Tashi. 'Do you think he is a spy?'

'Maybe. But probably not. He is probably just careful. He is probably quiet not because he is a spy, but probably because he is scared spies might be listening.'

I noted the 'probablies' in his speech.

'So why do you trust me?'

'I don't. But I think you are probably OK. I fear the Chinese first, the Tibetan spies next, the foreigners last. Perhaps I will have trouble for talking to you.'

'So why talk to me?'

'Because it is probably better I do. You might tell the PSB what I have said, but – even better – you might tell your friends at home.'

I thought of something the Dalai Lama once said. In a rough paraphrase it was: *Go to Tibet, and then tell the world about it.* It was the only antidote left against the domineering tactics of Chinese cultural dilution – experience Tibet yourself, and then disseminate, no matter what your outlook. This was perhaps why Tenzin trusted me: not because of the contours of my face or my body language, but because it was worth the risk. And, for my part, he could have been one of the very spies he decried, but I took the risk likewise, and asked him about his name.

'Tenzin is a very common name. Probably half of all Tibetan men are called Tenzin. When a Dalai Lama is made, many people name their sons after him. But probably now the name Tenzin is more popular than the others were. We know that Tenzin Gyatso is the most important Dalai Lama.'

'Even more important than Lobsang Gyatso?'

'Yes, the fifth Dalai Lama was very important. But I think the fourteenth is more so. He will be remembered for a long time.'

'I once read that the Dalai Lama said he will not be reborn in Tibet until it is free from Chinese control.'

Tenzin stared at me for a long time. 'Chinese control,' he muttered. 'China and Tibet have had problems for a thousand years. It is why the Chinese are here now. They think we have been a part of China since Princess Wencheng married Songsten Gampo. Have you been to the Potala Palace yet?'

I nodded.

'Then you will know that you were not allowed in the government sections.'

'The red parts.'

'Yes! These sections are closed to all tourists – especially Chinese – because they contain many documents and scriptures which prove that Tibet was once independent. It is a wash. They are trying to rewrite history. If they say Tibet was never independent for long enough, it will eventually become a truth. I know it sounds ridiculous, but speak to any young Chinese. The education in China is so powerful, that all young Chinese do not know that Tibet was its own country.'

'So how do you, the Tibetans, get past that?'

Tenzin laughed. 'We speak to people like you, Charlie. Perhaps you will report me but, like I said, it is worth the danger. Language is so powerful. Let me teach you mine.'

We spent the next hour perfecting my pronunciation of the lamentable amount of Tibetan phrases I knew, and my one to ten. Tenzin was a good teacher, encouraging and positive, though he could not help laughing at my British inflections. 'You know Hugh Richardson?' he shouted so loud the whole cafe must have heard.

'Sure,' I replied. 'The British representative who was here in the thirties. What about him?'

'He learned Tibetan! Why can't you?'

The sun had set by the time I left the cafe, and I navigated my way along alleyways towards my hostel to avoid walking anticlockwise around the Barkhor *kora*. On the way, down one cold backstreet, a middle-aged Tibetan woman with her *chuba* wrapped tightly around her spotted me from a distance and called, 'Helllooooo!'. With the force of her greeting, she casually bounced off the wing of a parked car, setting the alarm off, giving a little scream of surprise, and then bursting into deep and throaty laughter. Sticking her tongue out at me as we passed, I laughed myself, and realised that could have happened anywhere.

5

Dawa drove us to the Drepung monastery on the outskirts of the city. It was the first time I had seen him since the train station. Stopping at a restaurant for a breakfast of noodle soup and sweet, milky tea, he sat with us outside and I tried out some of my Tibetan on him.

'*Hur-hur-hur,*' he laughed in answer to each of my questions, nodding happily whether it was an appropriate response or not, and tipping his teacup at me.

'Your Tibetan is very bad,' Tashi informed me, and Dawa laughed again.

The Drepung monastery is one of the largest and most important in Tibet and, in its heyday, was one of the biggest religious establishments in the world. Over ten thousand monks used to live here, arriving from as far afield as Russia, Ladakh, Burma and Japan. They were organised into different colleges and subdivisions depending on where they were from and, when Palden Gyatso – who studied here in the 1950s – visited Oxford University in 1995, he was struck by the organisational similarities of the two disparate places of learning. Though the Drepung never quite suffered as much from the destruction of the Cultural Revolution as its brother-monasteries, such as Ganden and Sera, almost all the monks who lived there were turfed out or subjected to *thamzing* or jailed or killed in the late 1960s, so that today the monastery which once held ten thousand monks now houses only six hundred.

Drepung means 'a heap of rice', for from a distance the dotted white buildings which fill the nook of the mountainside look like a bowl of the food. As we arrived, the first thing I noticed was the snipers, perched on the rooftops, overlooking the entrance.

Unlike the Potala, we had as much time as we wanted here, and Tashi seemed content to let us wander off on our own. I skipped aimlessly about the buildings and pathways, dipping in and out of doorways to follow pilgrims on their mini *koras* about the dark rooms. The place was labyrinthine, as easy to get lost in as Venice, and just as enjoyable. Inside the chambers it was dark and quiet, but outside the pilgrims and visitors were loud and happy, some eating picnics and others sleeping on slabs of stone with their faces turned towards the warm morning sunshine. On one rooftop, a group of labourers worked on the construction of a new floor in the traditional building process known as *arka*. This involved three lines of twelve, most of them women, wrapped in shawls with headscarves or hats, flattening the fresh surface at synchronised intervals with smooth stones placed at the base of long sticks, and singing to the rhythm. This was not a ceremony or event, just work, and no one else stopped to watch except me, but I loved the way even the labour on this monastery seemed to be an expression of joy.

I found Tashi in a large chamber near the entrance. He was staring at the intricate mural which adorned an entire wall, so engrossed that he did not notice me when I stood beside him.

'What's this a picture of?' I asked, and he turned, startled, at the sound of my voice, before breaking into a smile.

'Charlie! You do not know what this is? This is the story of our creation!'

I tried to make some sense of the painting, a vista of grass, hillocks and mountains – possibly Lhasa – peopled with small, semi-naked men and women, and hosting sparse buildings and wells. The centrepiece, where most of the men and women clustered, seemed to feature an orang-utan and a huge and exceptionally ugly woman.

'This,' Tashi said, majestically raising his arms, 'is the monkey and the ogre. *Jigten chag-sul*. The creation of the world.'

According to Tibetan Buddhism, the first land to rise from the water which covered the earth was Tibet. Here, the Buddha of Compassion, Chenresig (the same Buddha all Dalai Lamas are said to be a reincarnation of) was reincarnated as a monkey. Pure and idealistic, the monkey was seduced by an animalistic, strong and cunning ogress, and the two gave birth to six children with long hair and tails, who encapsulated the virtues and vices of both parents. As the six children became adults, their hair and tails receded, and they became the first Tibetans, and thus the first humans. (There is also a Sherpa version of this story in which some of the children maintained their long hair and tails, took to the Himalayas, and became the ancestors of today's Yeti.) Patrick French once noted the similarity this story has with evolution, and Sun Shuyun has described it is a marriage of Darwinism and Creationism.

It is important to note that this is not the creation story of Buddhism, but of Tibetan Buddhism, which is very different to its parent – something of a conglomeration of Mahayana Buddhism and Bon, the ancient religion of the Tibetan people. Bon was the faith of most Tibetans until Songsten Gampo introduced Buddhism to the region in the seventh century. It is a distinctly Tibetan belief, a one-letter extension on the Tibetan word for Tibet, Bo; an animist religion much like the primitive faiths of many ancient nomadic ethnic groups which involve sacrifices, spells, superstitions and the elemental beat of the chant and the drum. When Buddhism came to Tibet under Songsten Gampo, it did not so much replace Bon as absorb it, and Tibetan Buddhism – unlike the traditional Theravada and Mahayana Buddhisms of the Indian subcontinent – flanked itself with the gods and protector deities of its predecessor. As a result, Tibetan Buddhism is more a sect of traditional Buddhism, and one of the most complex and intricate versions of the religion.

In the three hours which had passed while I wandered the Drepung monastery, Tashi had only come this far, just a few feet from the entrance. He wanted to stay longer, and gave me directions to the cafe where I could get some lunch and meet the others while he continued his personal tour, something he did once every couple of months, but which necessitated a thoughtful slowness. I told him to take as long as he wanted; I was content here. The sky was cloudless and the sun glorious, and I liked the thought of spending the whole day here, peppering it with reading, writing, the odd wander, and the occasional *momo*.

My group met me in the cafe, and they were similarly infected by the light and pace of Drepung. We decided not to set a time to meet again; we would find each other. I walked out through some low scrub and up a sandy hill next to the monastery, passing the few settlements where families sat beneath stretched sheets of canvas, enclosed by flimsy drystone walls. At the top of the hill were four thin, upstanding slabs of rock, adorned with chalk pictures of the sitting Gautama, or Sakyamuni as he was appellated here, and webbed with prayer flags. I applied sunscreen to my bare arms and face, and finished *Bleak House*. And then I fell asleep.

gye

'We could stay here. In Delhi.'

'I don't want to.'

'Neither do I.'

They had walked through this conversation once a week for the past three months. Its cycles were endless and maddening, for they never found their conclusion. The one thing they agreed on was that they did not want to remain in Delhi.

'I've liked it here,' Drolma said. 'I've *loved* it. But three years is enough. I'm still not used to the stink of piss.'

Lobsang laughed. 'No one ever gets used to that. Not all India's like Delhi, though. We could go somewhere else, further south perhaps.'

'Or Dharamsala,' Drolma said. Lobsang understood that this was going to be the version of the conversation where Drolma briefly entertained remaining in India and moving to McLeod Ganj. 'We could rent that room you had and live there together.'

'We'd need something a bit bigger than that.'

'All right, then we'll get something a bit bigger. With our qualifications and our heritage, it would be easy to get work with the Office of the Dalai Lama. Then we could stay as long as we wanted.'

At the end of their second year, Lobsang had planned to return to Dharamsala for the summer and take Drolma with him. She longed to meet the Dalai Lama and his sister, Jetsun Pema, who was a hero of hers. But Drolma's parents had forbidden the journey, calling it a waste of their money. When Drolma threatened to go anyway, her parents reciprocated in kind with their own threat: if she did not return straight to Lhasa at the end of her second year then they would not finance her third. Lobsang did not see her at all that summer.

'Or I could become a teacher,' she continued. 'And you could be a speechwriter for His Holiness.'

Lobsang was beginning to tire of this version of the conversation. He knew how it ended. He decided to speed up its demise.

'You know the last thing His Holiness said to me,' he mumbled. 'It would be the first thing he said to you.'

Drolma nodded sadly. 'Return to Tibet,' she said. 'And I would.'

'And you *should*. And so should I!'

The conversation had morphed into the incarnation Drolma despised. She put her hand up to stop Lobsang, but he had already set upon the particular monologue he liked to use at times like these.

'Imagine, you and me in Lhasa. It's the only place either of us truly wants to be. We'll live together in the Tibetan Quarter, an apartment above a shop or teahouse, something big enough to have friends over when we want, but small enough to keep warm through the winter. We could do that thing couples do – get a dog to practise for when we have children! I'll save money for the first year and buy a motorbike. We'll get a tent and make pilgrimages to Kailash and Manasarovar, or north to Kokonor. We'd just *be* in Tibet, *be* Tibetan. You can't do that properly in Dharamsala, it's not real there, and it's not real in Kathmandu, either. Thousands of people cross the border on foot every year. I did it when I was *five*! I can do it again!'

'No, Lobsang!' Drolma cried, unable to bear any more. 'Yes, thousands cross, but hundreds die, too. They starve or they freeze or they collapse from exhaustion and they never get up again. Or they're shot.'

Lobsang fell silent. Drolma hated herself for uttering that last sentence – of course Lobsang knew people got shot on the Tibetan border; who knew that better than Lobsang? – but Dorje's death had haunted her ever since Lobsang had first told her about it, and she categorically refused to even entertain the idea of Lobsang making that journey again. She could cope with some time apart, with a temporary separation, but she could not cope with his death.

'I was hoping we would have worked this out by now,' Lobsang mumbled. They had both graduated a week before, delaying movement and decision with each passing day. Drolma's parents were growing increasingly insistent that she return home soon. Lobsang knew she would.

'We *have* worked this out,' Drolma replied quietly. 'We're both going home: me to Lhasa, you to Kathmandu. It's all we can do for the moment.'

'That's not working things out,' Lobsang said. 'That's just procrastination. What happens once we're home? What then?'

'We stay in touch. We call each other every day, and we email when we can't. We find a way to make this work, to be together again.'

Lobsang took Drolma to the airport two days later. They made jokes about the bulk of her luggage and avoided any mention of the future, though their hands remained locked tightly together until she stepped through the gate. Lobsang returned to the city, found Ji at his usual spot with his street-artist mentor, and together they got horribly drunk.

Lobsang woke late the next day and wandered down to his nearest Internet cafe. Drolma had sent him an email just hours after landing. It ran on for pages and said nothing new. He should return to Kathmandu to be with his family, they must remain in contact, she would do whatever she could to help him back into Tibet, but he must not attempt to re-enter the country illegally. She repeated this last sentiment so many times and in so many different ways that it took up almost half the email.

Lobsang left the message without replying and navigated to another website to buy a ticket to Kathmandu. There, in a highlighted advertisement at the left of the screen, an airline offered discount rates to Lhasa. He clicked on it. There was a flight from Delhi in three hours, a flight cheap enough for him to afford. He could be in Lhasa that evening.

Except, of course, he could not. Lobsang had left Tibet illegally, and it followed that the only way he could return was illegally. If he booked on to that flight, he would not merely be turned away at Delhi airport, he would be arrested, handed over to the Chinese authorities and put in prison, where he could feasibly remain for much of his adult life. The same would happen if he returned by road or rail: all these avenues crossed the border where it was manned. His own country had shut him out and would not let him back in.

Lobsang bought a flight to Kathmandu, due to depart the following day. Then he went back to the apartment, which seemed so empty now Drolma had left it, cried until his ribs hurt, and lay on the floor in a stupor. He became lost in a daydream, more a series of images than a consistent narrative: his feet deep in snow; mountain-shadows; Drolma stood before the Potala Palace; him asleep in the back of a truck and surrounded by chickens, starscapes over Himalayan silhouettes; the street he had played upon at the age of four.

Lobsang opened his eyes and smiled, the decision made. He was already walking over the Himalayas towards Drolma.

Goddess Water

|

It was early in the morning and, on the way to Nam-tso Lake, we were stopped at a security checkpoint a few miles from Lhasa. A policeman circled the Landcruiser twice, clockwise, and came to a halt in front of the windscreen. Launching himself around to the driver's door, he wrenched it open, pointed at the dashboard, shouted something at Dawa's face, and then grabbed him by the arm and yanked him from the vehicle.

My palms began to sweat, and an uneasy silence settled in the car. Dawa was marched into a nearby building and a second policeman came out to stand before the car. In both hands he held a gleaming gun; his gaze often settled on Tanya for unnerving durations. I looked about me. There were no other cars on the road; just us, this policeman, and his gun. I nervously began to remove yuan notes from my wallet, hoping that, whatever happened, I might be able to bribe our way out of it. With my other hand, I pushed my journal deep into the folds of my daypack and, for one bizarre moment, considered eating its pages.

'Tashi,' I said, leaning forward towards our guide. 'What's going on?'

The policeman heard the question and his gun twitched noticeably.

'I don't know,' Tashi mumbled.

I looked ahead and along the thin road. As new as the tarmac was, it was already potholed, and ice melted in its dents as the sun fired up the sky even this early in the morning. I was beginning to learn about the extreme changes in weather on the Tibetan plateau at this time of year, with frozen nights and brilliant, cloudless days, and I peeled off the layers of clothing which had seemed necessary when I awoke.

Dawa had been taken into the security building: a long one-storey concrete block topped with red flags and flanked by pylons. A large car park had been cut into the earth behind it, but I could only see two cars there. The road stretched out, pencil-straight, towards a wall of mountains, the highest peaks daubed with snow which spangled in the morning sunlight. Three policemen appeared, milled about the periphery of the building, and then walked across the road to check the position of the four orange-and-white traffic cones which stood along the yellow lane-markings. One peered through the driver's open window; my companions looked away from him.

'*Tashi delek,*' I said in Tibetan.

'*Ni hao,*' he replied in Mandarin, and then sauntered away to stand behind the vehicle.

An hour passed before Dawa returned. When he did, he climbed into the Landcruiser, waited for the policeman to wave us on, started the engine, and then pulled out on to the highway.

'Is Dawa all right?' I asked Tashi, for our driver had not spoken a word since returning.

'Of course,' Tashi said. 'This is normal.'

But there was none of Dawa's characteristic laughter as he navigated away from the checkpoint, and the single cassette he had of Tibetan pop music remained unplayed on the car stereo as we drove on in a fuggy silence. I watched his face in the rear-view mirror, certain that, each time he steered right, he winced.

2

We were sightseeing. I had no illusions as to the terminology employed. I was no longer a traveller up here on the roof of the world, but a tourist, a sightseer, and though I tried whenever I could to break away from the itinerary that had been designed and bought in China, its tight time frame left little room for manoeuvre. This was a package tour: a trip generously handed me from the Chinese government, which did not so much marginalise the Tibetans as disenfranchise them. I could have been on a minibus in New Zealand to visit the Maoris, or on a coach in the States to go stand at the edge of a Native American reservation and watch the indigenes play at their primitive ways, as if I were some super-species of our Brave New World. The strictures of our itinerary made me itch, and, as Tashi turned in his seat from the front of the Landcruiser and exclaimed, 'Perhaps we will see some nomads!', I became conscious of my own part in this disenfranchisement, of how my money was funding it. It seemed like the entire Tibetan system of culture, spirituality and fashion was being used as a means of showing off – *look how diverse and accepting we are!* But I knew of the massacres and indoctrination which belied this Tibetan Disneyland, and I knew Tibetans were not an attraction to be gawped at.

'How about Drapchi?' I asked. 'Will we be seeing that?'

'No,' Tashi replied.

It was around here somewhere, I knew, on the outskirts of Lhasa: Drapchi prison; Lhasa Prison Number One; the largest prison in all Tibet. Built as a military garrison, Drapchi was transformed into a prison by the Chinese following the 1959 Lhasa uprising and used almost exclusively for the detention of those who had committed political crimes. The prison is not just reserved for male inmates, there are plenty of women (nuns, in particular) who have been sentenced to a spell there, and many of both sexes have died within its walls or been subject to unspeakable atrocities. When the Dalai Lama's personal physician, Dr Tenzin Choedrak, was imprisoned in Drapchi in 1959, he was told he would be released if he confessed that the Dalai Lama had been sexually active. He refused, and spent the next twenty-two years there, enduring hard labour, torture and what he called 'brain- and soul-washing'.

One of the most famous of Drapchi's former inmates is the monk Palden Gyatso, whose book *Fire Under the Snow* documents the thirty-three years he spent in Chinese prisons – among them, Drapchi – until 1992, when he was released and escaped Tibet into India. In this book he recounts the horrors he saw and experienced in Drapchi. He witnessed countless executions, when prisoners were forced to kneel at the edge of a trench and then shot by firing squad until their lifeless bodies toppled into the trench; their families were subsequently charged for the bullets. Some of these executions were for offences as implausible as leaving a fingernail mark on a portrait of Mao. Gyatso himself survived countless tortures, even at the age of sixty, when he was beaten with an electric baton as a Chinese guard smacked it about his body and shoved it into his mouth, causing him to lose consciousness and wake later in a pool of his own urine and vomit. Nuns he had known were raped with the same kind of electric baton.

He also experienced the resilient will of the prisoners in the face of such terror and pain. In the winter of 1990, in response to the death of their friend Lhakpa Tsering, who had been beaten so severely by guards that he died a slow and painful death from internal haemorrhaging, Gyatso and a group of other political prisoners held the first ever demonstration inside Drapchi. They did not riot, merely held up a banner on which was written in Tibetan script: 'We mourn the death of Lhakpa Tsering. We demand improvements to the conditions of political prisoners', and then marched it to the main office building. It took some days for the guards to react, but when they did, it was with characteristic immoderation. The demonstrators were beaten with the electric batons, and those who tried to flee were either stabbed with bayonets or shot. Gyatso remembers being beaten about the back and legs with a rifle butt.

Though Palden Gyatso's testimony ends in 1992, the atrocities of Drapchi have continued. In 1996, the monk Jampal Khedrub – who was serving time for printing and distributing leaflets on democracy – was beaten to death by a guard. And, in 1998, when a European Union delegation visited the prison to evaluate its accordance with the Universal Declaration of Human Rights (of which 1998 was the fiftieth anniversary), five young nuns imprisoned there shouted pro-independence slogans at the visitors. When the delegation left, the nuns were taken away and tortured, and all five were dead within a week.

3

We were climbing all the time, deep into the Tangula range where snow collapsed in chunks from the mountainside walls and splintered into powdery bursts on the road. Thin and white high-altitude clouds streaked the sky, so close to us that a mist trickled on to the windscreen and Dawa had to turn the wipers on. It all seemed so unusual, like an early morning fog, but a perfect white rather than the hanging grey I associated such weather phenomena with back at my sea-level English home.

Riding the crest of the 17,200-feet Kyang-la pass, we began the descent towards Nam-tso. At 15,520 feet above sea level, Nam-tso is the highest lake in the world, and the second-biggest saltwater lake in all China. As the road levelled, giant, black, nomad tents spun from yak hair dotted the plains on either side, topped with curling smoke, ringed by dogs and the occasional horse or motorbike. Herds of yak roamed between them, black dots on a sea of grass; and one ageing nomad man clad in a cowboy hat, huge spectacles, and a snow-leopard-skin *chuba* which reached down to his shins, stepped out from his tent to watch us as we passed.

Across much of northern Greater Tibet, as the plateau extends from the TAR up into Kham and Amdo, there are few towns, and fewer cities. These huge expanses of wilderness are inhabited by Tibet's nomads, or *drokpas*, tribes of Tibetans – most of them Khampas and Amdowas – who sweep across the plains following the migratory patterns of their herds of yak, and who live transient existences based on movement rather than topographical permanence. Their homes are their tents, which can be packed up and transported to their next destination with the ease of a campervan. These Tibetan nomads have journeyed back and forth across the plateau since the birth of human time, one of the few true nomadic groups of people left on the earth, and they have continued to wash like tides over the grasslands while most of the rest of us on this planet have eschewed our nomadic origins and, instead, built, and then fixed.

There are currently two million nomads who live and walk across the Tibetan plateau, though this is only half as many as there were before 1950. Such a reduction in numbers is in part due to the younger generations of the past sixty years feeling and responding to the lure of the city which perpetrated the globe in the twentieth century, decimating the rurality of most countries in that most swift and modernising of eras. But such reduction is peanuts when compared to the diminution of nomads during the Cultural Revolution, when the Chinese government sought to settle and collectivise such wanderers in the hope that doing so would produce a greater agricultural yield. Such tactics were quelled in 1981 when the communes set up across the plains were dissolved, but today the nomads are still feeling the pressure of the Chinese government, who continue to encourage them to settle, and their numbers are dropping every day.

The traditional Tibetan nomad family is large, and the smaller immediate family which occupies one tent is often composed of the elders, their children, and all their children's children, the latter usually numbering double figures. But their non-immediate family will spread into other tents, and many tribes travel together, moving around their chosen pastures and pitching their homes in turtle-shell-shaped groups of twenty or more. It is important that the tents form the shape of a turtle shell, as this is a symbol which will protect the nomads from the water and earth spirits. Likewise, all the tents will face south, though this has no spiritual connotations and is purely methodical – as the sun moves from east to west, the shaft of light which penetrates the door of each tent allows the inhabitants to effectively tell the time. Most tents – for they are huge, and the spatial likes of them are rarely seen on English campsites – have at their centre an ever-burning fire, and from this fan out the basic accoutrements of any house: seats and cushions, cupboards and hanging pots and pans, a kitchen area and a sleeping area, sacks of food, a stock of fuel (usually yak dung) piled in a corner, and an altar or shrine. Today, many nomads have embraced solar energy, and most families own at least one solar panel which they place on the roof of the tent during the day to power their stereos at night.

Another mainstay of the nomad camp is the Tibetan mastiff: dogs as large and hairy as bears, and as fierce. These mastiffs, called *dhoki* (meaning 'watcher') by the Tibetans, were first introduced to Tibet by the Romans along the Silk Road. Since then, they were kept and bred by the Tibetan nomads, who recognised their innate protective virtues. As loving to their owners as any dog is to its master, they have been conditioned over the centuries to protect their keepers with an unremitting savagery, and are considered to be one of the most ferocious breeds (and, outside of Tibet, one of the most expensive). Sometimes they are kept chained outside the tents during the day, but most of the time they are set loose to roam like sentinels about their turf, particularly at night, and any trespasser will be met by them in a deathly duel. For many nomads, these mastiffs are a necessity as cheap security guards which protect their families from any outsiders: be they Chinese, Western, or just the rival tribe from over the hill. In Kham especially, where banditry has never been uncommon, such patrolling mastiffs allow a comfortable night's sleep for those within the tent.

There is no use appealing to these dogs: to anyone save the human pack which they protect, they are wild and will kill. Just a few years ago, a lone Tibetan woman on a pilgrimage to the holy Mount Kailash was mauled to death by mastiffs when she chanced too close to a nomad tent. As we drove down the mountain towards Nam-tso, three mastiffs broke from their *kora* of a tent close to the road and raced along beside the Landcruiser, barking madly at the windows. I stared out at one, his eyes wide and yellow, spittle flying from his mouth, as he sprinted along beside us, his tangled fur like dreadlocks as it slapped against his muscled haunches.

A few hundred feet from the tent, they stopped as one and pulled away to walk three straight lines back to their posts. I watched the one who had got closest, looking for traces of excitement or exhaustion, but there were none. With his tail and head low, ignoring the two other dogs who forged their own lines on either side of him, he reached the tent and lay down, his head following our Landcruiser as it pushed on towards the lake.

4

We pulled into a shingled and bumpy car park on the fringe of the water. Ten shipping containers sat in a right angle in the middle of the gravelled space, rusting and undecorated. A few doors were open, and I peeked in to see a makeshift cafe in one, a souvenir shop in another and a row of bunk beds in the last. Even here, in the most desolate place I had ever been, tourists were catered to, and, as I looked out to the shores of the lake, I noticed five Chinese groups taking photographs of each other beside the water.

The wind was bitter as I stepped out of the Landcruiser, sucking salt from the lake's surface and driving it into my eyebrows. Like most holy Tibetan sites, there is a *kora* around the lake which takes eighteen days to walk, and it is a popular pilgrimage circuit for many of the nomads who come here. But I saw no Tibetans on their circumambulations as I walked down on to the shingle beach at Nam-tso's shore, only the few Chinese tourists wrapped in ski-jackets and hiking boots. I realised I was dressed the same.

The lake was not calm, was more of an inland sea as a half-foot shorebreak slammed relentlessly against the sand and its chopped face pushed out to the horizon, as blue as the clear and close sky it reflected, the fierce sun dappling the swell-lines with dancing, golden fireflies of light. I followed the beach as it skirted around the edge of the lake, away from the tourists and my companions, as the shingles turned to pebbles and then to clumps of black rock. Perched atop an overhang above the surging and carving water, I removed my hat, lowered myself on to my gloved hands, and plunged my head into the next wave. It felt like diving into a bonfire.

Around a headland, I became the only person on earth. Perhaps the Antarctic was like this. I could see no people on the ground, no birds in the sky: just stone, ice and crashing water. The only lives apart from mine were the occasional feral mastiffs, who wandered through the hazy desert stretching out from the lake, their bellies low to the ground, their movements slow. The closest spotted me, and began to track me as I walked further, easing itself closer and closer with each step until I threw stones at it and it sloped away. Further on, the pebbles diminished and in their place stood hand-sized tablets, smooth and rounded, and it took me some time to realise that many of them had been shelved into man-made walls and were inscribed with the Tibetan script for *Om mani padme hum* – the *mani*-stones which pilgrims carve laboriously and then leave behind to accrue merit until such stones are weathered to shingle thousands of years from now. Among one clump rested a perfectly preserved pair of yak horns wrapped in a white *kata* scarf and, among another, a skinny, brindled cat lay low and stared at me. I marvelled at how it had ever survived up here alongside all those huge and hungry mastiffs.

I came to two towering buttes of sandstone which rose from the ground like big toes, just a few feet apart and wrapped in prayer flags, their bulbous heads teetering unnaturally atop spindly bases. They were the gateway to the Tashi Do monastery built into the cliff-face behind: three small temples which peered over the wall of monks' quarters. I followed the line of stones which trailed into the central quadrangle, where a monk hurried past to one of the temples, trying not to spill the cauldron of yak-butter tea which he hugged to his body. Calling *'Tashi delek!'* as he shuffled along, he laughed, and perhaps it was at all the thick and stifling layers I had piled on to protect myself against the below-freezing temperature up here. His shoulders and head were bare.

I could have struck on further, but found myself mesmerised by Nam-tso itself, and so moved back towards it, where I sat down at the edge and breathed in the air thick with salt. Around me were miniature towers made from pebbles, as tall as my knee and as fragile as life. These were handmade, easily erected *chortens*, a three-dimensional symbol as sacred in Buddhism as Christianity's cross, and a common feature of Buddhist architecture (known as *stupas* outside of Tibetan Buddhism), which appears in all temples, monasteries and shrines. But these were made by pilgrims: nomads and peasants without the money for grandiose structures, who build them as their own temples-in-miniature. Wherever the land is stony and traversed in Tibet, there will be thousands of these tiny, impromptu *chortens*.

Across the lake, the Tangula mountain range divided the water from the few clouds in the sky. Iced with snow, smooth and conical unlike their spiny Himalayan cousins, they seemed at once inviting and unforgiving: just gradual hills on the horizon, though some of their peaks reached 23,000 feet. Heinrich Harrer and Peter Aufschnaiter crossed these mountains on foot in the winter of 1945 on their way to Lhasa, clad only in what scant clothing they had been able to borrow or buy from Tibetans along the way. As I watched the mountains and shivered in the cruel blasts of icy October winds, I marvelled at the pair's tenacity.

Theirs is one of the great travellers' tales. Trapped in British India whilst attempting a Nazi-funded mountaineering expedition at the outbreak of World War Two, they were interned in a British prisoner-of-war camp. After a daring escape, they crossed into neutral Tibet and spent the next two years trekking a long and circuitous route, over passes and peaks just as magnificent as these at Nam-tso, to Lhasa, where they lived for the next five years.

While Harrer's account of this time – the classic *Seven Years in Tibet* – is one of the few Western records of 'pre-liberation' Tibet, there had been a number of expeditions up and on to the roof of the world by Westerners long before his. The earliest known visit to Tibet by Westerners dates as far back as the 1600s, when another Austrian (Harrer and Aufschnaiter were both Austrian), Johan Grueber, and his Belgian companion, Albert d'Orville, spent three years walking from China to Lhasa. They were Jesuit missionaries, on their righteous path of spreading The Word, and a hundred years later a band of Capuchin missionaries entered Lhasa with the same intentions. Their attempts met with little success – only seven Tibetans were recorded as converting to Christianity before 1745, when Tibet expelled all foreigners from its soil – and today there are no churches in the country.

The British, who began to filter into Tibet from India just thirty years after the ban on foreigners (the first British man to enter Tibet was the Scot George Bogle, who reached Shigatse and eventually married one of the Panchen Lama's sisters), were slightly more successful, creating an Anglo-Tibetan link which was to endure to some degree until the 1950 invasion by the Chinese. By the early twentieth century, Russia had also begun to dispatch their own delegations to the Tibetan interior, and Britain responded by sending in a military expedition, led by Colonel Francis Younghusband. The war Younghusband's brigade waged on the Tibetan town of Gyantse was both unnecessary and unfair, but perhaps it consolidated Britain's relations with Tibet to some degree, for by 1936 Hugh Richardson was appointed as the British ambassador in Lhasa – the first Western ambassador in Tibet – where he remained, off and on, until 1950. Richardson was forced to leave Tibet when the Chinese entered, but he remained for the rest of his life a vociferous supporter of the Tibetan right to self-determination, and frequently remarked upon the shame he felt that his own country – mine, too – had stood by and allowed China to annex what he saw as a truly independent nation.

Perhaps the only other Westerners to have mounted such successful expeditions to the forbidden city of Lhasa were the Nazis. Before his seven years in Tibet, Heinrich Harrer was himself a member of the SS, and any quick Google-image search will show the infamous photograph of him standing beside Hitler. One of the greatest explorers of Tibet, the Swede Sven Hedin, was likewise a Nazi, and gave the opening speech at the 1936 Olympic Games in Berlin. Two years later, just before the war, Himmler commissioned Dr Ernst Schäfer and five German scientists and filmmakers to travel into Tibet. Reaching Lhasa in 1939 and spending a month there, records have it that they did not make themselves welcome: they shot footage of the swastika symbol (known in Tibetan as *yungdrung*, and a vital symbol of Buddhism which signifies good luck) and then claimed a kinship between it and their own totalitarian policies; they irreverently hunted wildlife for meat; and they even took photographs at a religious festival, for which action they were stoned by the crowds before running away.

Following the 'liberation', China all but closed Tibet, and it has generally remained so for the last sixty years. The borders have momentarily opened, and people have slipped in and out here and there, but even in the twenty-first century the opportunity to reach Lhasa remains as dubious as it ever has been over the last four hundred years. I marvelled at my own luck for getting in, but I marvelled more at the thought of such travelling stories from those 'pre-liberation' years, when travellers had no recourse to locomotives or combustion engines, but used only their feet and their will. Here at Nam-tso, wrapped in thick twenty-first-century clothing and yet still shaking like a foal, I wondered how anyone had ever traversed this high-altitude land without a Landcruiser and hostels. Back home, I knew I would gloat over my trip to friends in pubs, but I also knew my journey to and through Tibet had in truth been a breeze.

5

Yamdrok Lake, on the road to Gyantse, seemed a world away from Nam-tso: sunk deep into the valley through which it curved; freshwater; placid; immaculately turquoise.

'This lake is very holy,' Tashi explained as we stepped from the car and walked across the grasslands to stare down upon it.

'Can I swim in it?' I asked.

'No!' Tashi was shocked by the suggestion. 'All large waters in Tibet contain divine spirits, often goddesses. They are kind goddesses, unless they are angered, and the way to anger them is to enter or disturb their water.'

I urged Tashi to elaborate.

'Yamdrok, for example, is the physical manifestation of a goddess who argued with her husband, who was an angry god. To leave him forever, she turned herself into this lake. We believe that, if you swim in the lake, you are swimming *in* the goddess. If you sail a boat across it, it is like you are slicing a knife through her skin.'

I spotted a Chinese fishing boat moored up on the shore not far from where we stood. I remembered the Potala, at the foot of which stands a small man-made lake. Though not as holy as Yamdrok, it is sacred nonetheless, and today it is filled with pleasure-boats and pedalos, owned by a Chinese company, run purely for profit, and abhorred by the Lhasans.

Here at Yamdrok, whose liquid goddess is a protector deity of Tibet, an age-old myth has it that, if the landlocked lake ever dries up, all Tibetan people will die. It is therefore of much consternation that Yamdrok has begun to drain. From where I stood, the drop in the waterline was visible and obvious – gathered around the shore were plains of grey sand streaked with salty lines where once water covered.

The lake is draining because, in the 1980s, the Chinese built a hydroelectric plant, funnelling the lake's waters out through a four-mile-long tunnel to feed the huge turbines which stand by the receding shore, and supplying power for the growing populace – most of them Chinese – of Lhasa. The government have claimed that the lake can be replenished by diverting the flow of the Yarlung Tsangpo (the Brahmaputra) river, but such a scheme would irrevocably upset this area's delicate ecosystem. The goddess of Yamdrok survives on snow-melt, not the detritus of a muddy and fast-flowing river, but such rationality appears to have escaped the Chinese, who have run the hydroelectric plant since 1997, slowly draining the lake, and slowly murdering its goddess.

While China continues to perpetrate the social degradation of Tibet, it would be churlish to suggest that the concomitant natural degradation of this country is their fault alone. Granted, their environmental policy is shocking – Yamdrok is a fine example – but the whole globe has contributed to the ecological changes the Land of the Snows is today enduring. When we stopped at the Karola glacier near Gyantse, Tashi explained how he had watched it diminish year by year, so that now it was barely half the size he remembered from his childhood.

I walked out across the shingle which spread to the base of the mountains, a rough and slippery moonscape which undulated in banks and dunes. The glacier trickled down through rivulets which fed a white stream, and I found the narrowest point to leap over. Climbing a few feet up a mountain wall alongside the thin waterfall which plinked down into a perfectly circular basin, I reached out my hand to touch the lowest point of the glacier, and a rock of ice broke away from its root, plunging into the pool below and then bobbing about before reluctantly being dragged down to the stream. I wanted to climb higher, but feared the fragility of the glacier, imagining one gentle tap might bring it all crashing down.

As a popular stop-off point for non-Tibetan tourists, the semblance of an industry has grown up around the road beneath Karola, manifesting itself in two stone buildings which stand either side of the tarmac, flanked with ladders and prayer flags. There is even a lavatory, sheathed in four walls of corrugated iron and balanced on a precarious platform to allow greater space for the small mountain of frozen excrement which sits beneath the hole in the floor.

Tiny children tumbled about the roadside, their noses thick with snot, their hats and hands grubby and unwashed. A few mastiffs basked in the sunlight, growling at me if I got too close, but docile and compliant to the kids, who sat on their backs, tugged at their ears, and screamed with delight when the dogs stood up and took them for a ten-second ride before flopping back down on to the gravel again.

A woman stepped out of one of the buildings and approached me.

'Hello,' she said.

'Do you speak English?'

'Yes!' she replied proudly. 'Lookee lookee. Nice stone.' She held a smooth fist-sized stone in her hand, and I wondered what was so nice about it.

'Nice stone,' she repeated. 'Real. You want?'

'No,' I said.

She dropped the stone on the floor and clapped her hands. 'Fuck you,' she said, turning her back on me and walking away to tenderly pluck one of the children from the back of a mastiff. The boy giggled as she wiped the snot from his nose with her sleeve and kissed his fingers.

gu

'You won't get shot,' the man said. 'That hardly ever happens anymore. It's more likely you'll be arrested and thrown in prison.'

'What's the sentence for an illegal border crossing?'

'Without an identity card? Indefinite. But, realistically, you'd probably do three to five years. Unless you knew someone who could vouch for you and buy your release. Do you know anyone like that?'

Lobsang sighed, for he did know people like that: Drolma's parents. But he also knew they would never extend such sympathy to him, and this understanding was even more deflating than knowing no one at all. He shook his head.

'It's a risk. I won't lie to you about that. Much more for you than for me. If they catch us, the worst I'll get is a few weeks in prison and then deportation. That's the *best* you'll get. Have you told anyone what you're doing?'

Lobsang had not mentioned a word of it to his family, with whom he had spent the last week. His father and Chogyal were oblivious to his intentions, seeming to accept without even asking him that he was back in Kathmandu for good. Jamyang had become suspicious of his late nights, though her morning-after questions revealed that she believed him to be drinking and therefore that she was far from the truth, which was that he had used the nights to hunt down the portion of Kathmandu's underground which dealt with smuggling Tibetans across borders. That hunt had led him to this man, with whom he was sharing a pint-bottle of beer in a dimly lit bar somewhere in the south of the city.

'No one here knows. I have a friend in India,' Lobsang said, meaning Ji, 'who I've told. He's the only one.'

The man nodded approvingly. 'That's the best way. One person is enough, and it's better if they're not family. You should tell this friend of yours that, if he doesn't hear from you within two months after you leave, that you've probably been arrested.'

'What good will that do?'

'Perhaps none at all, but perhaps a lot. One voice asking questions from the outside – especially if they're the right questions aimed at the right people – can do more than you might think.'

Lobsang agreed to pass the information on to Ji, and the man nodded his approval again, taking a gulp of beer. Lobsang looked at him. He was not the kind of person Lobsang had expected. His looks were thoroughly average, and if they tilted in any direction it was towards geekishness. He was well spoken and had a fine complexion, and he looked neither strong enough nor bold enough to lead a party of illegal immigrants over the Himalayas. There was nothing about him which gave any indication of the character Lobsang had spent six nights hunting for – and that character was a 'criminal'.

Nevertheless, that was exactly what he was. He specialised in taking groups, usually monks, across the Tibetan border, to (and usually around) a sacred mountain or temple, and then back to Nepal again. He had a number of different routes into the country which he swore by and which he alternated between depending on the destination, and he insisted that his passengers dress as traditional Tibetan pilgrims, ordering them to buy *chubas* and wooden paddles for their hands (pilgrims use these when they prostrate themselves along the ground), because wearing these outfits would reduce the likelihood of them being stopped and questioned by the police once they were inside the Tibetan Autonomous Region. A group of monks in red robes wandering along the Friendship Highway stood out like *tsampa* in a bowl of rice; a group of prostrating pilgrims snaking their way to Mount Kailash did not.

His reputation was exemplary – seven or eight separate individuals had suggested him to Lobsang as a man who would be able to help him – and the odds of him getting Lobsang into Tibet were better than most others, but his fee was extraordinary. Lobsang had even had to pay a small amount just for the privilege of this meeting.

'I'm only going one way,' Lobsang protested. 'I won't be returning to Nepal. I should only pay half price.'

The guide shook his head. 'Fixed rate,' he said.

His next 'expedition', as he liked to call it, was two weeks away. Twelve people, who were all related to each other in some way, were paying him to take them to Tingri (where they had even more family) and the nearby Langkhor monastery (where some of the older men of the group had studied as novice monks), sixty miles or so north of the border. Tingri lay near the end of the Friendship Highway and, once there, Lobsang could leave the group and use the road to navigate his way to Lhasa alone. This seemed Lobsang's best option. The next expedition was not leaving for another four months, and that was to Mount Kailash, far out in the west.

Lobsang spent as much as he could of the next two weeks with his family. He made sure to reveal nothing to them, but he soaked up their love and broadcast his own with enough subtlety to escape suspicion. He wondered what they would make of his disappearance. It was likely they would guess the truth. They knew Drolma had returned to Tibet and, being tactful, they had not asked him where his relationship with her was heading now that it had become international, so he had not been forced to lie. He considered leaving them a letter explaining his actions and reasons, but even this could endanger his family should anyone come knocking. He knew from his guide and a number of others that spies had infiltrated the Tibetan areas of Kathmandu in the same way they had infiltrated Dharamsala and Tibet itself, knew that there were officials and agencies in Nepal in cahoots with the Chinese who relocated illegal refugees into prisons and arrested those connected to them. No, he had no need to tell his family; they would know immediately what he had done and why. He only hoped they would also understand, and forgive.

The two weeks did not pass quickly, but when they finally had Lobsang walked out to the edge of the city at night to meet his group, feeling faintly ludicrous and overheating in the second-hand *chuba* he had bought from a street market.

The *chuba* was immense and dotted with pockets, which Lobsang had filled with as much food as he could carry. His sporty rucksack contained the typical accoutrements of a Tibetan on pilgrimage – wooden paddles, prayer beads and a hand-held prayer wheel, more food – along with writing paper, pens and an assortment of printed maps and information which he hoped would help him skirt around the many police and military checkpoints on the road between Tingri and Lhasa. His three most prized possessions, the same three his guide had recommended he not be thrifty while purchasing, were his brand new shoes, sunglasses and broad-rimmed cowboy hat.

He was the first to arrive at the meeting place. Within the hour, his twelve companions appeared together, followed by their guide and then the four cars which were to take them to the Sagarmatha National Park below the border.

'Enjoy this bit!' the guide laughed at them as they squeezed into the cars. 'From Sagarmatha it will all be on foot. This bit is luxury in comparison!'

It did not feel luxurious to Lobsang. Squashed on a back seat between two others, the thick clothing of all three had wedged them into a sweaty stasis which no amount of polite jostling could bring any comfort to. The car was old and reeked of dirty petrol fumes; the suspension was either damaged or absent, and every pothole on the road sent jolts of pain into Lobsang's knees. He found himself remembering the truck his family had hidden inside during their flight from Lhasa, the little den he had made amongst the crates and plastic sheeting and the folds of his mother's skirts, and this led him to remember his mother. Had it really been three years since she had died? And had it really been seventeen since Dorje had died, transforming his mother into the bedbound ghost she became? It surprised him that he could still remember so vividly how his mother had once been – so loving, so playful, so merry, so pretty – and he found release from the journey's discomfort by thinking about that young Dolkar, his mother, for the rest of the way.

When they arrived at the limits of the Sagarmatha National Park, the sun had risen. Stepping from the cars and shouldering their belongings, the thirteen Tibetans followed their single Nepali guide up and along the zigzagging mud paths of a small and terraced village. The local men who passed them offered them fruits and dried meats from the sacks they carried on their bicycles or backs; the local women smiled and called out to them in a dialect Lobsang could not understand.

'They like to see Tibetans going in this direction, going home,' the guide explained to Lobsang. 'They're not so friendly on the way back.'

Lobsang had fallen into step with the guide for the other Tibetans rarely spoke to him. Eye contact was allowed, as was a smile, a nod, a greeting and perhaps one or two cursory sentences, but communication ended there. They were a close group, all family, from a town no bigger than a village, and Lobsang knew it would take them some time to trust him, that they perhaps even suspected him of being a spy, and so he refrained from any meaningful conversation pieces such as the whens, hows and whys of their exile.

'Up up up,' the guide muttered. 'This is the worst bit. Thousands of metres we have to climb. Coming back is much easier.'

Lobsang craned his neck back to take in the vast mountain range before him: a skyline of shark's teeth; a barrier as impassable as an ocean. It seemed illogical to even contemplate walking over it.

'How long will it take us?' Lobsang asked.

'If we're lucky,' the guide replied, 'two weeks.'

Two weeks? Lobsang had imagined it as perhaps three or four days, not an entire fortnight, and that was if they were *lucky*. Plus, following that, he then had to walk all the way to Lhasa. By the time he arrived, it would be winter. A plane flew high overhead, its white trail settling over the Himalayas like a plume of spindrift. Lobsang watched it disappear behind the serrated horizon and felt resentment deep in his bones.

It took them all day to reach the snowline and, once there, they set up camp below it. The guide disappeared while the Tibetans collapsed to the ground and rubbed their feet, returning an hour later with enough wood for a healthy fire.

'Our last fire until we cross the mountains!' the guide intoned, raising his arms to celebrate the flames.

This seemed absurd to Lobsang. 'Why can't we have fires up there? Surely it'll be much colder and we'll need it at night.'

'No fuel in the snow,' the guide replied.

'We can gather some here before we leave in the morning. If we share it between us all we can carry enough to last us.'

'Fires mark us out. The mountains are crawling with guards. At night, they look out for flames, by day they look out for smoke.'

The guide explained how things would have to change once they stepped into the Himalayas. This would be their last long sleep. During the day, they would break every two hours for a one-hour rest; during the night they would break every hour for ten minutes. Any sleep they got would have to be snatched during these breaks. It was too dangerous to remain still for any longer without shelter: that was how people froze to death. They should eat small amounts regularly whilst also ensuring that they rationed their food to last them until they arrived in Tibet where they could buy more. Any belongings not absolutely necessary should be discarded here for their weight would soon become a glaring burden once in the mountains. Fingers, toes and – here he looked at the men – genitals should be checked regularly for frostbite. They were likely to be stricken by altitude sickness and they were also likely to recover from it, but if any of them needed to turn back they were welcome to, though they would not get a refund and he would not accompany them unless the whole group wished to turn back. As the fire waned, Lobsang curled up inside his *chuba* and listened to the guide explain why they should all remain as close together as possible. Slowly, he drifted into sleep, and the guide's descriptions of hidden crevasses, the insidious creeping of snow-blindness, and the damning and relentless cold, all melded together to colour his dreams.

The group set off into the snow the next morning on an ascent which lasted days, though Lobsang soon lost track of how many. He grew suspicious of time, did not trust it, for the short bursts of walking followed by the even shorter bursts of rest – most of which brought a fitful and unsatisfying sleep – made him feel like he was living his life on fast-forward. He had imagined that, when he saw Drolma again, he would boast of his time in the mountains, of the glory of his journey and the splendour and beauty of his surroundings, but – in reality – he was consumed by the treachery of this frozen world, and he loathed it. The peaks which loomed above him seemed to threaten to crash down on to his head at any given moment; the glaciers beneath his feet would swallow him whole if he stopped for too long; the monotony of snow everywhere was sending him mad; the act of walking for eighteen hours a day filled him with an exhaustion which was only surpassed by the fear of freezing to death; the ever-increasing altitude left him reeling from fits of dizziness; and then there was the cold, which plummeted and plummeted to he did not know how many degrees below zero, which rode the wind and pierced his clothes, which settled on his eyebrows and froze them solid, and which numbed him so thoroughly that he seemed to lose the ability to think.

He was grateful for his guide's sartorial advice: the *chuba* which had seemed such a burden in Kathmandu was appropriately thick up here in the snow and could double as a sleeping bag during the moments of rest, and he could not have imagined this walk without his shoes, his sunglasses and his hat. Yet he still developed blisters on the soles of his feet, sunburnt and cracking skin across his face beneath the rim of his hat and a permanent squint against the blinding white even through his glasses. His *chuba* was good, but he would have gladly worn three more. It was not, by any definition, *warm*.

A morning arrived, a bright and fresh morning which Lobsang guessed was a Thursday, though he could not be sure. The snow seemed extra hard underfoot, the air crisper.

The Tibetans had been walking for over three hours and, their body clocks already attuned to the expedition's timetable, were beginning to complain that it was time to rest. The guide, however, urged them on.

'Just a little further,' he called from the front. 'I want to show you something.'

Lobsang took a tube of processed meat from the many which lined his pockets, split it open and gnawed at it as they walked. He, too, craved a rest period, but he was intrigued by the guide's determination to continue. Over a ridge, in a thin valley between two cliff-like walls stood a cairn of *mani*-stones amongst a web of prayer flags. The guide walked beyond it, turned back to face his group, waited until they reached him, raised his arms into the air and called out: 'Welcome back to Tibet!'

It was the border: the Nangpa La pass. Lobsang looked at his companions, some of whom had fallen to the snowy ground to pray or to laugh. He felt a sense of familiarity with the scene. Had this been where he crossed the border at the age of five? He did not know, for he could barely remember the journey. Chogyal could have told him, but the door which led back to his family had in the last few moments become more firmly shut than ever before.

Somehow, the going became easier from there on. The first stretch was a welcome descent from the Nangpa La peak which some of the younger Tibetans ran gleefully down, passing far ahead of the guide. The sun felt warmer during the days, and the wind at night seemed to drop as they walked beneath the light of the stars. The other Tibetans grew more relaxed around him, and one in particular began to walk with him as they passed under the shadow of Mount Everest.

Her name was Pema: she was both pretty and overweight, and she reminded Lobsang of those women he had seen in India with their proud bellies bulging out over their saris. Lobsang had at first wondered if she would survive the strenuous journey, but she had proved herself to be as strong and as reliable as anyone else there. She was a little younger than Lobsang, and he suspected that she might have a crush on him. He made sure to mention Drolma whenever he could, but this made Pema fawn over him even more, for she thought that his walking over mountains to reclaim his love was the most romantic thing she had ever heard. Nevertheless, she was good company, and Lobsang enjoyed her conversation as they pushed farther into their homeland, crossing the rivers and streams which had started to pop up between the stone and ice.

'Do you remember much about Tibet?' she asked him the morning they were due to descend from the Himalayas on to flat Tibetan plains.

'Not much at all,' he admitted. 'There are a few photos up in here –' he pointed to his head ' – of my old house, my old street. But, mostly, when I think about Tibet I think about my mother and my brother.'

Pema nodded silently. Lobsang had not told her his history, but she guessed that his mother and brother had died. She knew many Tibetans in Kathmandu and each of them had lost at least one close relative.

'What about you?' asked Lobsang. 'Any memories?'

'Me?' Pema appeared startled by the question. 'No, I was born in Kathmandu. This is my first time in Tibet.'

'OK,' Lobsang replied, 'so how does *that* feel? The first time here?'

Pema looked about her at the brown wilderness, the cloud-cased sky, the mountains shrinking behind them and, in front of them, growing slowly closer and larger, several clustering herds of yaks. 'My mother said it would change my life, that I would finally feel at home, that I hadn't known what home felt like yet.'

'And do you?' Lobsang asked.

Pema put her hands to her two plaits, one per hand, and tugged gently at the cords of hair. She breathed the thin air in deep, and then sighed hard. 'No,' she finally said, before changing the subject and demanding more information on Drolma.

There was no road from where they left the Himalayas to Tingri, and so the group spent the next three days walking through a sky-wide expanse of rocky desert. The guide allowed them longer rest stops, particularly at night, and even treated them to a fire made from yak dung which he scooped from the ground, but the group found themselves less inclined to rest now that the end was so close in sight. This was due in part to their dwindling food supplies. Few had paid attention to the guide's rationing advice at the start of the journey, and those who had eaten all their own food were now dependent upon what remained of others'. The encroaching hunger spurred them on, and before long they arrived in Tingri to, Lobsang noticed, no fanfare whatsoever. Quietly and one by one, they slipped off into houses where the celebrations could begin clandestinely behind closed doors and away from prying eyes.

Lobsang was offered a bed for the night before he continued on his journey alone. He gratefully accepted the lodging as well as the abundance of food that came with it which, he guessed, was the doing of Pema, who did not leave his side all evening. When she came to him in the middle of the night, he felt guilty for turning her away, but she only giggled and whispered something he did not catch before tottering back to her own bed.

His many pockets were filled with food the next morning as he prepared to leave, and all twelve of the Tibetans he had crossed the mountains with – some of whom he had not exchanged one word with along the way – appeared in the street to give him an emotional and heartfelt send-off. Pema did not cry, though her mother did, and the guide found the whole situation immensely funny.

'The local celebrity,' he laughed. 'The wandering hero, ready to face anything to bring back his lost love.'

'I'm not bringing her back,' Lobsang corrected him. 'I'm staying in Lhasa with her.'

'That's if you make it there,' the guide said, laughter fading into solemnity. 'You need to be *very* careful, you know. The Himalayas were dangerous, but the road to Lhasa is dangerous for different reasons. Stay as far away from checkpoints as you can, even if it means taking a whole day to circle around them. And any time you see a vehicle coming towards you, get down on the ground and prostrate, even if it's not a military or police vehicle. Don't expect to get to Lhasa quickly. You won't. And don't talk to anyone, because you sound more like me than like these people.'

Lobsang thanked him for the advice and vowed to stick to it. The guide's suggestions had proved invaluable for the Himalaya crossing, and Lobsang saw no reason why his tips for the rest of the journey should not be considered as equally important. Tying the *chuba* tightly around his waist with one of the sleeves and pulling his hat down over his hair, Lobsang bid one final farewell to his companions before setting off on the road to Lhasa, his steps light and his countenance bold and blithe.

It did not take him long to realise how woefully underprepared he was. His legs and his heart had grown strong from the mountains and so following the undulations of a highway were easy, and he had enough food secreted around his person to last him two weeks; but he had not brought nearly enough water, and the materials he had gathered in Kathmandu to guide him along were lacking. He had a number of maps of the regions the Friendship Highway passed through, which he had printed off from websites and photocopied out of guidebooks, as well as what he considered to be his core text for the journey: a hand-drawn map of the road which showed the location of every single checkpoint between Lhasa and Zhangmu and which listed out the distances between each. This map had cost him a lot of money in Kathmandu.

What Lobsang had not brought along, however, what he had not even considered the necessity of until he was firmly posited within the Tibetan plateau, was a compass by which he could direct himself away from and back to the road again to avoid checkpoints, or any kind of device by which he could measure distance, thus rendering his maps fairly useless and leaving him perpetually unsure of exactly how far behind or ahead of him each checkpoint was.

It was the lack of both these items that caused Lobsang – not two days after leaving Tingri – to become hopelessly lost. After spotting a shape on the horizon that he assumed to be a checkpoint, he set off what he assumed to be north for what he assumed to be about six miles, arcing around towards what he assumed to be the east for another six miles to meet back with what he assumed to be the road. He had no idea whether it was one of his assumptions which had been incorrect or all. A panic set in and, for two hours, he darted about in erratic directions, changing angles like a bluebottle, at times trying to retrace his steps and at others trying to broach new ground, but he never retrieved his goal, the road, and soon had lost all perspective of where it could possibly be or, more importantly, where he could possibly be in relation to it. Resolving that resolve was needed, he picked a single point on the horizon and began to walk towards it. He had no idea that the point he had chosen lay in entirely the opposite direction to the road, and even less idea that, a few miles beyond that point, a Tibetan mastiff would catch his scent on the wind.

Hero Town

|

'Becoming a Buddhist is like finding gold', Tashi said. 'You must study it deeply to make sure it is real. If you do not think it is real, you throw it away. It is the same with Buddhism. You must study it. And if you do not think it is real, it is not for you, then you should look elsewhere. You can be Christian, that is OK. You can be Muslim, and that is OK, too. You have had many, many lives, and you will have many, many lives. Perhaps in one of these, you will study Buddhism, and you will see it is right for you. Perhaps it will happen in this life, perhaps here, in Tibet. But that is up to you.'

We had stopped a few miles outside of Gyantse at a *Petro Bluesky* service station. While Dawa filled up, Tashi had walked away from the forecourt to smoke a cigarette. His habit seemed to increase the further we got from Lhasa. I had sauntered behind him, looking for conversation.

'Why aren't you a monk?' I asked.

'You do not have to be a monk to be a Buddhist.'

'But why did you choose not to enter a monastery when you were young?'

'I did not choose. My parents sent me to China to learn instead. But I am glad for it. My grandfather's brother was a monk. He died last year with no wife or children, no house and no money. I do not want that life this time. One day I will be reborn and *will* want that life. Then I will become a monk. But now I am enjoying this world too much.'

'You sound like me. Maybe you will always enjoy this world too much.'

Tashi flicked his cigarette on to the tarmac of the road where, free of squashing traffic, it smouldered to the butt and then blew off into some scrub on the light breeze. He lit another, and crouched low.

'This is a good story,' he said, exhaling smoke from his mouth and sucking it back up through his nostrils. 'A shepherd and a lama both lived on the same hill. The lama spent every day and every night on top of the hill meditating. The shepherd spent his days lower down the hill with his sheep. Every day, he killed a sheep to sell or to eat himself. After one thousand days, the shepherd suddenly realised he had killed one thousand sheep, and was horrified. 'I have taken the lives of a thousand innocent animals,' he thought. 'I am a bad person.' Thinking this, he walked to the top of the hill next to where the lama sat meditating, and threw himself off the hill to his death. At the moment of his death, he was suddenly enlightened, and he achieved Buddhahood. The lama saw all this and was confused. 'This shepherd has spent his days killing animals and has become enlightened,' he thought. 'While I have meditated for a thousand days and have not become enlightened.' He decided the shepherd must have achieved Buddhahood by throwing himself off the hill. He desired the same, and so he copied the shepherd, jumping from the hill and falling to his death. He was reborn as a sheep.'

Flicking his current cigarette in the same direction as the former, Tashi smiled at the ground, stood, and walked back to the Landcruiser.

2

From a distance, Gyantse looked like a Peloponnesian town: arid and brown, set at the foot of gentle mountains with its own acropolis and an elevated fortress. A troop of dusty labourers worked on the roadside with rusting tools, and one peered up at the passing Landcruiser from beneath his fading red cap, across which was emblazoned: 'I love U'.

I was looking forward to Gyantse. The further we travelled from Lhasa, the more Tibetan the country became, and the less Chinese. No one I knew had heard of Gyantse, for the images one pictures when imagining Tibet are often Lhasan. Even the cover of Sun Shuyun's book, *A Year in Tibet*, which documents the author's twelve months in Gyantse, is illustrated with a photograph of the Potala Palace. Nevertheless, Gyantse has its own share of architectural icons. It was the third-largest town in Tibet for most of the past five hundred years, thanks to its integral position on the trade routes between Tibet and India, Sikkim and Bhutan. Yet today it has been surpassed by at least ten other Tibetan cities, and remains, by any standards, tiny – little more than a village nestled in the Nyang-chu valley at the base of a low, protective mountain. A high wall creeps up the spine of the mountain, culminating at the top in the fourteenth-century fort, or *dzong*. Directly below it sits a beautiful and pyramidal Buddhist temple, or *kumbum*, built in the shape of a tiered *chorten*, which reminded me of Indonesia's ancient Borobudur.

'You know, Charlie,' Tashi said as we entered the town, turning around in his seat and shouting over at me. 'The British were very bad here. You have heard of Colonel Younghusband? He killed many Tibetans.'

For once, it had not been the Chinese who had done the greatest disservice to a Tibetan enclave. It was, in fact, the British; and the atrocities committed by them in the early twentieth century are remembered to this day. For the locals, Gyantse still retains the colloquial moniker: 'Hero Town'. There is an 'Anti-British Museum' here.

In 1903, Lord Curzon, the British viceroy of India, set his sights upon the previously impenetrable plateau. Reacting to disputable intelligence that the Russians had their eye on Tibet, Curzon struck the next move in 'The Great Game', commissioning Francis Younghusband – an intrepid military explorer already famed for his expeditions into Manchuria, Ladakh and Turkestan – to invade the country and march on Lhasa, where it was hoped he would encourage the thirteenth Dalai Lama to sign a treaty with the British. Younghusband entered Tibet from India in 1904, taking with him a 3,000-strong army, 7,000 servants and 4,000 yaks.

When the Tibetan government in Lhasa got wind of Britain's intentions, it sent its own army division south to meet Younghusband and stop him. The two platoons met a hundred miles south of Gyantse, at Chumik Shenko. The Tibetans, armed with matchlock rifles, knives and trinkets blessed by the holiest throughout the land, advanced upon the imperialists, assured that their victory was preordained by the gods. Most wore talismans which they believed would protect them from bullets. The British opened fire from their machine guns, killing 628 Tibetans and wounding 222 in less than four minutes. The Tibetans, confounded by the kind of firepower they had never before experienced, became doubly confused when the British then set up temporary hospitals to tend to their wounded, and buried their dead for them (the Tibetans later unearthed the cadavers and gave them a proper sky burial).

Younghusband advanced on Gyantse, where he and a division of Gurkhas massacred thousands of Tibetans and shelled the *dzong*, commenting at one point, 'It is great sport.' Tibet's spiritual army was no match for the greatest empire on earth, and Younghusband continued from Gyantse to Lhasa, where he was met with applause. What he did not know at the time was that, when Tibetans clap their hands, it is not an expression of commendation, but of disapproval.

What he also did not realise was that the thirteenth Dalai Lama had fled to Mongolia – the only time a Dalai Lama has exiled himself from Lhasa due to a Western power – and was not present to sign the treaty Curzon was demanding. Younghusband stayed in Lhasa for the next month, eventually convincing the Tibetan regent to sign Curzon's treaty, and commandeering the renowned Lhalu House (one of the most opulent country estates around Lhasa) as his headquarters. During this time, the London newspapers – effusive with praise for the empire's latest conquest – christened Lhalu House 'Younghusband House', the Potala Palace 'Windsor Castle', and the Barkhor *kora* 'Piccadilly Circus'.

Tibet never became part of the British Empire, but it became a close ally, accepting and accommodating British representatives for the next five decades, and then despairing when their supposed ally stood back and offered no support as China invaded in the 1950s. Such was the double-edged sword of British influence, manifested especially by Colonel Francis Younghusband and his murderous expedition on to the roof of the world.

But perhaps Younghusband had his comeuppance of sorts. On the eve of his departure from Lhasa, he experienced a moment of profound philosophical transformation, deciding then and there that his life no longer lay in the military, but in spiritualism. Twenty years after his arrival in Tibet, he renounced the army, becoming instead a mystic who believed all humans were controlled by cosmic rays from divine beings on a planet called Altair, and who spent his November years writing weird books with titles like *Life in the Stars: An Exposition of the View that on some Planets of some Stars exist Beings higher than Ourselves, and on one a World-Leader, the Supreme Embodiment of the Eternal Spirit which animates the Whole.* Some call his Lhasa moment an epiphany; I prefer to think of it as a fracturing of the mind. But whatever strange literary output it may have afforded, it at least led to one positive outcome. Francis Younghusband came to regret his invasion of Tibet, an invasion which led to the deaths of some three thousand Tibetans in and around Gyantse for the sake of a piece of paper.

3

I stood atop the highest level of the *kumbum*, gazing down from over 100 feet at the streets of Gyantse below, and then wended my slow way down the spiralling concourse which encircled the temple. The walkway passed doors which led to single-room chapels where paintings of monstrous deities leered out from the gloom. The contrast between the interior and exterior was startling: inside, all seemed to be mauve and varying shades of black, while outside the fierce sun bounced off the white and gold walls, sending my pupils into whorling kaleidoscopes of confused expansion and contraction.

I left the *chorten* in a daze, bumbling down Gyantse's streets and narrowly avoiding the stray dogs flat on their sides and asleep in the pounding sun. They sprawled out in clusters upon the road, twitching with dreams, and ignorant of the few cars and tractors which bore down upon them, knowing perhaps that, no matter how violently the horns sounded, the drivers would always swerve to avoid them, for no devout Tibetan Buddhist will ever willingly take a life, no matter what form it manifests itself in. These dogs were not mastiffs, but the lean mixed-blood mongrels which fill the developing world's streets like pigeons, belonging to no one. One shuffled towards me and I knelt down to stroke her scarred head. She was calm and amiable, had to be, for she, like all the street dogs there, lived off the charitable scraps of shopkeepers and pedestrians. Seeing that my strokes came without the promise of food, she pushed her crusty nose into my palm one last time, and then collapsed in a shard of sunlight which spread from the gap between two houses, encasing her closed eyes in her front paws, and snoring noisily within seconds.

'You like dogs?'

I turned from the mongrel to look at the man addressing me. He was tall for a Tibetan, and wore jeans and a shirt with three buttons missing. The faint trace of a moustache hunkered above his lips: the bumfluff of one of my Year 11 students, though he was well into his forties.

'I do,' I replied.

'Dogs are nice. I have one. A Tibetan mastiff. He cost me many dollars. But he will be a good friend to my son.'

'How old is your son?'

'I do not have a son yet. But when I do my dog will be his dog. His protector. I am Sonam.' He held one hand out for me to shake; with the other he wiped his thin, black fringe out of his eyes. 'And you are, I think, British.'

I nodded.

'So you are like Colonel Younghusband,' he said.

'And you are the hero,' I replied.

He laughed. 'No, I am not a hero. Would you like to drink?'

'Absolutely.'

'Good. We will go to my cousin's bar. He has Lhasa beer. The best.'

Sonam led me out and around the base of Gyantse's solitary mountain until we progressed on to a multi-laned highway which fed into a fenced-off roundabout, out of which protruded a tall, steel pole holding a striped red-and-white platform with a camera which denoted the speed of each passing vehicle via foot-high digital numbers. A small and dirty tractor towing an empty trailer spluttered along the road, and the speed camera clocked up the number 3.

Sonam took in my incredulous gaze. 'Ah, it is not so bad,' he said. 'At night, many of the young boys ride their motorbikes too fast here. This helps to stop them. Look.' He pointed to the tall concrete plinth which presided over the roundabout, its front daubed in red Mandarin characters. 'The Monument to People's Heroes,' he said.

'Chinese?' I asked.

'Of course. Tibetans would never build something that...' he sought for the word, '... that *shape*.'

Clean and bright, it stood like a phallic dagger thrust into the heart of Gyantse: as striking and alien here as all its counterparts across the country; the ugly symbols of Chinese and Communist rule in a Tibetan and Buddhist land.

We came to Sonam's cousin's bar: one of a line of terraced white and red Tibetan buildings, indistinguishable from the outside as anything different to the homes it lay between. Sonam ordered two pint-bottles of beer from the teenager behind the bar, and then took them over to a corner table while I paid. Three Tibetan men in their fifties sat silently at the table next to the one Sonam had chosen. There was no one else there.

'They cannot understand English,' Sonam told me, noticing my looks at them.

'But you do,' I said. 'Very well.'

'I am a businessman. English is the language of business.'

'Not Mandarin?'

'What?'

'Not Chinese?'

'I speak Chinese, too. Better than English.' He launched a volley of Mandarin at me, and I noticed the three men to my right stiffen. 'Look at me,' Sonam said. 'I am not Chinese. I am Tibetan. You can see this.'

I had imbibed little beer since the train into Lhasa and, matching Sonam for each of his gulps, my first went down quickly. Sonam ordered another round. I paid again. Halfway through the second pint-bottle, I was feeling drunk already, and Sonam noticed.

'It's the altitude,' I explained. 'I'm not used to it.'

'Maybe the altitude. Maybe the Lhasa beer. It is good for you. Strong. Being drunk is OK. I like it.'

'Yeah,' I admitted. 'So do I.'

'But *chang* is better. The traditional Tibetan beer.'

'Why aren't we drinking *chang* now?'

'*Chang* is for families. Inside the house. Tonight I will drink *chang* with my father. At home. When I am the father, I will invite you to my house to drink *chang*. Now, I cannot.'

'Why?'

'You would not be welcome.'

'Because I'm British?'

'No. Because you are a foreigner.'

Sonam lit a cigarette, and his eyes grew rheumy. 'Another?' he asked.

'No,' I said.

Sonam stood from his chair and lurched towards the bar for a third beer. With it came a large shot of something brown and cloudy, and Sonam drained it in one swift motion. He came back to our table with the fresh bottle of beer swinging from his hand. He was suddenly and perceptibly drunk.

'My mother's father, you see,' he said, 'he was part of the Tibet government. When the Cultural Revolution...' his English was beginning to fracture, '...when the Cultural Revolution, his job was taken. He was given a white hat. Had to wear it everywhere.' He took a long draft of his beer, four or five gulps, and then his voice quietened. 'He had a large house, and many possessions. They were all taken. All. In days, he was begging on the streets with my mother's mother.'

He drank more. I was both enthralled by and fearful of the change which had transformed his countenance from smiling to dour in a matter of minutes. 'But my father's father,' he continued. 'My father's father. He joined the Chinese army.'

'What did he do?' I asked.

Sonam looked at me, took a long, final swig from his bottle, and then knocked it to the floor. 'He joined the Chinese army,' he said again.

In the space of three beers (and a swift shot), Sonam had transformed. He had become irascible and foul-tempered. He had become drunk. I sympathised with his bitterness, with the righteous anger which intoxicated him far more than the alcohol he had consumed, but the rancour which flowed from him left me both uncomfortable and ashamed of it. I made my excuses and left, though it didn't matter. Sonam wasn't listening. Walking out the door, I turned to see him move from our table to sit with the three silent men. His presence went unregistered.

chu

Lobsang knew the stories about these dogs. They were just one step away from the call of the wild: as strong as wolves and as reckless. They would die in defence of their pack, whether it was canine or human, and they would kill for it, too. This particular mastiff had not yet bared its teeth, but it was on its feet, its fur and back and tail were up, and its eyes had not left Lobsang. Frozen to the spot, he felt as if his body had calcified. The dog's shrill growls which fluctuated between a guttural roar and a flat whine drifted across the three hundred feet between them. Lobsang's inability to move was perhaps the only reason the dog had not advanced.

The black cone of the nomad tent stretched up behind the dog, the only living creature visible. Lobsang thought he could hear the sound of a radio and, once, a woman's voice, soft but insistent. He dared not call out to announce himself for fear the dog would take this as a cue to launch, though he longed for water, directions and conversation. He wondered if, were he to approach the tent, whoever was inside would hear his cries and call the dog off him before it inflicted any lasting damage. He did not have the courage to try.

Feeling miserable, he began to slowly step backwards. The mastiff seemed to approve, for its growling lowered and then ceased. This was a reprieve Lobsang knew he was lucky to get: had there been other dogs present they would have gladly attacked him as a club the moment he was spotted.

Another noise floated towards him. It sounded like the dog, but there was something unnatural about it, something mechanical. Taking his eyes from the mastiff for the first time since he had seen it, he turned to observe the speck of a motorbike as it danced across the desert void towards him. The growing noise of the bike and the presence of Lobsang sent the dog into excited confusion, and it began to charge in circles around the tent. A woman and a young girl appeared from the tent's doorway. When the girl spotted Lobsang, she darted back inside again, but the woman remained at the doorway, ample hands on ample hips.

The motorbike came to a stop alongside Lobsang. The rider did not wear a helmet, and Lobsang could see that they were roughly the same age. The rider smiled and launched a volley of questions at Lobsang, who could barely answer each before the next exploded from the lips of this excitable young man. Finally, Lobsang was afforded enough time to explain that he was on his way to Lhasa and had become lost, and this seemed to satisfy the man, for he grabbed Lobsang by the elbow and ushered him past the yelping dog and inside the tent, where he insisted Lobsang drink *chang* and eat stew with him. The woman silently placed yak-dung on the fire; the little girl had hidden somewhere.

'I'm very grateful for your hospitality, but all I need are directions back to the road,' Lobsang said, feeling uncomfortably caught between the young man's loud attention and the older woman's quiet hostility.

'Don't be silly!' the man barked. 'You won't get back to the road tonight. It will be dark in a few hours. You must stay with us tonight. Here, have some more *chang*. Drink with me.'

His name was Nyima. The older woman was his mother and the young girl his sister. They lived in the tent with the rest of their family – a large web of uncles, aunts, cousins and grandparents – but their particular nuclear unit had been chosen to stay behind with the tent while the rest went to a large festival some three hundred miles to the west. This caused Nyima a great deal of anger and resentment: since his father had died, he often felt that he, his mother and sister were excluded from many of the family's affairs. It would have been easier if his mother had remarried one of the men her own age who lived in the tent, but she could not, for they were her brothers.

'I don't think she likes me,' Lobsang whispered to Nyima when his mother left the tent to go to the toilet. 'She hasn't spoken to me once.'

'And she won't,' Nyima replied, laughing. 'Why would she like you? She would have been fine if you were just an average pilgrim, but you're *dangerous*. Walking over the mountains to get back *into* Tibet. Who does that?'

'Plenty of people.'

'None I've heard of.'

'I won't be any trouble.'

'That's not what I mean. You think she's worried about that? No one's going to come all the way out here to check up on you. No, she's worried about you being a bad influence. You could put ideas in my head.'

'Ideas?'

'She may not be talking to you, but she's listening. She's heard you talk about your Drolma, about what you've done and what you're going to do to get her back, about all the world you've seen so far. It's exciting stuff.'

'So is it putting ideas into your head?'

'Just one. But it doesn't include leaving my mother and sister. I will never do that.'

'What's the idea?'

'I'll tell you later. First, let's have another drink.'

Nyima was right: his mother did not speak to Lobsang for the rest of the night, and he never saw that little girl again, though he sometimes thought he heard her skulking about the edges of the tent's yak-hair walls. The two young men were left alone, and they used the opportunity to drink far more *chang* than they should have.

'So my idea,' Nyima finally said, and it startled Lobsang somewhat because he had drunkenly forgotten that there had ever been such a thing, 'is about you and Lhasa.'

'Me and Lhasa,' Lobsang slurred.

'You're doing it wrong. If you keep on the way you are, trying to walk around the checkpoints, getting lost at every second one and only finding your way back again because some nomads took pity on you, if you keep on like that you'll never get to Lhasa. You need help, my friend, and I can give you that help.'

He outlined his idea. With Lobsang riding pillion on his motorbike, Nyima could take him all the way to Lhasa. They would go off-road (Nyima knew the way, he had done it a number of times before) which meant they could avoid any police or military checkpoints between here and the city. If they left early enough in the morning, Nyima was certain they could make it to Lhasa in the space of just one day. It would be far quicker and far safer. Lobsang thought it was a marvellous idea and said so.

'Of course, you'll need to pay for the fuel to get there, and perhaps a small fee for me,' Nyima said.

'No problem,' Lobsang replied, his head swimming from the combination of alcohol and the possibility that he might see Drolma the following day. 'I've got plenty of money.'

'Have you?'

'Loads. I made sure of that when I left. How much will you need?'

'We can decide that tomorrow,' Nyima replied. 'If we want to leave early enough, we should go to sleep now.' And, with an abruptness which surprised Lobsang, Nyima did.

The next morning, clutching on to Nyima's waist while the motorbike bounced painfully through the dark, Lobsang's sense slowly came back to him. Had he really, he questioned himself, given Nyima *all* his money?

Nyima had woken him with a soft kick to his back. Lobsang, eyes crusty and head throbbing with a high-altitude hangover, pulled himself up into a sitting position.

'We need to leave now,' Nyima said. Lobsang marvelled at how fresh he looked. 'How much money do you have?'

Without thinking, Lobsang took the entire wad of *yuan* notes from his *chuba* and held them out. Nyima took it all.

'That should do,' he said. 'Come on, let's go.'

Lobsang obediently followed Nyima out of the tent and climbed on to the back of the motorbike, which roared into life at a kick of the foot and a twist of the wrist.

As sobriety began its resurfacing act, Lobsang looked back over the last twelve hours through glasses of a different colour. Everything seemed suspect to him now. Perhaps Nyima's hospitality was nothing more than a means to ensnare him and perhaps he had been plied with *chang* to make him suggestible. The frequent mentions of the military vehicles seen on the road, the careful avoidance of outlining his grand idea until Lobsang was well and truly drunk, the demand for money when Lobsang was at his most vulnerable and compliant – all this pointed to a manipulation on the part of his host which first made Lobsang angry and then made him paranoid. What if Nyima wasn't taking him to Lhasa? What if he was taking him further out into the wilderness where he would deposit him, alone and penniless? What if his intentions were baser? What if he was going to kill Lobsang, murder him in cold blood somewhere out in the Tibetan plateau where nobody would ever find his corpse? Was that why Nyima's mother had been so quiet? Had she known what was going to happen? Had Nyima done this before?

During the times when the bike veered towards and then on to a road and into a garage for a fuel top-up, Lobsang considered running from Nyima and hiding himself until this new and mortal enemy of his left. But he did not. Rationality bubbled beneath his paranoia, and he knew that, as much as he resented and feared Nyima, he was his only chance. With no money left, he would never make it to Lhasa alone. He had to trust in the man who had ripped him off so effectively.

Nyima did not speak to Lobsang for the whole journey, confirming Lobsang's impression that he had only ever been interested in the promise of money, but he kept to his word nonetheless, and Lobsang disembarked the bike on the limits of the city.

'Good luck with finding your Drolma,' was all Nyima said before he sped off back towards his tent, his mother and sister.

Lhasa. Lobsang had not noticed the city's approach from the bike: his view had been filled by the back of Nyima's head. And, even now, he saw only one thing, the Potala Palace, which rose up from the mire of urbanity and left him aching with emotions he did not have the language for. Feeling both timid and dizzy, Lobsang started to walk towards the Potala, for he knew from her thousand descriptions to him in their Delhi bed, when he would urge her to talk about Lhasa, exactly where Drolma's district lay in relation to the palace. He could ask directions to her house once he got to the district, he thought, pulling a scrap of crumpled paper with her address written across it from a pocket.

Walking the city's streets, following the Potala like a lodestar, Lobsang recognised nothing. It seemed like a skin had grown over the Lhasa he remembered. There had been Chinese high-rises when he was a young boy, but these which he ambled between seemed like glass and steel Himalayas; there had been Chinese police and soldiers on the streets, but there seemed even more now, and they were smaller and stockier, little marching bundles of power. At first, he shrank from each uniform as it passed – if just one asked to see his identity card, it would all be over – but when they paid him no heed he grew bolder and began to observe them. The uniforms especially fascinated him with their rainbow of tones from light green to dark blue, each denoting whether this young man was Public Security Bureau, People's Liberation Army,

Lhasa Security or the People's Armed Police. Those in light green walked in pairs, their steps so synchronised and their bodies so close they could have been lovers, and when not walking they stood pencil-straight, feet together, chest out, immaculate in their discipline. The dark greens and the blues seemed more languid and relaxed, leaning against walls and fences, chatting, occasionally stopping passers-by for an invasive but passionless bag-search. Lobsang kept away from these wherever possible.

As the sun passed behind the mountains, the light began to fade and Lobsang knew it would not be long before darkness fell. He hurried on. A lone man wandering the city at night was too conspicuous. He came to Drolma's district. Most of the faces he passed were recognisably Han – this was, as Drolma had explained to him, a Chinese district, after all – but soon he came across a young Tibetan couple who he stopped, enunciating to them in a quiet and careful voice Drolma's address.

They knew it and listed out the five right and left turns he would have to make through the district to find the place. He thanked them, unable to stop a hint of excitement from spilling into his words, and marched along the streets until he found exactly what he was looking for. A door. The correct door. Taking a deep breath, he raised a fist and knocked twice.

Panchen

I

The mistake had not been to drink those beers with Sonam; the mistake had been to continue drinking that evening with Joe at our guesthouse in Gyantse. I woke the next morning to a high-altitude hangover, groaning in the back of the Landcruiser on the way to Shigatse, my body bouncing between fluctuating episodes of jarring headaches, immaculate breathlessness, and fierce attacks of white-hot panic. At Shigatse, Tashi insisted yak-butter tea would make me feel better. It did not.

I needed to walk, to shake off the hangover with exercise. It would be painful, but it would work. With suncream on my arms, sandals on my feet and a large bottle of water in my daypack, I set off into the city.

A long and open-plan market which filled an undeveloped square the size of two football pitches drew me in with the lure of shade from the close sun. I sauntered along beneath the lines of hoisted canvas sheets, so low and drooping that I walked with a perpetual stoop as I passed the rows upon rows of stalls, so many of them selling shoes or fur-lined boots.

The Tibetan keepers behind their tiers of footwear or sweets or hand-tools grinned out at me from their chairs, but few tried to entice me in like they had on Lhasa's Barkhor, and the jovial but reserved atmosphere here was closer to that of London's east than the world's. I spied a pair of slippers just right as a gift for one of my brothers, and used my sparse knowledge of Tibetan to attempt a bout of haggling with the seller. He laughed when I suggested a price 100 yuan below the one he had set and then walked off to drink a cup of tea with one of his neighbours. I paid the full price, and he offered me some tea, laughing when I took the proffered cup, and then attempting to sell me a pair of bright red trainers.

Leaving the market, I opted to walk the mile or so to the Tashilhunpo monastery. Shigatse is only about a quarter of the size of Lhasa, but it maintains its city feel with floods of traffic, convoys of Chinese tourists, and sprawling and increasingly affluent blocks of new developments which push outwards from the crescent of wood-brown mountains hovering protectively over the Tibetan quarter. Its roads are wide and well paved, its pavements busy and populated with grocery stores, Internet cafes, bars and restaurants whose exterior blackboards announce global cuisines in Tibetan, Mandarin and English. Street dogs lurch anxiously in the hidden alleyways, nervous cousins to the lazy Gyantse mongrels or proud nomadic mastiffs, terrified of the feet and wheels which fill the main thoroughfares with rapid charges. There seemed to be an absence of children and birds in Shigatse and, with that, an absence of song and delight. Instead, each passing face appeared grim and hurried, and for a moment I fancied myself in winter-city England.

Detouring out through a park, I bought grey rice from a mobile food stall and ate it on the grass. It was another hot day, devoid of cloud or wind, and I felt my arm-hair blonding in the flushing sun – the perfect day for an afternoon in the park with friends or a book; but the few souls who traipsed the slim concrete path did not stop, and where there should have been birdsong to send the weary traveller to sleep and children's screams of play to wake him up again, there was only the noisy throb of traffic drifting over from the main road, punctuated by the claps of backfiring engines. A straight-backed man in an olive uniform ambled in a wide circle around me, stopping far enough away so that I could not work out if he was police, PLA, PSB, or any of the myriad acronyms which I was growing tired of trying to remember. I waved at him, and he shifted his gaze to the horizon, staying in position. Rising from the ground, I walked towards him to say hello, but he casually sauntered away so that the same distance remained fixed between us. It would have made a pleasant game, I thought, to idly pursue this man for the next few hours and waste his afternoon, but in doing so I would suffer the same consequences.

2

Built in 1447 by the first Dalai Lama, Genden Drup, the Tashilhunpo monastery later transformed Shigatse into Tibet's second city when the great fifth Dalai Lama, Lobsang Gyatso, nominated the first Panchen Lama in the mid 1600s and instructed that Tashilhunpo be his Potala for eternity.

Since then, Tashilhunpo grew in size and importance, and it has been one of the few monasteries in Tibet to escape the all-pervading destruction of the Cultural Revolution and the Red Guards. Today, Tashilhunpo remains as huge as it has ever been, and is similar in design to Drepung in Lhasa and Longwu in Repkong: a town of temples and monks' quarters cut through by narrow, dusty pathways where protruding and uneven paving slabs poke from the dirt, inscribed with Tibetan characters, polished by the slippers of a million monks, and weathered by the burning days and frozen nights. Flights of steps connect the paths as they rise up the hill: some cracked into diagonal vertices by natural and dislodging turf; others heavy and flat, but deceptive, so smooth they are as slippery as scree.

There were no signposts or directions at Tashilhunpo, no Ikea-esque footprints emblazoned on the ground to follow. Instead, one meanders like a nomad along the haphazard paths, and I enjoyed the lack of system, ignoring the occasional group of tourists who blindly followed their tour guides if they had them or huddled around printed maps and cross-checked them with the GPS systems on their smartphones if they did not. To get immaculately lost seemed appropriate here, and each dead end revealed a collapsing stable inhabited by skinny goats or chained dogs, leaning *chortens* made of dried mud, or amateur and fading wall-paintings of Sakyamuni. I stumbled up perilous steps into a cul-de-sac of flat-roofed bungalows, each seeming to lean on another, where a boy no older than six sat in red robes poking a tiny black kitten with a stick. The kitten lay on its side, its eyes glassy and its breathing laboured, while its front leg twitched back and forth like an involuntary and mechanical animatronic. Thirty minutes later, I unwittingly arrived back at the same cul-de-sac, and the kitten had died, lying still and in a slim pool of yellow, miry liquid. The young boy sat beside it crying, the stick at his small feet. It was a tiny scene of horror, one which my tour guide Tashi would have guided me away from.

I had with me my guidebook, but I kept it lodged inside my daypack, choosing instead to continue through Tashilhunpo with an aimless yet curious abandon. The lower levels seemed reserved for the single-storey monks' quarters, but as the complex rose towards the mountains which backed it, homes gave way to temples, their golden roofs and plastered walls starkly juxtaposing the simple and collapsing bedrooms and kitchens below. I followed the pilgrims and Chinese tourists up the thin stairways on the left, and then exited along those on the right. Between them were carpeted and wider stairways, but these were only to be ascended or descended by the Dalai Lama or the Panchen Lama, and nobody else used them, not even the monks. Each of the monastery's chapels was confoundingly similar: dark and smoky with incense; signs at the entrance demanding in both Mandarin and English that photography was forbidden; a walkway – in effect, a *kora* – around the centrepiece which, be it a statue, shrine or tomb, was always towering and golden.

The biggest buildings were the prayer-halls, filled with monks who sat on large cushions, pored over scriptures and chanted melodies which jumped and trilled with the musical intervals of the east. Stairways ascended to the balconied tiers which overlooked them, and the vocals of the monks bounced about the rising walls, looping with their own echoes. A ten-foot-long photograph of a plump and smiling face hung above the main hall, the same face – the same picture, in fact – I had seen throughout Tashilhunpo, in Repkong's Longwu monastery, and throughout all Tibet: the face of the tenth Panchen Lama.

3

Secondary only to the Dalai Lama, the Panchen Lama has been one of the most supreme spiritual leaders in Tibet since the fifteenth century. As the Dalai Lama is and always has been the incarnation of Chenresig – the Buddha of Compassion – the Panchen Lama is and always has been the incarnation of Amitabha – the Buddha of Infinite Light. The story of the Panchen Lamas throughout the twentieth century and throughout China's annexation of Tibet is perhaps more fascinating, more suspicious, and more tragic than even the story of the fourteenth Dalai Lama.

In his younger years, the tenth Panchen Lama sided with the Chinese, and it was the PLA who enthroned him in the Tashilhunpo in 1952 to the reluctant approval of the Tibetan delegates. The Chinese installed him as a puppet, a way of controlling the Tibetans through their own religion, and reports filtered through China and Tibet of the Panchen Lama's support for the Communist takeover, with Beijing Radio announcing telegrams sent to Mao by the young Panchen Lama stating such things as: '*On behalf of the Tibetan people, we respectfully plead for troops to be sent to liberate Tibet, to wipe out reactionaries, expel the imperialists and liberate the Tibetan people.'*

For the next ten years, the Panchen Lama remained as an active voice for China within Tibet, spending his time between the two countries, and rallying support for the Chinese and for communism. When the Dalai Lama escaped into exile in 1959, the Panchen Lama was moved to Lhasa where the Chinese authorities hoped that he, as the head of the Preparatory Committee for the Tibetan Autonomous Region, would lead Tibetans into a new Marxist era.

It was around this time, however, that the tenth Panchen Lama began to have doubts about his superiors, about Mao, and about his own role beneath him. Tibetans saw him as a traitor, but he had been young and impressionable, enthroned at the age of eleven, and there was still time for him to make a change. He began clandestinely, asking the Chinese for the restoration of the religious buildings shelled during 1959 and for the return of the religious artefacts removed or stolen at the same time. His public speeches and teachings began to contain implications and insinuations that the true spiritual leader of Tibet was the departed Dalai Lama.

Then, in 1960, while he was away on an official visit to Beijing, the PLA arrested 400 of the Tashilhunpo's monks, executing some of them and imprisoning the rest in Qinghai's emerging gulag. This was to be the Panchen Lama's turning point. A year later, on his next visit to Beijing, he stopped in many parts of the Tibetan countryside on his journey from Lhasa to experience first-hand the sheer volume of Tibetans suffering from the persecution of the Chinese. By the time he reached China's capital, he had put together a now legendary

70,000-word petition which he delivered to the Chinese premier Zhou Enlai in Beijing, requesting it be passed straight on to Mao Zedong.

The document was a brave, reckless and emotional plea for the Tibetan people, which espoused in detail the religious persecution and political cruelty of the invading Chinese, and the suffering, starvation and mortality rates of the hapless Tibetans. Though the Panchen Lama was careful to couch his protests in Maoist phraseology, few who read it doubted his bravery in attempting such a critique of the Great Helmsman and his projects – particularly the Great Leap Forward – and many of his entourage pleaded with him to destroy the document, for fear it endangered their spiritual leader's life.

The Panchen Lama was not to be deterred, however, and the document soon found its way to Mao, who immediately declaimed it as a 'poisoned arrow' and the Panchen Lama as a 'reactionary feudal overlord', seeming to forget that his government had installed and enthroned this feudal overlord in the first place. What came next was considered by many of the Panchen Lama's followers and friends as inevitable – he was held in Beijing and subjected to numerous struggle-sessions and public beatings (in one especially harrowing example, he was 'struggled' before a full stadium in Beijing, and denounced by his sister-in-law, who had been persuaded to claim that he had once raped her), and then put under house arrest in the capital for the next fifteen years.

Though he was released after Mao's death following a decade and a half of torture and 're-education', the Panchen Lama never ceased in his protests against Chinese rule, changing irrevocably from a puppet of the Communists to a figurehead of Tibetan autonomy. The Dalai Lama – who states in his autobiography, *Freedom in Exile*, that he had never doubted his second-in-command, but instead felt only remorse at the fact that he had been pinpointed and indoctrinated by the Chinese at such a young age – gave him his full support from India.

Some within Tibet still have it that the tenth Panchen Lama remained a traitor, though they seem to base that on the fact that, following his release, he married a Chinese woman called Li Jie and had a daughter with her, thus betraying his sacred monastic oaths. But most allow him this discrepancy, for he remained a tireless campaigner for Tibetan rights until his death in 1989, which occurred in his rightful home of Shigatse during one of his allowed visits to Tibet.

'He *chose* to die in Shigatse at that time,' a Tibetan told me later. 'To die in Tibet was important for him. It meant he could be reborn in Tibet. And continue his work.'

But the reincarnation of the Panchen Lama has, in the last two decades, only opened the leader's story to more intrigue and controversy. Just like the Dalai Lama, the new incarnation of the Panchen Lama must be sought out and officially approved, and that he was. In 1995, the Dalai Lama and Tibet-in-exile government announced that, six years after the death of the tenth, they had discovered the eleventh Panchen Lama: a six-year-old boy called Gedhun Choekyi Nyima. Three days after his discovery, the child was placed in protective custody by the Chinese and spirited away and, to this day, nobody but those in the highest echelons of the People's Republic government know where or exactly who he is. In his place, the Chinese installed their own choice for the eleventh Panchen Lama: a five-year-old boy called Gyancain Norbu, the son of two Tibetan Communist Party members.

Gyancain Norbu is still the eleventh Panchen Lama. Gedhun Choekyi Nyima is still an enigma, at the time of writing in his mid twenties and very probably some clerk or accountant in a small Chinese city with no idea of his spiritual lineage, or of the terrifying story which precedes him. Such mystery is a constant source of woe for Tibetans, who feel that, as their culture is being diluted by the increasing levels of Han immigration into Tibet, so too is their heritage swiftly disappearing. Each year, more and more lamas and abbots flee for the safety of India, and those who do stay to live and some day die in Tibet can never be sure whether their reincarnated selves will be nominated by their fellow Tibetans or by the Chinese Communist Party, the kinds of 'overlord' which Mao and his cronies so decried on 1 October 1949.

chu-chig

Drolma's eyes told Lobsang that she had known for some time; her kiss told him she had feared for his life during every moment. After the kiss, she pushed him hard in the solar plexus, part in anger and part to get him off her doorstep. Another kiss, the single word 'parents' whispered in his ear, and she was gone behind the slam of the door, reappearing minutes later in a denim jacket and grabbing Lobsang by the arm to drag him down the street towards a small and hidden teahouse. He grinned all the way.

The tea was so sweet and milky it made Lobsang's gums itch. He gazed across the low table at Drolma. Throughout her angry tirade, flecks of spittle had flown from her lips and attached themselves to strands of her hair. Lobsang thought she had never looked so beautiful.

'I'm not the only one, Lobsang! Everyone knows! Jamyang emailed me, of course, and she had worked it out the first night you were gone! I even called Ji! Think of that! *Ji!* And it really made me and your sister feel wanted when we found out you had told him and not us! Thank you, Lobsang, thank you so very much! I have been *ill* worrying about you, we all have! You're a stupid, selfish, ignorant man, and if you'd been killed I would have...'

Three other patrons sat in the bar. They watched without inhibition while Drolma ranted, laughing quietly at Lobsang whenever he made eye contact with them, as if to say *you'll be paying for this for a while.*

'And the worst part is that I can't tell you to go back home – which is *exactly* what you should be doing, by the way – because there is no chance I am ever going to let you cross those mountains again!'

This fury of Drolma's persisted for the next two hours, dissolving slowly with tear-filled giggles and wet kisses. She maintained that she saw no romantic gesture in what Lobsang had done and held no sympathy for any part of his ordeal, but her fundamental delight in seeing him again began to outweigh it all. After those two hours, the catharsis seemed complete and Drolma was ready to move on to more pragmatic matters.

'You can't stay with me. There's no point even asking my parents.'

'I guessed that, so I was hoping we could get a place of our own, like we had in Delhi.'

'Out of the question. My parents don't know about you. What would they think if I suddenly moved in with a boy when they think I've been single for the last three years? That would raise a lot of questions. You don't want that here, not from anyone.'

'It's OK,' Lobsang said. 'I can find my own place.'

'How are you going to pay for it?' Drolma challenged him. 'You told me that nomad took all your money.'

'I'll get a job.'

'Where? Doing what? No one will employ you without an identity card.'

'Would your parents help me? If you told them I was just a friend?'

'They'd find out you were illegal, and then they'd report you to the police, and then you'd find yourself locked up in Drapchi. Have you really not thought about any of this, Lobsang?'

Lobsang admitted he had not, and a gloomy silence descended. He stared at the backs of his hands as they lay flat on the table: they were as brown as the deserts he had crossed, with rope-like veins furrowing between dry and cracked knuckles. Drolma had been right, his stupidity *was* unsurpassed – he had fatally beached himself on the Tibetan plateau.

'If you had told me what you were planning,' Drolma continued, 'I could have sorted things out for you: found you a place to stay, helped you get a job, put back a little money for you. But you didn't think about that, either.'

Lobsang remained focused on the back of his hands, glum, willing to concede that no, he hadn't thought about that, either.

'So you're lucky I did.'

Drolma placed her hands over Lobsang's. Hers seemed twenty years younger than his, lightly freckled, soft as her hair.

'It's lucky Jamyang emailed. It's lucky I called Ji. It's lucky I did it all in enough time to find you a room and save up some money for you. It's lucky I was able to ask around a few people, to find out the kinds of jobs an illegal immigrant might be able to get. What I'm saying, Lobsang, is that you're very lucky to have me.'

Lobsang grinned. 'I am.'

Drolma grinned back at him. 'While you are a terrible burden on me.'

'That, too.'

Drolma had been networking hard on Lobsang's behalf. The offer of a room came from a man twice Lobsang's age called Norbu, which Lobsang decided was fortuitous since this was his father's name. Norbu gladly welcomed the young man into his home, but he did not like it when Drolma joked that Norbu could be Lobsang's 'Lhasa-father'. Norbu was single and childless for a reason, he explained – he despised families and wanted nothing to do with them. He would have gladly become a monk if he didn't despise them so much, too. But Norbu did have one guilty pleasure, which Drolma whispered to Lobsang later at a small and crowded bar: he had a passionate crush on Drolma's best friend, Yangchen, and Drolma was convinced Norbu had agreed to rent his spare room to Lobsang in the hope that this would give him more opportunities to see Yangchen.

Norbu could afford an apartment large enough for a family without actually having one because he owned a fleet of taxis, Landcruisers, motorbikes and rickshaws which he leased out to various individuals in return for a portion of their fares. 'Your Drolma tells me you need a job,' he said to Lobsang in the bar, for Drolma had told him Yangchen would meet them there later and he had insisted on joining them. 'You can work for me, if you like.'

'I'd love to!' Lobsang shouted above the loud pop music blaring from the bar's substandard speakers. 'I could run tours all over Tibet in a Landcruiser.'

Norbu laughed. 'You can start on a rickshaw. Then maybe we'll see from there.'

Yangchen arrived at the bar, as did other friends of Drolma's. Norbu laughed and flirted and bought drinks. Lobsang was introduced to everyone – they already knew all about him, Drolma having told them everything, and they treated Lobsang with such deference that he felt like a king. The clock above the bar passed through midnight and one day slipped into the next, and life, for Lobsang, kaleidoscoped. He had a room of his own, a job, enough money to buy food and books and clothes, a brand new gaggle of friends who drank with him and played pool with him and who, within a few days, stopped asking him searching questions and instead involved him in their meaningless cycles of babble and the kind of small talk which breeds familiarity and comfort, and, more importantly, he had Drolma again.

This new Lhasa still felt unusual to him, alien and synthetic – it made him think of an American film he had watched once where a man's DNA had been spliced with an insect's – but his place inside it felt more natural than he had felt in Kathmandu, Delhi or even Lhasa as a boy. New Lhasa, with its wide roads juxtaposed with the Barkhor, with its cuboid high-rises facing down the Potala, suited him. Lobsang was, he felt, similarly hybridised himself: simultaneously Tibetan and not. His friends thought him the most cosmopolitan person they knew, more so even than Drolma, for many of them had left Lhasa before, but few had ever left the Tibetan Autonomous Region.

A year passed so swiftly that when his friends threw him a party for the anniversary of his arrival – 'We should call this Lobsang Day and celebrate it every year!' Norbu joked – he had to ask if it was somebody's birthday. It seemed to him impossible that a full twelve months had passed since he had arrived at Drolma's door in that dirty *chuba*, penniless and footsore. It seemed to him impossible that not only had he escaped the detection of every single military and police officer in Lhasa, but also that he had succeeded in sneaking out a number of clandestine missives which informed his family and Ji that he was alive, well and ludicrously happy. Above all, it seemed to him impossible that this was the absolute truth – that he *was* alive, well and ludicrously happy, and that he had been for a full year.

Lobsang's whole life had been filled with a longing so acute and omnipresent that he had only come to notice it through its absence. It had never necessarily been Tibet which was the source of his longing – it played a part, that could not be denied, but there was more to it, acceptance perhaps, love certainly, and he had never satisfied it in Kathmandu nor Delhi, even at the bedside of his mother or in bed with Drolma. Yet, for the last year, the longing had vanished. He adored his life in Lhasa.

He had remained with Norbu, who was a pleasant housemate and, as time passed, grew to become a good friend, despite their age difference of twenty-five years. Unlike Lobsang's other friends, the vibrant crowd of young men and women who had adopted him not just as Drolma's boyfriend but as one of their own, Norbu never tired of hearing Lobsang's stories about what he liked to call 'the rest of the world'. At least once a week, he pressed the young man into telling him again about his summer in Dharamsala, a place he longed to visit, but knew he never would, for he feared the Himalayan crossing too much.

'That's the only good thing about having a family,' Norbu would say. 'They force you to do exceptional things you would never do just for yourself.'

Lobsang kept up the rickshaw-riding. It did not pay especially well, but he was able to cover the meagre rent Norbu asked for and still have ample funds left over for food, clothes and drinks at the many bars he, Drolma and their friends seemed to frequent each week. It helped that Norbu did not charge him for leasing the bike. Besides, he enjoyed the job: it kept him fit and out in the open air which he inhaled like a tonic, and he was able to spend his days on the roads and streets, rediscovering and relearning the city of his heritage.

Drolma spent her days working in an office for a tour company and her nights at home with her parents, but every hour they could snatch in between she spent with Lobsang. Their time was coordinated, always prearranged and mapped out: evenings with friends in bars and teahouses, on the streets and in the town; and days off in Lobsang's room, rarely leaving, the door closed. If she gave her parents enough notice and had primed a believable lie sufficiently, she could pretend to stay the night with a friend and spend it instead with Lobsang, but these occasions were rare. Though she promised and promised him that she would, she never told her parents about Lobsang.

The first time Drolma failed to meet him after work in the usual teahouse, Yangchen told him not to worry, that she probably either had to stay late at work or her parents had demanded her home early for family matters. When Lobsang saw Drolma the next day, she did not even allude to the fact that she had stood him up for the first time in over three years, and so he chose not to ask her about it. Later, he regretted this omission for, as her disappearances became more regular, sometimes even for days at a time, he still found himself unable to ask where she had been and what she had been doing, as if he had already left it too late.

Nangma

|

This Shigatse cafe was a wide second-floor space with small windows, a threadbare and beer-stained carpet, and a dozen young Tibetans spread about the wooden tables playing cards. I had entered it alone for a quiet beer and some time to write in my journal, but Jigme sat down next to me and offered a game of cards before I could put pen to paper. It was not long before I found myself losing each hand, and I was grateful I had declined his offer to play for money.

'My girlfriend can play better than you, Charlie,' he said as I suffered my twelfth defeat.

'Then maybe I should play her,' I sulked.

'You can soon,' Jigme replied. 'She is meeting me here.'

On cue, a petite Tibetan woman with plaited hair entered the cafe. She wore thin jeans, heavy boots and a thick, red hooded jumper, and as she sat next to Jigme her score of metal bracelets jangled against the table. They smiled at each other, but did not touch.

'Nguyen,' he said. 'Please meet my friend Charlie.'

'It is very nice to meet you, Charlie,' she said, smiling.

'You, too,' I replied. 'Nguyen's a beautiful name. Is it Thai?'

'Vietnamese. My father is Vietnamese and my mother is Tibetan.'

'Her father doesn't like me,' Jigme confided.

'He likes you!' Nguyen laughed.

'Every time I go to their house, he begins to talk in Vietnamese so I don't know what he's saying.' Jigme mimicked a stream of Vietnamese syllables, curled one hand into a fist and punched it into the palm of the other.

'This man!' Nguyen sighed. 'Always exaggerating!'

'Your English is excellent,' I said admiringly.

'I hope so!' she laughed. 'I am an English teacher!'

'Then we have something in common. I'm also an English teacher.'

'What kind of school do you work in?' Nguyen asked.

'Secondary schools,' I replied. 'With teenagers. Some good, but some not so good.'

'Is that why you are sitting in a cafe in Shigatse rather than working?' Jigme asked, and Nguyen laughed, slapping him gently on the shoulder.

'Yes. But only temporarily. I had a difficult year last year. Some tough schools. I needed a break. When I go back to England I'll teach again, though I might try to find a good school for a while. How about you, Nguyen? What kind of school do you work in?'

'Like you, I work with teenagers. But mine is a private school.'

'Is that better than a public school?'

'It is better for me.'

'In England, teachers who work in private schools say they like the freedom of them.'

'What do you mean?'

'They don't have to do what the government tells them.'

She laughed. 'It is very different here.'

'Are there things you can and can't say in the classroom?'

'It is better for me because I teach a foreign language, so I do not have to worry about things like history or geography, where there are lots of rules about what you can and cannot say. But I must never talk about politics.'

'What would happen if you did?'

'Probably nothing,' she conceded. 'It would be between me and my students, and they would understand. But if one student told their parents.'

'Intentionally, or by accident?'

'It is the same in all Tibet. You never know who is a spy.'

'Even children?'

'Sometimes, especially children. They do not know any better.'

'Do you think any of your children are spies?'

'Like I said, you never know. Maybe, and maybe not. But if I did talk about politics, and a child told their parents, and the parents told the school, I would lose my job immediately. I would also be arrested and asked a lot of questions.'

'And then?'

'That would depend on how I answered the questions.' Nguyen was beginning to look uncomfortable, and I feared that perhaps my conversation had itself become something of an interrogation. Jigme confirmed my suspicions.

'Charlie has as many questions as the Chinese!' he laughed. 'Let's drink some beer and play some more cards.'

I agreed, feeling awkward and appreciating the change of subject for Nguyen's sake, though it was a topic I would have liked to pursue. It is well documented that during the Cultural Revolution, in all China and Tibet, teachers had been especially persecuted. Mao's Red Guards were by design young, and he encouraged them to question and then overthrow all authority figures save himself. The Cultural Revolution was Mao's attempt at the decimation of all hierarchy, a Marxism refined not just to politics and the economy, but to all aspects of sociological and psychological life. The ensuing malevolence, permitted by none other than the Great Helmsman himself, became directed at and then telescoped on to immediate authority figures. For that mad decade, the Red Guards rose from their school desks and took their impetuous revenge on the instigators of all those homeworks and detentions: the closet fantasy of the teenager, and the nightmare of the teacher, actualised.

In China, teachers became the ironic subject-matter of the Red Guards' first lessons in how to revolt: the model frogs there to be dissected to see what applications the Cultural Revolution could have outside of school walls. Some were held prisoner in their own classrooms or locked into the supply cupboards, starved of food and water, their only sustenance the beatings bestowed on them from students they had once humiliated before their peers or kept behind to rewrite unsatisfactory coursework. More fortunate teachers simply had their lesson-planning and marking supplemented by new work: to clean their students' shoes, or perhaps even the school toilets.

Many teachers – declaimed as 'The Stinking Ninth' (as intellectuals, they were perceived as the last of Mao's nine categories of cultural enemy – among the other categories were landlords, rightists and foreigners) – died from the more severe forms of treatment meted out by their students, and many others committed suicide.

In Tibet, teachers were treated in much the same way, not just by the Chinese Red Guards who flooded into the country, but by their own Tibetan students, who paraded them about the streets wearing dunces' caps, their arms bound into the crucifix position with such force that often their shoulders became dislocated, and their bodies scarred with the fresh wounds of torture.

During the Cultural Revolution, Nguyen would have been one of the first to have endured *thamzing*, not because she was a woman or half-foreign, but because she taught English – an imperialist and therefore traitorous subject. Now, she displayed no obvious physical wounds, but her silence as we played cards was indicative of the clandestine control of the Party.

We ate dinner together, and then Nguyen stood and announced it was time for her to leave. 'I have marking,' she explained.

'I should go, too,' I said.

'Why?' Jigme asked.

I had no answer.

'It is Saturday,' Jigme said. 'I am going to a Tibetan dancing club later. I think you should come. You want to see Tibet? This will be a unique cultural experience for you!'

'Oh yes, Charlie,' Nguyen giggled. 'You should *definitely* go.'

2

It was 10 p.m.; the streets were silent and unlit. A single military truck circled Shigatse's centre, its red flag billowing in the scant breeze, but I seemed the only other person alive. The market stalls with their wheels of rancid yak butter had been covered; the workforce of sweating men who dug into the road and shovelled rubble on to towering slag heaps by day had gone home; the dogs had disappeared for the night.

A car approached as I neared the cafe where I had arranged to meet Jigme. It was a small and dirty hatchback and, as it slowed, I saw Jigme inside gleefully winding down the window.

'Get in, Charlie!' he called, swinging the door open and hustling me inside the car, where he introduced me to his friends: two men and a woman. They were, like Jigme, in their mid twenties. Unlike Jigme, who worked in a grocery store on the outskirts of the city, they were tour guides, and were looking forward to a night out during their brief spell of leave.

We coasted along Shigatse's lifeless streets, coming to a stop outside a detached and windowless building. A bass-line throbbed out from the building's walls and dictated our steps as we clambered out of the car and towards the small, single doorway. Two men stood on either side, and I took in their puffy, black jackets and flabby jawlines with the happy realisation that they could have been bouncers anywhere in the world. They broke into wide grins when they saw Jigme, and seemed to smile perhaps further when they saw me behind him.

The club was large and open-plan with a score of tables clustered around the central dance floor. As we took our seats at a corner table, the barman appeared within seconds, placed a crate of cans of lager on the table and carefully positioned a small glass in front of each of us. Jigme cracked open the first can, distributed it evenly amongst us, and then topped us up with a second.

All our chairs pointed vaguely towards the dance floor, polished and sparkling under the rig of lights and their flashing rainbow display, out of tempo with the slow beats of the thumping music. Young men appeared on the dance floor one by one to grab the single microphone and wail out angst-ridden love songs to the backing tracks of sweeping synthesisers and digital drumbeats, each finishing to a rapturous applause from the audience and the ceremonial march of the club owner, who would rise from his seat and wrap a white *kata* scarf around their bowed necks after each number. The singer would then disappear, to be replaced by another, never the same, and the pattern would repeat. One sang a song slightly different from what appeared to be the proscribed genre, its distorted guitar power-chords lifting each major-scale chorus into the realms of the epic ballad, above which he sang the repeated refrain: *Om mani padme hum*, soaring to a drawn-out, falsetto scream on each *hum*.

'Is this song about Buddhism?' I shouted at Jigme, who sat next to me.

'It is!' he shouted back, leaning in so close that his lager-sodden spit bounced off my earlobes. 'But it is also about Tibet. The words have two meanings. The first is a love of Buddhism. But really it is about a love of a free Tibet.'

'Isn't that dangerous?'

'Very. But the words are in a local dialect, so Chinese do not understand the second meaning. The second meaning is hidden. But all Tibetans will understand it – Lhasans, Khampas, Amdowas, those in exile.'

The song came to an end while Jigme elaborated, and his friend Yeshe joined in our conversation. Together, they explained that the song – and a multitude of other songs like it – represented an artistic call to defiance and self-expression against oppressive forces, one which connoted a free Tibet not so much through vocabulary, but through the evocation of imagery which all Tibetans, no matter where they were from, would recognise as sovereign and autonomous.

'We call this *nangma*,' Jigme said, topping up my glass with lager and lighting a cigarette. 'There are many Chinese bars here in Shigatse. More in Lhasa. They are like the bars in China and, I think, in your country. Bars to get drunk in, nothing more. But here, in *nangma*, we drink second. First, we enjoy Tibet. If you had come to Tibet before the Chinese and I had met you, I would have taken you to my house, and we would have had a night like this. But this is not possible any longer. It is difficult for us to do this at home now. So we do it at *nangma*.'

'And the Chinese are OK with this?'

'This beer is Chinese beer,' Yeshe said. 'These cigarettes are Chinese cigarettes. They get their money, and they are happy. But they do not come here.'

'Because they wouldn't be welcome?'

'No,' Jigme replied. 'Welcome is no concern for the Chinese. They do not come here because they do not enjoy it. They go to their own bars. Have too much drink. Have a fight. That is why this is good for us. We are watched all the time. *All the time.* But not here, not in *nangma*. Here is Tibet. It is why I wanted to bring you.'

The music started as Jigme sat back and necked a can of lager.

'Charlie!' he shouted above the thudding roar. 'This is a good one! You must watch this!'

The music was a simple but loud accordion riff which rose chromatically after each eighth bar, the kind of playful music one associates with the cadences of a circus. And, matching the Barnum-esque tonality of such a tune, two little people shuffled out on to the stage to enact a weird mime-show for us.

'It is the dwarf number!' Jigme shouted. 'This is the best!'

The man – a Tibetan who looked in his forties – danced about his stage wife with cartoonish grimaces as she cradled a baby doll and refused to pass it to him. The tempo of the music increased, the 'mother' dropped the baby doll on to the floor and kicked it into the wings, and a tall woman clad in biker's leathers appeared on the stage. She started a mock fight with the 'mother', ripped the bundles of cloth from her arms, and then swept up the 'father', wrapping him in the sheets, and carrying him offstage while she kissed his forehead. As the audience cheered, I searched for the metaphor, and gave up when a wave of dizziness swept over me. A new song started, all bass drums and tinny, syncopated happy-hardcore melodies, and three young Tibetan women bounced on to the stage and mimed their vocals into silent microphones whilst pumping out energetic and synchronised dance routines. I looked over at Jigme, who rolled a can of beer across the table towards me and smiled.

3

We left the *nangma* bar at two o'clock in the morning and climbed into the hatchback, inebriated and giggly. Yeshe, as drunk as the rest of us, had decided he would drive, and started the engine. Jigme placed his hand on Yeshe's arm and said something in Tibetan to him, then turned around to face me in the back seat.

'Did you enjoy the *nangma*?' he asked.

'I'll suffer tomorrow, but it was worth it.'

'Good. But I would like to show you one more thing before we take you to your hotel. I like you because I know you are interested in Tibet. In the *real* Tibet. Your tour guide would not have brought you here tonight, but I did, because I wanted you to see the good side of modern Tibet. But now I would like to show you the bad side.'

'I want to see *all* sides of Tibet,' I replied.

'Good. Then we go.' Jigme turned back to Yeshe and spoke in Tibetan again. Yeshe angled the car out away from the centre of Shigatse, stopping at the mouth of a dark alleyway.

'This is a bad street,' Jigme said. 'But it is important for you to see it.' His eyes were growing cloudy: partly from the drink; but perhaps more from some emotion brewing inside him, something which transcended rage, but which fostered ill regard nonetheless.

'Is it dangerous?' I asked.

'No. It is very safe. But here life is bad. Come with me.'

I stepped from the car with Jigme and Yeshe while their other two friends stayed inside, the engine still running. The alleyway was thin and unlit, devoid of pavement or road, just a network of deep and wide potholes which had sunk between the lines of crumbling houses, and we navigated them by jumping from one pile of rubble to another. A small cluster of beggars huddled communally about the remains of a fallen wall, ignoring us as we passed. We came to a wooden door coming off at the hinges.

'We will have one beer, and then we will leave,' Jigme said.

He knocked on the door. A young girl, perhaps fourteen years old, opened it, grinned broadly, and let us in. We found ourselves in a living room, where eight girls surrounded us and pressed us on to the wobbling chairs which circled the room's lone table. The girls seemed to range from fourteen to eighteen years old, though it was impossible to tell: all looked as if they had a decade of the wrong kind of experience. They were dirty and poor, and they squeezed up against us with hopeless desperation.

'Jigme,' I said. 'Is this a whorehouse?' My tone was that of the questioner who dearly hopes for the opposite answer to the one he expects; the one that is, in fact, already known.

'Yes,' Jigme replied grimly. 'But we are only here to drink a beer. Then we will leave.'

The youngest of the girls, the one who had opened the door, appeared with three warm cans of lager. She opened them for us while Jigme paid and then settled herself down next to Yeshe, rubbing herself against his leg. Another sat by me, picked a malnourished kitten up off the floor, and asked if I would like to buy it. The oldest, though she could not have been more than eighteen, took my other side, sneezed into her hand and then pointed to the fraying pictures of scantily clad American celebrities Blu-tacked to the wall. She reeled off their names mechanically.

'Angelina Jolie. Christina Aguilera. Paris Hilton. Megan Fox. Lady Gaga.'

I drank my beer hurriedly and told Jigme that I wanted to leave.

'Of course you do,' he said. 'So do they.'

It would be naive to suggest that the Chinese brought prostitution to Tibet; the stories of the carousing sixth Dalai Lama are proof enough that the ancient trade has prevailed in this country as long as it has anywhere in the world. But the proliferation of prostitutes in the larger cities such as Shigatse and Lhasa has almost certainly increased since the Chinese invasion, and especially after the Cultural Revolution, when many young nomad girls fled the persecution of their families to seek refuge in the cities. With no learned skills to offer – for many nomad daughters are lucky to attend school for just three years – money-making alternatives became narrowed down to either begging or prostitution. And, as the cities grew with the exponential immigrant Han populace – a large number of them young, single men – so too did the monetary rewards of prostitution, and many Chinese women have also moved to Lhasa to supply the demand. There they can earn twice as much in one night as they could in a month of factory work back home.

As a result, prostitution has grown into a huge and viable business in Tibet's cities, with high-class escort agencies and myriad red-light districts filling the developing urbanisations. This place Jigme had brought me to, however, this place was the very bottom of the barrel.

I followed Jigme and Yeshe back to the car sober and silent, perhaps more moved by the night's experiences than by my first glimpse of the Potala Palace. Inside the car, his friends looked hard at me, and then seemed to nod in approval. Had it, I wondered, been a test? Had they expected me to succumb to those unfortunate prostitutes, those children with streaming noses? Perhaps Jigme sensed my cerebral queries, for he sat next to me in the back of the car and unexpectedly put his arm around my shoulders.

'The Dalai Lama has something he likes to say to foreigners,' Jigme said. 'He says they should go to Tibet, and they should tell everyone what Tibet is really like. I am so pleased you have come to my country, but your tour guide will not show you some things. I wanted to show you these things. And I want you to tell everyone what Tibet is really like.'

Since leaving Tibet, I have tried to fulfil Jigme's request, am still trying. I tell anyone who will listen. But it is ironic that, of all the episodes and experiences I relate – of my first sight of the Potala; of the Norbulingka zoo; of a feral mastiff tracking my steps on the shores of Nam-tso; of Lobsang himself – those fifteen minutes in that brothel are usually left out of my pub-table narratives. There is, of course, the anxiety of misunderstanding, but underlying that rides a tide of nauseous sadness which grips me fiercely each time I contemplate the recollection of that quarter-hour. In Tibet, I saw poverty, squalor, the day-to-day squeezing of fundamental human rights and civil liberties, the constant reminders of the wholesale destruction of an entire culture, and a thousand guns. But those eight girls with their shabby clothes, old hands and pleading eyes disturbed me far more than anything else I saw on my journey to and through Tibet, and perhaps more than anything else I have ever seen.

4

I met Jigme and Nguyen the following night in a small bar in the centre of Shigatse. Jigme was his usual effervescent self, but Nguyen seemed quiet and reserved. A friend of hers, a monk, had been arrested two days ago, and nobody knew what had happened to him.

'Why was he arrested?' I asked her.

'I don't know. Nobody does.'

'He will be OK,' Jigme said to her in English.

She snapped back at him in Tibetan, and then turned to me. 'This is Tibet, so this is China,' she said. 'And it is the twenty-first century. That is what the Chinese tell us. It is the twenty-first century, it is time to join the rest of the world.'

'Indiscriminate arrests don't seem very twenty-first century to me,' I said.

Nguyen sneered at me. 'Unlike Jigme, I have a passport. I visit my family in Vietnam regularly. I have seen the newspapers. Your government can arrest and do what they like, because of the war on terror. China has the same policy, but it is called a war on splittism.'

'Is your friend a splittist?'

'Of course not! He is a monk. He lives for his faith. But that is not important. Do not tell me this is an Asian problem, when your country supports Guantanamo Bay.'

I sat back and sipped my tea, suitably chastised, but Nguyen was not to be assuaged by silence nor timidity.

'Why are you here, Charlie?' she asked. 'What do you expect to see on your short journey?'

'I want to see Tibet – as much of it as I can within what the Chinese allow me.'

'And then what? You will "tell the world"? You are immature if you think they will listen. And you are a hypocrite if you think your country will do anything. Britain did nothing when the Chinese invaded. Nothing. And they will do nothing. You will go home, tell your friends about your little holiday in Shangri-La, and then you will go back to your job. Maybe boast about climbing Everest. You want to see Tibet? Next time, learn Tibetan first.'

Nguyen had risen from her seat with her last question, and was thrusting her arms into her denim jacket with the closing sentence. Jigme looked up at her, but she avoided his eyes and marched out of the bar, leaving behind an awkward and hanging silence as we stared at the circular ripples in our cups of tea caused by her banging footsteps on the wooden floor.

'I am sorry,' Jigme said.

'No, I'm sorry,' I replied. 'She's right. I've got no place here. I'm not helping.'

'I love Nguyen, and I agree with her on many things,' Jigme said thoughtfully. 'But on this, I do not. I think it is better that foreigners come here and see Tibet, not just hear what the Chinese media tell them. If no one ever came here, then we would be in trouble. The Chinese would spread their lie that Tibet has always been a part of China, and in time the lie would become truth. Let me ask you, do you believe Tibet has always been a part of China?'

'No,' I replied.

'Why not?'

'Because I know it's not the truth. I know that there have always been issues of control and issues of sovereignty between China and Tibet, but I also know that Tibet was truly and legally independent before 1950.'

'And you know this because you have been here, because you have read about Tibet and learned about Tibet?'

I nodded.

'I would be very interested to hear your opinion, Charlie.'

'On what?' I asked.

'All of this. Why do you think China invaded Tibet? Why do you think they are still here?'

I sipped slowly at my tea as I thought about the question. 'In all honesty, I don't think I know the answer to your second question. I don't know why they're still here or why they're still pushing so hard for full integration. But I think I can understand why China colonised Tibet in the first place – aside from the historical context, the battles for territory which had gone on for a thousand years, I think Mao was flexing his muscles, showing off about what he could do, and any dictatorship seems to revel in the notion of expanding itself. Particularly communism, which has an ideology like religion.'

My English was becoming too idiomatic, and Jigme seemed confused.

'What I mean,' I said, 'is that those who believe in extreme politics never seem content with just believing it. They need everyone to know, and to convert. And when these people, like Mao, win over their own country, they seem to feel the need to expand, to push their politics out on to the rest of the world. Like it's not just about changing their country, but changing the globe.'

Jigme laughed, a deep and sonorous laugh which trembled our table beneath his hands. 'You think this is about politics, Charlie?' he guffawed. 'You think China keeps Tibet because of Marxism?'

'That's what they've sold it on,' I rejoined. 'It's the twenty-first-century Iron Curtain.'

Jigme laughed so hard at this one that he knocked over his tea and had to pour himself a fresh cup from the communal flask. 'Maybe Nguyen was right! Maybe you are naive!' he grinned, gulping from the cup and belching loudly.

'So educate me,' I said.

'China never invaded Tibet because of Marxism, and certainly not because of nationhood. It is much more simple than that. It is much more practical than that. China just wanted, and still wants, Tibet's resources. We are a gift to the Chinese: a big mass of land with only a few Tibetans on it. Really, Charlie? You did not know this?' He laughed again, swinging out his arms with such arcs that the waiter walked over, supposing we wanted to order another drink.

'Yes!' Jigme told him in English. 'My friend Charlie needs a beer. Me, too.'

Cowed by Jigme's shouts and gesticulations, I retreated into my cushion, enticed out by the offer of a game of cards, which we played for the next hour, punctuated by Jigme's sniggers.

In part, Jigme was, of course, right. Tibet is a mine of natural resources, and the Chinese have plundered their Western Treasure accordingly. In the last fifty years, conservative estimates have it that 50 million trees have been felled in Tibet and millions of the country's acres cleared of vegetation, most of them for the benefit of Chinese timber companies which, according to the Dharamsala Information Office, have earned over 33 billion US dollars from the sales of Tibetan wood since 1959. By the early 1980s, the Party had set its sights upon the vast quantities of uranium, borax and iron ore hidden beneath Tibet's mountains, and today mining companies spread throughout the land. Even my trusty but biased companion, *China's Tibet*, spoke adoringly and unashamedly of the conquest of Tibet's resources. Wordy paragraphs detailed Tibet's dominance in all China when it came to the reserves of copper, chromite, magnetite, boron, lead, zinc, gold, petroleum and iron which she held locked away within her plateau, culminating in a beige-and-white table which showed that, between 1978 and 2003, exports of timber rose from 1,491 to 26,480 tonnes, chromite from 4,193 to 74,342 tonnes, and all 'Materials Transported Out of Tibet' from 20,724 to 173,508 tonnes. Nationalism, dogma and ideology aside, Tibet has been and continues to be a gargantuan material resource for China.

'Please tell Nguyen I'm sorry,' I said as we stood up to leave. 'I didn't mean to offend her.'

'Charlie, she will be sorry,' he said. 'She has had a very bad day.'

We agreed to meet the next day for lunch, and I looked forward to it. But, when I arrived at the restaurant at the accorded time and then waited there for the next two hours, neither Jigme nor Nguyen showed up, and I ate lunch alone.

chu-nyi

Lobsang felt he could cope with Drolma's early disappearances, for they were short, they were irregular, and they never impinged upon her behaviour towards him. She remained as loving and as passionate as ever, her moods swung but only marginally, and they continued to spend much of their time together finding something in life which could be laughed about and then doing so until the subject had been wrung of all comedic value, at which point they settled on something else and squeezed that for joy, too.

Once, he rode his rickshaw to her office and spotted her through a small window two storeys up. This was enough for him, and he cycled away through the streets before she could see him. When, a few days after, she did not meet him at their usual spot and he found himself playing pool with Norbu when he should have been with her, he wondered what had led him to Drolma's office, what he had hoped to discover, and what he would have done had that discovery been made. He could not answer any of the questions. He might have sat there all day and not seen her through the window – he had never been inside her office, he did not know how close to or far away from the window she sat, what the plan of the office was, how frequent and via which trajectories movement existed there – and this would have proved nothing. He had built that image himself, the one of her pressed up against the windowpane with masculine arms caressing her back, and he understood now how ludicrous it was.

It was much later, perhaps a whole two months after her first disappearance, that Drolma was away for three days at a time: longer than Lobsang had been without her since walking into Lhasa. When she returned, popping up at his elbow in a bar while he drank beer with their friends (who did not mention her absence, and so neither did he), she seemed quiet and anxious, prone to a nervous and staccato laughter Lobsang did not recognise. She let him have sex with her that night – that was how it felt: she *let* him – and he surreptitiously checked her naked body for scratches or any other kind of mark which might have suggested the presence of a third party, but he found none.

Her absences increased, tipping her time for Lobsang downward like scales. Once, she was away for a week, and Lobsang cycled his customers to their destinations at furious speeds which he hoped would exhaust his jealousy. Twenty days later, she disappeared again, and this time she did not return.

One week passed, then two, and Lobsang began to loiter: by day, outside Drolma's office; by night, outside her home. Sometimes he rode his customers miles out of their way so that he might pass either, and when the customers complained about the detour he charged them nothing. He never saw her. He questioned each of his friends – where was she? who was she with? – breaking a silence which had hung about them all for months, but none of them knew or, if they did, they would not tell him. He became fixated on nationality. Since he could not conceive of her with a Tibetan other than himself, he illogically reasoned that her new lover must be foreign – an Indian was feasible, but he could be a Nepali or a Muslim from the north; and it was unlikely, but a Westerner, a white man, or even a Chinese could not be ruled out. It would explain where she had gone, spirited out of Lhasa, out of Tibet, and into the seductive lap of a stronger, richer nation.

Fifteen days after Drolma's final disappearance, Lobsang vanished, too. He was found two days later by Norbu in a filthy and vampiric bar, more drunk than Norbu believed a man could be short of alcohol poisoning, and Norbu carried him back to their apartment where he threw Lobsang on to a bed to vomit and moan while he himself ran back out on to the streets. Fuelled purely by worry and not an ounce of lust, he scurried to the door of Yangchen. She agreed to visit Lobsang the next morning. She agreed she could be a comfort. She agreed that she might have some information which Lobsang would want to hear.

When she arrived at Norbu's apartment, he left her alone with Lobsang, quietly sneaking out the door and pointing her towards the stove, where Lobsang was boiling up a huge cauldron of yak-butter tea.

'I used to hate this,' he said, passing her a cup which she raised to her lips. 'Now I love it. So there you go. Feelings can change.'

'I know where Drolma is.'

Lobsang emitted a grim chuckle. 'You're lying. Norbu told you to come and cheer me up. With lies.'

'I'm not lying. I know where she is.'

'She told you?'

Yangchen paused. 'No.'

Lobsang gave the same laugh. 'It's all right, Yangchen. *I'm* all right. I just need some time.'

'You're wrong about her, you know. Norbu told me what you think.'

'What do I think?'

'That she's on a beach in Thailand with her new Australian boyfriend.'

'I never said Thailand.' Lobsang considered it. 'Possible, though.'

'You shouldn't be so flippant,' Yangchen replied. 'You'll feel guilty for it later.'

'*I'll* feel guilty? For risking death by gunfire or frostbite so that I could be with her? For having it all thrown back in my face? I don't feel guilty. I feel stupid.'

'She only did it because you outshone her when you did all that. She used to be the worldly one, the wise and brave one, then a man walked over the Himalayas to be here, a man whose own brother was killed the last time he did it, a man who speaks four languages and met the Dalai Lama! The one thing she had never felt in Lhasa was inadequacy, but you made her feel it. Everything she had ever achieved was overshadowed by you. *And* you were poor and an exile. How could she top that? That's what she told me. She said she was doing it to reassert herself. But I think she was doing it because she wanted to make you proud of her.'

Lobsang let his cup rest on the edge of the table. Yangchen's speech – delivered, it seemed, on that hysterical border between tears and laughter – had left him confused. He tried to make sense of the concepts, tying his pride with her inadequacy and creating knots from them that he could not unpick.

'She isn't cheating on you,' Yangchen said. 'She never has. You were the first thing she told me about when she came home from university in her second year. She had only known you a month or two, but her amazing new boyfriend was all she could talk about. When she came here at the end and you went back to Nepal, she wouldn't leave her house for a week because she had no control over her tears. And when your sister told her you had gone missing, I genuinely thought that she might do something... stupid. I promise you, Lobsang. There's no other man.'

'You just said you don't know for sure!' he howled.

'No, I said it wasn't her who told me where she is now. But she told me what she was doing when she started. And others have told me what's happened since.'

Lobsang refilled their cups and they sat opposite each other while Yangchen laid out Drolma's story like a pack of cards across a table. Long before Lobsang arrived in Lhasa, before even Drolma came home from university, a small group – mostly boys – from Drolma and Yangchen's school had formed, calling themselves 'Stone and Ice'. One of them was an ex-boyfriend of Drolma and, when she graduated, he asked if she would like to join the group.

'He asked her because she was the one who came up with the name,' Yangchen explained. 'A long time ago, back in school. Did she ever tell you her "Stone and Ice" theory?'

'No,' Lobsang said, aware that there were many things he still did not know about his love.

'I'll try and explain it, but I won't be able to do it justice. Not like the way Drolma tells it. Basically, she used to say that the symbolism of Tibet as a snow lion and China as a dragon was wrong. She believed that there was a better metaphor: Tibet as stone and China as ice. Right now, we are in an ice age, and China is covering Asia with its thoughts and people. But stone, you see, is resistant to ice. It can get chipped and broken and eroded, but it will always exist, sustaining itself from beneath. Ice, on the other hand, is a temporary condition, not like stone, which endures. Drolma used to say that we needed a new stone age, that in fact there would be one – for no matter how long an ice age lasts, it will always melt in the end, and the stone will always win.'

This, Yangchen explained, became the core philosophy of 'Stone and Ice', which sought to 'end the ice age by ushering in global climate change', and the prospect of joining the group both tempted and excited Drolma, but not enough. She had ordered Lobsang back to Kathmandu for fear he would put himself in danger; how could she then justify putting herself in danger by joining an illegal anti-Chinese group?

'And then I crossed the border anyway,' Lobsang said. 'I gave her a free pass to join.'

'Don't be stupid,' Yangchen snapped at him. 'Drolma didn't join until a few months ago. You were here a whole year before she even considered it.'

'So why did she do it?'

'You know what she's like – full of hot air. She goes on about freedom for Tibet, but does she ever really do anything? Come on, how many marches or protests or demonstrations or whatever did she take part in at university?'

'None.'

'Exactly. She was all talk. But then, after a while, it was, well, like I said, I think she got *jealous*. You're an outsider, you don't get it, but this group of friends we have, we've been like this since school. It takes a long time for new boyfriends and girlfriends to be accepted, if they are at all. But then you sauntered in and suddenly everyone wants to spend more time with you than Drolma. She used to be the interesting one of the group.'

'That's no reason to...'

'But it wasn't like she even cared that much,' Yangchen interrupted. 'She was more happy that you had been accepted, that everyone loved you as much as she does. She just wanted to show off, just once. To show you what she was capable of.'

'I still don't understand why she needed to keep it all a big secret from me.'

'Involving you in "Stone and Ice" would have put your life at risk. Drolma is a Lhasa citizen with respectable parents. You are an exile with no identity card. An arrest would have held very different outcomes for you and Drolma.'

There was a sickness growing in Lobsang's stomach. It was yet small, but he recognised it intimately, from the way it ached at his ribs to the way it trembled up through and along his arms. It engulfed and absorbed the bitter jealousy of another man, made that seem feeble by comparison, and instead brought up images he did not want to remember.

'They got this idea that 2009, this year, would be a big one for the Tibetan independence movement.' Yangchen's words came through muffled and distant as blood rushed to his blazing ears. '1959. 1989. The biggest Lhasa uprisings always happen on the 9s. They began to plan something. At first, they wanted it on the anniversary of the Dalai Lama's flight, but then they decided it would have more impact on National Day.' The floor beneath Lobsang's feet became a bank-burst tributary of the Kyi Chu, wood-brown water coursing and gushing. '"The People's Republic of China will be sixty years old in October," that's what she told me. "It's the perfect time to begin the new stone age."'

'What were they planning on doing?' Lobsang managed to utter.

'A poster campaign followed by a demonstration on the Barkhor. They were recruiting well. Into their hundreds, Drolma said. Perhaps one of them was a spy.'

Lobsang lost all feeling above the neck. The sight of Yangchen before him blurred, mingling with a long-distance image of armed border guards surrounding a young man, and to say anything more was impossible.

'The police came,' Yangchen finished. 'Drolma and twelve others from "Stone and Ice" were arrested. They were taken to Drapchi.'

Pilgrims' Progress

|

It took a day to drive from Shigatse down through the arid plains of southern Tibet to the small town of Shegar, where the Himalayas begin and, behind them, Nepal. We stayed on the China-Nepal Highway – the Friendship Highway – the 435-mile single carriageway which runs from Lhasa all the way to the border town of Zhangmu. Few other vehicles passed ours. The road seemed characterised by stillness, silence and heat. It could have been desert Australia or Afghanistan. The only telling symbols that this soil was Tibetan were the *mani*-stones and makeshift pebble-*chortens* heaped precariously along the sides of the road, or the thin threads of prayer flags which fluttered from hillocks somewhere in the distance: their collective and unremitting presence evidence of human hands and human feet, yet also a marker of human absence, like faded gravestones in a derelict churchyard.

The prayer flags increased in number as we rose up and conquered each high pass, draped over boulders and signposts, trailing down into the valleys below. These flags – always one blue, one white, one red, one green, one yellow, then one blue again – are blown by the wind, and the woodblock-printed prayers upon them are thereby released to spread the world with peace and compassion. Unlike the Tibetan flag, as illegal in the TAR as a picture of the Dalai Lama, these prayer flags are the true emblem of Tibetan nationhood, and they outnumber the Chinese red flags which hang limply from official buildings by a million to one. Fundamentally, they are a testament to the resilience of the Tibetans themselves, who scramble up to these peaks and tie the lengths of string over passes which seem insurmountable, so that all those in the villages and towns and cities below may have a skyline capped with spirituality. At one pass, a third-of-a-mile-long line of prayer flags was strung taut over a 650-feet drop, and I wondered how anyone had ever managed to achieve such a feat. Perhaps a stone had been tied to one end and then lobbed and reeled back in again and again until it found the waiting catcher's hands at the other end; perhaps, like a spider, they had merely been cast on to the wind, to find purchase wherever.

Dawa stopped the Landcruiser at each mountain pass, launched himself from the vehicle and screamed '*La Gyalo!*' at the sky. It meant 'Praise to the Gods!': a phrase Tibetan pilgrims call each time they cross a summit to appease the protective deities who guard each pass. Dawa would then hurry us out into the cold winds and urge us to take photographs while he did the same on his ageing mobile phone camera, even though he had driven this country his whole life. It was clear that his nudges were that of the boaster, the man proud of his land and desperate to show it off. His good humour at such high points was infectious, and he was never the first back in the Landcruiser.

Travelling is good when the journey is as exciting as the destination. This was to be my last long foray through Tibet, and, from my entry at its northernmost point down along the railway line and then all the way by road from Lhasa to Zhangmu, I never ceased to remain in awe of the roof of the world and its striking landscapes. I have never spent so many hours in one country staring from the window, and I loved it. This was Tibet in perpetuity for me: a sky-wide and lonely land of delicate-brown deserts, fierce-white mountains, and milky-blue rivers fed by snowmelt, which coursed through stone and ice.

Such long periods of staring, of pure reliance on visual stimuli, trained my eyes, and I began to see that, in fact, life out here on the plains was not as rare as I had earlier supposed; it was just camouflaged. Marmots blended into the earth, birds of prey hovered in the halo of the sun and, perhaps most surprising of all, those fields of black rocks were in fact huge herds of grazing bovine beasts.

'Yaks!' I shouted involuntarily the first time I realised.

'No,' Tashi said. 'Not yaks. Dzo.'

Despite his sneering tone, I was grateful for Tashi's correction. Yaks, which used to number over a million in pre-Chinese Tibet, are in the twenty-first century an endangered species, with only fifteen thousand left. All I saw throughout Tibet were dzo: a cross between a yak and a cow, a sturdy and worthwhile livestock, but nonetheless an indicative metaphor of the Sinicisation of Tibet.

It is impossible to overestimate the importance of yaks for Tibetans. Without them, it is arguable that Tibetans never would have been able to thrive upon the plateau. So perfectly evolved for their high-altitude environment that they will die if taken too close to sea level, yaks supply Tibetans with an astonishing array of necessities: far more than simple beasts of burden, their milk is drunk and churned into butter, which is in itself used to drink in tea or made into lamps or statues; their meat constitutes most meals; and their hair and hides are woven into everything from clothes to the canvas of nomad tents.

When one has identified the dzo, it does not take long to make the next leap of recognition and spot, amongst them, the people. Or, more often, the single person. Deep in the midst of each herd I began to notice the shepherds: sometimes just a head poking above a throng of black, hairy shoulders; at other times a full body sat low on the ground, looking at me as I looked back at him. These, too, in their yak-skin robes or *chubas*, blended immaculately with their environment, perfecting the camouflage of movement, and such solitary figures began to pop up so frequently that I wondered with alarm how I had ignored them at each previous stop, when I had pissed happily into the wind.

There were others, of course, who I had seen all the way from Lhasa: the roadside pilgrims on foot or, more often, on their bellies, who were snaking their long ways to the capital and its myriad sites of worship. It can seem that everything in Tibet offers the opportunity for pilgrimage, from the mini *koras* of each tomb, statue or temple to the larger *koras* of the Barkhor or Nam-tso Lake, yet the true pilgrimages are those which do not take minutes or hours, but weeks or months. The most famous of these is the pilgrimage to and then around the holy Mount Kailash in far-western Tibet, but to travel from anywhere in the country to Lhasa, or to a lesser extent Shigatse, is a pilgrimage most Tibetans try to make at least once in a lifetime. It is believed that such a pilgrimage will enhance one's karma, and the harder the journey the greater the accumulated merit.

Before leaving England, I joked with a friend of mine that these pilgrims reminded me of backpackers. Both he and I had spent large portions of our early twenties backpacking around the globe, and had ourselves succumbed to the peculiar delight backpackers find in retelling their most challenging travelling-stories. The tougher the journey, the greater the ooohs and aaahs of those other backpackers around the hostel table, and my friend and I had competed with each other at home after bouts of travelling over who had endured the most difficult journey.

These Tibetan pilgrims put us to shame. It is an age-old tradition, one which precedes the advent of roads in Tibet by a thousand years, when pilgrims would follow the songlines of mountains and sacred rocks to navigate their way to their destinations. Today, the roads are used by the pilgrims, though most still ignore the comfort of vehicles and instead prefer to use their own bodily mobility. Some walk the hundreds of miles, but others see even this as too easy, and instead prostrate themselves along the entire length of their journey. This involves lying flat and face down on the ground with arms and legs outstretched, then standing up, stepping forward to the spot your fingertips reached, placing your toes upon them, and lying back down again. By prostrating, the pilgrim is moving one careful body-length at a time. I had seen such movement by those on their hardy *koras* around the Potala or Jokhang, which could take them all day, but had never imagined that some would do this all the way along the Friendship Highway. Wearing wooden paddles to protect their hands and thick aprons to protect their bodies, they inch their way along the road, progressing as little as three miles a day, and sometimes taking over a year to reach their destination – at which, they will then return to the ground, and prostrate themselves around it.

To see this ardour from the window of a comfortable Landcruiser is humbling; and to consider it from the window of an atheistic mind is perplexing. Such devotion to the intangible, to the incorporeal, is a concept as alien to me as the Crusades. My idea of a hard journey is a thirty-hour bus ride or a night sleeping rough, but there will always be a beer and a conversation at the end of it. Even in my poorest, hardiest days, I could never last more than a week without civilisation or company. What must it be like to slither on your belly for a year, with nothing save a few rolls of *tsampa* and a blanketless, desert bed at the end of each day? What must it be like to travel so light you cannot even carry a book, and to have your own recitations of *Om mani padme hum* as your only experience of the human voice? Such repetition is anathema to me. Give me variety to live. How can one possibly endure such an existence?

Such an existence is, I suppose, endemic to the entire belief system of Tibetan Buddhism, which states that, while I claim the need for variety, for earthly pleasures, it is exactly this which is holding me back from ever achieving enlightenment. The Chinese dissident writer Wang Lixiong puts forth the theory that, for Tibetans, such subservience to their beliefs, and indeed such a rigorous belief system, is a product of the Tibetans' hostile natural environment. Tibetan Buddhism, and its forbear Bon, have been so successful up on the plateau because they not only offer an escape from such an unforgiving environment, but moreover they embrace the hardships of life on the roof of the world, and state that those who suffer the most (by all natural accounts, surely the Tibetans come close to the top of the poll) are those who are rewarded the most in the next life. This is why, Lixiong theorises, Tibetans will leave their already precarious existences in nomad tents or crumbling houses to prostrate themselves 500 miles towards the opulent palaces and temples of their god-kings, why they sacrifice most of their earnings to monks and monasteries, and why they continue to live in such remote and demanding landscapes.

I considered Lixiong's ideas as we sped past two pilgrims who sat by the side of the road munching *tsampa*. They waved at us. I remembered that the great Tibetan historian Tsering Shakya had already criticised Lixiong for allowing Chinese cultural imperialism to colour his thoughts, that even though he was considered an enemy by the Party for his dissident writings, Lixiong could still not escape the very education he had received as a Chinese national, and that such reliance on the notion of 'fear' amongst the Tibetans' ways and beliefs led to a fundamental prejudice within his theories. But, as I watched the next pilgrim a few miles down the road – alone and staring at the gravel an inch from his nose – I realised that Lixiong's theory made sense to me far more than whatever that pilgrim might have told me in his justifications for his chosen mode of journey. And I realised that, though I had to come to Tibet to try to understand the whole Sino-Tibetan issue and make some sense of it within my own head, I perhaps never would. I looked over at Joe to instigate a conversation, and realised I had nothing to say.

2

At Shegar we bought our passes for the Everest National Park and checked into a hotel for the night. There were still a few hours of sunlight left, and I wanted to walk before dinner.

Shegar is a small and narrow town huddled under the shadow of a green mountain, up which nimble goats creep and wooden huts cling. A large, Chinese-built bridge crosses the emaciated river, leading a single stretch of black road down to a dead end. This road is short, straight and seemingly alien here, but behind it the village exists in genuine: a lively and twisting maze of paths, shrines and low houses. Children huddled around me with outstretched hands and grinning, snotty faces while I bought some new socks from a stall in the street market, and then burst into joyous screams and scuffles when I moved to the next stall and gave the owner a few yuan for some sweets, which he distributed carefully amongst them, ensuring they all received at least one each. A few adults moved closer to me as the children scrambled away, offering stickers, cassette players and gloves. One waved a foot-long aerosol canister in my face, and I took it off him to study it.

'What is this?' I asked.

'Oxygen,' he said. 'You going Everest? You need this. Noooo oxygen up there. This help.'

'How much?'

'Three yuan. Two for five.'

I bought two canisters of the compressed oxygen, doubting I would need them, but reasoning that they might make a fun present (though little did I know that, later, at Kathmandu airport they would be pulled from my backpack and I would be marched into a small room to be asked why I had brought explosives into the airport).

Behind the street market, the pathways twisted and curved like those around a monastery, and I got lost navigating them. At the thin T-junction of one, two bulky dzo blocked my way and, as I turned to walk from them, I noticed that they had begun to follow me. I quickened my pace and made a few sharp turns around corners, realising as I did so the imbecility of such actions, as if I was trying to outfox the police, but the dzo remained close behind me – indeed, seemed to be getting closer. Then panic as I hit a dead end. I turned. The dzo were still there. This was ridiculous. Had I really just been cornered by *livestock*? As I contemplated vaulting the wall into somebody's back garden, an old woman half my size appeared from nowhere and shooed the dzo off. I smiled in gratitude at my diminutive saviour, who cackled at me, and then disappeared again.

There was a *kora* around Shegar's mountain, and I wanted to walk it, but the sun was getting low, and if I had just been stalked and outwitted by two dzo, I was clearly not suited to circumambulate a night-time mountain. There would be no septuagenarian women up there to rescue me.

3

That evening, I ate dinner with my group, our guide and our driver. Dawa inspected my new socks and nodded in approval at the purchase. He had a pen and sheet of paper on the table before him and, after filling my cup with yak-butter tea from his flask, he returned to the letter he was writing. Sipping my tea, I pulled my Tibet guidebook from my daypack and began to leaf through it. A photograph of debating monks caught Dawa's eye, and he gingerly plucked the book from my hands, flicking through it from the last page to the first, and then settling intently on one page. This was the preface, written by the Dalai Lama. The guidebook itself warned its readers not to reveal it to any officials in Tibet for fear they might find this page and confiscate it, for it was headed with the Dalai Lama's official seal: two snow lions beneath a wheel and three mountains. This was what Dawa had recognised.

At the bottom of the preface was the fourteenth Dalai Lama's signature, and Dawa traced his finger over it a few times before snatching up his pen, turning over his sheet of paper, and then practising the signature again and again until he had it perfect. He folded the paper up with a satisfied grunt, popped it into his shirt pocket, and then looked me in the eye, patting his chest twice.

Bowls of *tsampa* and yak noodle soup were laid out before us all. Tashi was in good spirits, and revealed that he was excited about visiting Mount Everest the next day.

'You must have been before,' I said. 'Surely all your tours end there?'

'Not all. A lot of my groups only like to go as far south as Shigatse. They are Chinese, you see, and in the very south of Tibet there is not so much for the Chinese to see and do. And they have to go back to Lhasa to fly. Everest is too far. But I have been five times. Tomorrow will be my sixth. Everest is not a very holy mountain, but I like it a lot. You will see tomorrow. It is a very beautiful place.'

I picked up a wad of *tsampa* and chewed on it. Dawa said something in Tibetan to Tashi.

'Dawa would like to know if you have enjoyed Tibet,' Tashi translated.

'I have,' I replied. 'Tibet is beautiful.'

Tashi relayed my words to Dawa, and the latter beamed at me.

'Do *you* enjoy Tibet?' I asked Tashi, who cocked his head to one side and smiled.

'You are asking me, I think, perhaps one question when really you mean a thousand. You want to know if I am happy here as a citizen of China, I think.'

'Perhaps I do.'

'*My* life is good. Next year I will buy a house. I could not have done this without the help of Chinese economics. There is perhaps one thing I am sorry for, however.'

'What?'

'You see there?' Tashi pointed his spoon at the framed photograph of a Gelugpa monk wearing a curved and conical yellow hat which hung on the wall above the bar. 'That is a very famous abbot from Tashilhunpo who has now left Tibet for India. There are many like him, monks, abbots and lamas who no longer live here. You know that I am Buddhist. And it makes me sad that I will never hear their teachings.'

'Because the Chinese drove them out.'

Tashi laughed. 'No, Charlie. The Chinese never exiled my teachers. My teachers *chose* to leave. They *chose* exile. That is a very important difference.'

Tashi was right: the Dalai Lama and all his Tibet-in-exile government had chosen to exile themselves. But they had not done so willingly. Their flight was reaction, the only option when the alternative of the defence mechanism, to fight, had been nullified by the volume and capacity of the 'liberating' forces. There were, of course, many lamas, abbots and high-ranking monks who stayed in Tibet following the Dalai Lama's 1959 flight, but by staying they became the first victims of the Cultural Revolution, and many of those who weren't executed or imprisoned were stripped of their robes and forced to work as labourers or butchers, or forced to copulate and marry. Many who survived the horrors of the Cultural Revolution found themselves fleeing Tibet anyway, and they still continue to. Today, nearly all of the major Tibetan lamas and abbots have left the country, leaving, in essence, no one behind to replace them but the Chinese bureaucrats themselves, who have embraced this top-down suffocation of the Tibetan theocracy. Such a policy is deceptively cunning in its longevity. It is a waiting game which the Chinese know they will win. Looked at as a chessboard, China has all its pieces, while Tibet is being systematically stripped down to nothing but its pawns, and those bishops and rooks which have been won back – the Panchen Lama, for instance – have been substituted by the opposition's players. As the Dalai Lama himself gets older, no one even dares think what might happen when he dies. What is certain is that, if he even is reborn as the fifteenth, he will be approved first by Beijing.

4

We congregated at the Landcruiser early the next morning. It was still dark, though the fingernail moon and plethora of stars lit our way. Tashi had encouraged us to leave this early, for in doing so we might see Everest at sunrise. The Friendship Highway directed us down through a checkpoint, where three Han policemen ordered us out of the car and checked our Tibet permits, Everest National Park passes, China visas, passports and faces with their torches. We were told not to get back in the car and left to stand in the frozen night air as they returned to their booth. Ten minutes later, a gloved hand appeared from the window and waved, and we were back on our way.

The road seemed to rise perpetually as we forged on, and our emotions with it. No one spoke in the Landcruiser, and even Dawa forgot to light a single cigarette. Out the window, the sky morphed from black to an ever-lightening blue, and the sun crept above the horizon just as we crept up and on to our final mountain pass. Dawa stopped the car, stepped from it and yelled '*La Gyalo!*' at the crest of the sun, and

I walked out on to the road and looked south. There, in a long, thin line across the horizon, were the Himalayas – jagged, mysterious, and terrifying. And, pushing up as their unmistakeable centrepiece, was Everest in the sunrise.

chu-soom

Lhasa grew dark in Drolma's absence. The streets narrowed; Han faces crowded them. Lobsang had never seen – or never noticed – so many soldiers and police and guards before, nor so many guns. The tips of the rifles which pointed out from rooftops filled the skylines, jostling for position with the closed-circuit cameras which hung and pivoted and watched. Lobsang saw a spy in every face, heard an informer in every conversation, and felt followed on every street. His friends had begun to avoid and ignore him. They did not congregate in their usual spaces. They did not answer their doors when he knocked.

'It's not you they're avoiding,' Norbu explained. 'It's the police. Each of your friends has had or is going to have a visit. That's how the police work. They start from one person, then they speak to every other person connected with them, no matter how tenuous the connection is. And, if what Yangchen says is true, they've got thirteen members of this "Stone and Ice". That's a lot of visits.'

'How long will it last?' Lobsang asked. 'I can't find out anything about Drolma without help.'

'*You* need to be more careful than anyone else.'

'Drolma won't say anything about me. And none of the other guys know me.'

'Didn't you listen to what I just said? They visit and they interview every person Drolma has even the remotest connection to. Only one of them has to mention a boyfriend, not even your name or address. Then they're after you. The boyfriend. The one person most likely to be complicit or have information. And if they do find you, they'll take you. For a long time.' Norbu paused and looked away from Lobsang. 'They'll take me, too.'

A month had passed since Drolma's arrest. That she was in Drapchi seemed to be the general consensus, but it had been impossible to confirm. With Lobsang's delicate status in Tibet, he had no official channels available to him by which he could secure information. It was all rumour, rumour which thinned each passing day as Drolma's friends locked themselves into hermetic lives. Lobsang did all he could to rally support for Drolma, but few would even talk to him about her, let alone help him campaign for her release.

'There's nothing you can do,' Yangchen told him in Norbu's apartment. She had asked Lobsang not to come to her home anymore. 'Drolma was breaking the law.'

'By planning a peaceful demonstration?' Lobsang asked.

'By planning an anti-Chinese protest,' Norbu corrected him, and Yangchen nodded.

'But the police have no proof of that,' Lobsang said. 'They were just meeting together. They were arrested before 1 October, before they got a chance to protest.'

'They made posters,' Yangchen said. 'From what I hear, the posters defamed Hu Jintao and named the Dalai Lama as the true leader of Tibet. That's a terrible crime in itself.'

A heavy silence hung over the three heads, tempered by impotence and the awareness of it.

'Someone should speak to her parents,' Norbu suggested. 'They've got more influence than any other Tibetan I know. They might be able to get her out.'

'Someone already has,' Yangchen said. 'They won't do a thing. They're ashamed their daughter had anything to do with a group like "Stone and Ice". They've disowned her.'

Lobsang stared hard at Yangchen, weighing her words carefully. Then he sprang to his feet, made a dash for the door and hopped on to his rickshaw before Yangchen or Norbu could stop him. He pedalled to Drolma's home, leaving his bike askew on the pavement and, for only the second time in his life, knocked on the door. A woman with long, straight and sleek black hair which fell to her waist answered, an older Drolma and just as beautiful, though her beauty was hidden behind a manifest misery. She had been, it was clear, crying.

'Sometimes I wonder if she knew us at all,' she whispered in incredulity while her husband, Drolma's father, massaged her hand. They sat together on a long sofa in the front room while Lobsang hovered awkwardly in a corner. 'She kept so much from us. What did she think we would do?'

'She thought you would disapprove,' Lobsang replied.

'We never disapproved of a thing Drolma did,' her father said. 'We were always supportive, always cared.'

'But not enough,' her mother added.

Lobsang felt miserable. He had charged into the house, barging past Drolma's mother on the doorstep. Drolma's father was in the front room and Lobsang confronted him with myriad accusations: none of which, he was to discover, had any grounding. The moment they had heard about Drolma's arrest, they had marched straight to the police station, where the mother had stayed for four days while the father petitioned every influential person he knew for help. None of it had mattered. They had been told that Drolma's crimes were too severe to warrant any kind of levity. They had been told to expect the worst.

'She shouldn't have kept you a secret, either,' the mother said, and the father nodded. 'You seem kind.'

Lobsang cycled the long route home: the route which avoided as many of the military posts dotted about the city as possible. With the admission of Drolma's parents, he felt more vulnerable than ever. If even they could not secure her release, how on earth could he?

The apartment was empty when he arrived. Norbu had perhaps walked Yangchen home, or persuaded her out for a drink. Lobsang did not mind the solitude. His thoughts whirled from the impact of the day's revelations and, for the first time since her disappearance, he contemplated the likelihood that he might never see Drolma again. It was a firm possibility, one he had not yet dared to entertain in the unconscious knowledge of the pain it would cause. That pain was immediate and overwhelming, and he spent the next four hours on his bed, wide-eyed, still, wrists clamped between knees, vacant and blunted.

Norbu did not come home that night. This would not normally be unusual, but since Drolma's arrest everyone

Lobsang knew had imposed a curfew upon themselves and not left their homes after dark. He wondered if perhaps the old lecher had finally seduced Yangchen and spent the night with her, but when she turned up late in the morning to check on Lobsang she revealed that she had not seen him since she had left the apartment the previous day. Norbu had not walked her home.

Yangchen agreed to ask after Norbu at some of his favourite bars and to speak to some of his friends and employees to find out where he was. Lobsang was thankful, agreeing with her that it was too dangerous for him to do the same and following her instructions by shutting all the windows, blinds, doors and curtains and staying inside until either she or Norbu returned.

When, two hours later, she did and he had not, Lobsang allowed himself the right to panic. She had gone to all the places Norbu was likely to have been and spoken to all the people Norbu was likely to have been with, but nobody had seen him for at least twenty-four hours. Yangchen offered to stay with Lobsang, but he insisted she leave. If Norbu had been taken, they would be back looking for him. There was no need for her to be there, too. Yangchen left. Lobsang moved to the kitchen, where he made cups of tea which he could not drink.

At 9 p.m., with black silence outside, the front door opened. It was Norbu. His clothes and hair were wet, though it was not raining outside.

'Where have you been?' Lobsang stuttered.

Norbu shuffled into the kitchen, steadied himself against the table and then sat down. Lobsang brought him lukewarm tea. Norbu downed it.

'Are you... are you all right?' Lobsang felt foolish asking such rubbish. It was clear Norbu was not, though he nodded. 'I've been with the police.'

'Did you see Drolma?' The selfishness of the question hit Lobsang the moment it left his lips.

'No. She's in Drapchi. It's definite. They confirmed it.' Norbu seemed to find it hard to meet Lobsang's eyes. Instead, he directed his clipped sentiments at the floor.

'Did they say for how long or what –'

Norbu interrupted Lobsang with a weak smack of his palm on the table. 'Lobsang, you have to leave,' he said, and Lobsang froze at Norbu's tone. 'They know Drolma has a boyfriend. They know he's illegal. Someone's said something. You have to get out.'

'Out of Lhasa?' The thought nauseated him.

'Out of Tibet. Go back to Nepal. Go back to your family. You're not safe here. They don't know you live with me. But it won't take them long to find out.'

'I can't leave Drolma,' Lobsang muttered, but there was no force behind his words, and he began to doubt himself. *Can I?*

'You can help her more there. You're incapable of anything here. Useless. But you have Chinese friends in India. You have Tibetan friends in Nepal. You could go back to Dharamsala. You could tell the Dalai Lama.'

Lobsang looked pityingly at Norbu, who believed that one summer in the land of the Tibet-in-exile government and a few minutes in the company of the Dalai Lama had given Lobsang some sort of sway over the man. 'The Dalai Lama can't even sleep in his own bed or shit in his own toilet. How is he supposed to get my Drolma out of prison?'

Norbu's face registered emotion for the first time since his entrance: it was shock, shock mingled with resentment and fear. Lobsang should not have said those things.

'If you stay here you *will* be arrested,' Norbu said. 'You *will* be sent to prison. Those are facts. That you will be killed is not, but it is probable. You will gain nothing by remaining. Drolma will gain nothing by you remaining. The only chance you have is if you leave. We can keep things going here – me, Yangchen, Drolma's parents – and you can work from outside. What was it you said your guide told you when you left Nepal to walk into the mountains?'

Lobsang had to think for a moment. He had told Norbu his entire life story five times over, each time with more detail, and it took a while to locate the specific memory Norbu had alluded to.

But then he remembered it. *One voice asking questions from the outside – especially if they're the right questions aimed at the right people – can do more than you might think*, the guide had said, referring to Ji. Perhaps he was right. Perhaps Norbu was right. Inside China's borders Lobsang could barely raise a fuss without fear of incarceration, torture and perhaps death. But on the outside he was legal, a free citizen of the world, and that gave him the right to shout and stamp his feet and make as much commotion as he wanted. Others had done it, had started with just one voice and one demand, and then they had been joined by like-minded folk, by fighters and the righteous, by crowds and then sometimes governments and nations, all joining together to apply pressure where it was needed. Lobsang began to imagine a long line of marchers spilling through McLeod Ganj, another filling every nook of Kathmandu's Thamel District and yet another flooding Delhi's Connaught Place, in and amongst them every religion and every colour, children and old men and monks and fashion models and film stars, Jamyang, Chogyal and his father, Ji, the Dalai Lama even, and uniting them all, two words, woven into banners and painted on to placards and hollered from every mouth – *Free Drolma!*

Norbu cut through Lobsang's reverie. 'It's the only thing you can do.'

He understood that Norbu was right. He understood that, for the second time in his young life, he was about to become a refugee again.

88-48, That's My Number

Before 1950, there were scarce hotels in Tibet, and the few intrepid travellers who conquered the foothills of the plateau and succeeded in forging out on to its wide and lonely plains often stayed as guests in local monasteries. Today, with Han tourism in Tibet bigger than it has ever been before, there is a bounty of comfortable and comforting accommodations on offer, and the few Westerners who make it here are herded towards them. Monasteries are off-limits except for quick daytime visits, and many of them can no longer support guests anyway, working as they are on skeleton crews of the few monks allowed to stay there, let alone travellers.

But there are some which still house visitors. The Rongphu monastery – a small cluster of buildings etched into a hill in the shadow of Everest – offers rooms for tourists. The Chinese have good reason for opening Rongphu to outsiders: the Everest National Park is a tourist hotspot, and many yuan can be made by providing the myriad trekkers, mountaineers and day trippers with a roof, a bed and a cup of hot tea. We paid our money to a young man in jeans and a fleece rather than monk's robes, and he walked us to our room with four beds and a six-foot-high pile of blankets. The rattling window looked out on to a gravelled courtyard, where two mastiffs snarled at each other and then took off as one as a single-cylinder tractor pulled in to the grounds.

We gathered around the large stove in the low dining room, imbibing yak-butter tea in preparation for the trek to Everest Base Camp. Gavril seemed nervous, itching to begin the walk as soon as possible. Tashi appeared in the canteen and sat with us.

'Maybe it is better if you wait for tomorrow,' he said. 'I have been talking to the monks. An Italian climber died here two days ago. He got stuck halfway up Everest and froze to death at night. The monks say the cold weather here is worse than it has been in years.'

'Perhaps we should wait,' Tanya offered.

Gavril resolutely shook his head. 'I'm going,' he said. 'You can stay here if you like, but I'm going.' He stood up, shouldering a daypack which seemed to me curiously empty and deflated.

We agreed to join him and stepped outside, away from the interior stove. The cold sunk in and penetrated my bone marrow. It was still mid morning, and the sun was low. I rushed back to the room to empty my backpack on my hard bed, wrapping myself in jumpers, jackets, hats, thermal leggings, gloves and a scarf. As we began the trek towards Everest Base Camp, I was just a pair of eyes and a mound of clothes.

On either side of the valley, the hills narrowed in with claustrophobic rises, but the sun crested over them so that, as

I walked, layers of clothing were peeled away one at a time. A river gurgled noisily beside the pathway, the thick crust of ice at its sides melting and breaking into its surging middle. The path rose as we approached Everest Base Camp, with it the frozen winds which came fresh from the Himalayas and whipped between my legs and across my face. One by one, the layers of clothing were replaced. A herd of antelope broke out from the peak of the eastern hill, racing down into the valley and then congregating about the edges of the burgeoning river to drink. They ignored our presence, as did the lean and solitary dog which nosed its way about a skip overflowing with rubbish, munching on the scraps of tinned meats and high-energy chocolate bars left behind by mountaineers.

The rubbish itself seemed to characterise Everest Base Camp. The climbing season was over, and along the plains which had just weeks before been filled with tents and camping stoves and humans hungry for the endurance test of a lifetime, there was now only detritus, spread across the ground like the shoreline jetsam of a receding tide. It seemed that those who had come here to conquer nature had done so not just by their exertions, but also by their litter: broken bottles and crisp packets, empty gas canisters and discarded clothes, pits of frozen shit. Everest Base Camp was ugly, nothing more than a photo opportunity, and I was dismayed to discover that, even here, there was an entrance fee.

Two harassed and sulky Chinese soldiers manned the sentry point, a small tent which bent and flapped in the wind, and we took turns to walk in and slap our notes on the metal table while the guards flicked through our passports. They came out to watch us as we climbed the shale hillock which would give us our closest view of Everest. We were not allowed any further.

Joe stood next to me and pointed towards another hill half a mile away. 'It used to be that you could walk all the way out to that one,' he said. 'This whole area from here to there is Everest Base Camp. But they've closed it down. This is as far as anyone who hasn't got a pass to climb the mountain can go. And that costs thousands, tens of thousands.'

'Why can't you go there anymore?' Tanya asked.

Joe grimaced into the wind. 'Some asshole American tourist walked out there and planted a Tibetan flag into the hill. The soldiers arrested him, his group and his Tibetan guide. Him and his group were driven straight to the Nepali border. The guide got six years in prison.' Joe spat on the ground.

A sudden shout pierced the air from behind us, and we turned to see one of the soldiers running forward. Gavril had broken the line, and was steadfastly marching towards Everest. The guard continued to scream as he chased Gavril. His companion had run back into the tent, from which he reappeared moments later with a rifle.

We watched in mounting horror. The two soldiers had placed themselves in front of Gavril, and were pushing him backwards. Gavril retreated a few steps and then stopped. The angles of his gesticulations suggested he was attempting to reason with them. The guards screamed at him and Gavril's voice rose in response. A current of Bulgarian and Mandarin invectives launched itself on to the wind and carried up the hillsides. Suddenly, Gavril raised his hands to protect himself from another push by the first soldier, and the second raised his gun. I started forward and, when the second soldier saw me advancing, the gun swivelled towards me. I backstepped. One of the guards took Gavril by the arm and led him into the tent. The other followed behind, his gun still raised and aimed at the back of Gavril's head.

'What should we do?' I asked Tashi.

'We should leave. Now.' Tashi turned and left the hillock, striding down the path in the direction of Rongphu.

Joe, Tanya and I remained. We told ourselves this was the closest we would ever get to Everest, that we had paid good money to be here, but we all knew we stayed out of concern for Gavril, and whatever might be happening to him in that tent. Soon, the icy winds heightened, the temperature plummeted, and Joe and Tanya left with a mumbled apology. I sat alone, alternating my gaze between the tent and the highest place on earth.

2

Mount Everest has only been known as Mount Everest for less than 150 years. Before that, it was simply known to Westerners as Peak XV, but once it was designated as the highest peak in the world by the Royal Geographic Society, it was assigned, in 1865, the name Everest, in honour of Sir George Everest: a colonial legend who mapped a swathe of the then-British Indian subcontinent. The fact that the mountain had been known by its Tibetan name – Qomolangma – for centuries was inconsequential to the imperialists, and the modern name has superseded the ancient ever since.

Tibetans still refer to Everest as Qomolangma: that appellation is chiselled into the two-foot-high stone tablet at 'Qomolangma Base Camp', and the towering, prayer-flag-strewn entranceway to the Everest National Park bears the English welcome: 'YOU ARE NOW ENTERING QOMOLANGMA NATIONAL NATURE PRESERVE'. This name comes from the amalgamation of the Tibetan words 'jolmo' (meaning 'queen') and 'glangma' (meaning 'on an ox'), for in Tibetan lore the mountain is the ox upon which the goddess Miyo resides. For Tibetans, Qomolangma is important in that she is one of the five Goddesses of Long Life (the other four are also Himalayan mountains), though she pales in comparison to the far holier mountains away from the Himalayas, of which Mount Kailash in western Tibet is the true queen.

Though Qomolangma is almost insignificant amongst the gigantic pantheon of gods and goddesses in Tibetan Buddhism, Everest holds a lure to Westerners unlike any other mountain. For Tibetans, a mountain's importance is heightened by the possibility of walking a *kora* around it (and Everest is nigh on impossible to circumambulate), but for others, it is the height itself which matters, and nowhere else on earth offers such a tantalising challenge. Over two hundred people have died attempting to reach Everest's summit. Edmund Hillary and Tenzing Norgay have gone down in history as the first to conquer the mountain in 1953, but there is a plethora of stories about others who have tried and failed. In 1934, Edmund Wilson decided the best way to get to the top would be by crash-landing his Gypsy Moth plane into the side of the mountain and then climbing the rest of the way up. He died during his second attempt, and his frozen cadaver was found at 21,000 feet decades later. In 1924, two renowned climbers of the era – George Mallory and Andrew Irvine – made their way towards the peak (which disputed evidence claims they conquered thirty years before Hillary and Norgay), and were last seen at 25,590 feet as clouds enveloped them. Their bodies were not found until 1999.

Since 1953, over three thousand people have stood upon our world's highest point of land. But how high that actually is remains a source of controversy. All around the Everest region, from the Tibetan plateau to the foothills of Nepal, 8848 is the totemic number which adorns all postcards, fridge-magnets and badly printed T-shirts. Mount Everest or Qomolangma, they say, is 8,848 metres (29,029 feet) high, and the tourists and travellers and trekkers who buy such tat adhere to the official number. But others claim the peak is in fact 8,850 metres high, while still others claim it is indeed lower than 8,848 metres, since – despite the tectonic-plate movements which are pushing the Himalayas ever upwards at a rate of 4 millimetres a year – the peak of Everest is measured not to the rock itself but to the snow and ice which caps it, and this is receding annually.

Whatever its true height, and despite the shitty effluence which streaks Base Camp in windblown lines, I found myself immersed in Everest, or Qomolangma, for close to two hours before the rising cold forced my retreat from the mountain. The sun had peaked over my valley, and was beginning to make its quick way towards the western hills. I still worried for Gavril, but it would get much colder, and dark, very soon, and I had an hour's walk back to the monastery's stove. With regret, I rose to my feet and shook the pins and needles from my legs. Turning my back on Everest felt like I was turning my back on Tibet, but all journeys are characterised by their end, or they would not be journeys. To live, to work, to *be* in Tibet meant stopping, and the impositional strictures put in place by the Chinese dictated movement through this country, this stolen Western Treasure of theirs, and dictated that I must return to Nepal or China itself.

Like so many other monasteries across Tibet and indeed China, Rongphu is a recent rebuild of the original destroyed during the Cultural Revolution. Centuries ago, monks used to make a pilgrimage to this spot to meditate in the place with the best proximity to and visibility of the holy Qomolangma. Gradually, individuals began to build small single-room huts from the stones of the valley so that when they or their fellows returned they would have shelter, for there were no caves here. Over time, more and more huts were built, increasingly elaborate, but always from the same material, so that an entire village which blended perfectly with its environment eventually sprawled some one and a quarter miles along the valley's eastern hill. The monks began to live in their shelters permanently, and as each new pilgrim came along, if they decided to stay, they would simply build their own hut, and Rongphu evolved from the earth.

Today, little remains of the original monastery and, when I had walked the 5 miles from the rebuild towards Base Camp, I had not even noticed it: it had always blended into the hills, did so more now than ever after its destruction, and I had been too enthralled with Everest herself. But, on the way back, I did. Wandering up to study an oddly shaped collection of rocks on a bank of the valley, it was only then that I realised I was at the edge of a ghost town. As I picked amongst it, I became increasingly surprised at how much was still intact: a large mortar and pestle set in the earth; a well; two-roomed houses with roofs and alcoves cut into the walls where icons would once have sat; a toilet. There was a semblance of glory still here within this hodgepodge of construction which had been moulded into and from the Himalayan stone, a perfect example of man and the environment working in harmony. But such glory was overshadowed, for the smashed walls and crumbling fireplaces spoke quietly and sadly of death.

Back at the new Rongphu, I circumambulated the large black *chorten* with a few of the sixty monks who lived where once hundreds had. They smiled and nodded at me as we walked, but I felt tired and irritable and frozen, and so retreated to the main building. One of the monks, perhaps sensing my blooming depression, hurried after me and caught me by the arm. Wordlessly, he guided me down to the walled entrance which led out on to the road to Base Camp, and pointed at a large, mirrored, concave dish sat on a makeshift tripod, with a cone of metal bars pointing out from its centre.

'Satellite dish?' I asked in surprise.

The monk looked at me with a half-smile, gesturing incomprehension with his arms.

'TV?' I said, making the charades-sign for the medium with my fingers, tracing a rectangle in the air.

The monk laughed and shook his head. He bent down to pick up the tiny kettle which rested atop the cone, pulled a mug from his robes, filled it with thick and salty yak-butter tea, and then offered it to me.

I drank deep and cursed my stupidity. I had seen these dishes across the TAR and Amdo, had even noticed the blackened kettles which rested in the centre of them, but had somehow never made the connection. My brain was too hard-wired towards decadence, for I had foolishly questioned how on earth these homes and monasteries could afford satellite television. They could not, and these were nothing of the sort, but were in fact solar cookers: heaters which reflected the rays of the high-altitude sun to boil a single kettle within minutes. The sudden understanding of all those dented dishes crested in my mind like the clichéd light bulb, and I fancied they were yet another product of the Tibetans' symbiotic relationship with their environment. It came as some surprise to learn, when I got home, that they had in fact been introduced to Tibet by the Chinese.

What is definitively Tibetan, however, is the cowpat stove. With wood a rarity up on the plateau and coal even more so, Tibetans learned to harness the excrement of their yaks and even of themselves for fuel centuries ago. Most of the food cooked and water heated in Tibet is done so over a smouldering fire of shit, and if that sounds disgusting, it is barely noticeable, for few bacteria can survive at an average altitude of 13,000 feet, and the burning excrement therefore gives off no nauseous smells.

After thanking the monk for my tea – which had warmed my blood, calmed my nerves and soothed my blistering lips – I hurried inside to join my friends around Rongphu's cowpat stove. Gavril had not returned, but Tashi assured me he would be fine. Joe and Tanya sat eating piping-hot noodles. I joined them in the dinner, which was tasteless, but never so satisfying. A bottle of Everest beer was attempted, but the altitude rendered it head-splitting, and I returned to tea as we played cards until it grew late. The food and drink hit my bladder and bowels simultaneously, and I forced myself towards the outdoor toilet: a jagged hole carved into three planks of wood, where a mini-Qomolangma of frozen defecate coned up from the ground with threatening proximity to my bare bottom.

Under a foot of blankets, I grew warm again in bed, but sleep drifted in and out with a maddening inconsistency, and I woke each hour to the barking of the feral mastiffs outside or the lung-squeezing lack of oxygen or the terrifying itches which engulfed whole limbs at a time or the singing of the monks and pilgrims outside, who sat along the pathway to Base Camp and wailed their vibrato chants at the stars, the glottal stops and staccato starts of their incantations melding together to form the antithesis of a lullaby.

More fragments of sleep, more periods of wide-eyed darkness, Joe snoring, and vivid dreams. Suddenly, an earth-shaking boom. Then another. Followed by the clattering of snare drums in rapid-fire succession. I was awake, out of my bed, standing and shivering in the middle of the room, and wondering where the fuck I was. The swift treble of the crashes resounded about the room again, and I tentatively made my way to the window, crouching low and raising my hand to the curtain. A thick snore from Joe seemed to rebound off my knees, and I almost fell to the floor. With adrenalin spiking through my blood and my fingers twitching with each crashing heartbeat, I pulled the curtain aside a fraction. There, on the outside, was Gavril, backlit by the stars, a thin frost across his beard. He knocked on the window again. Wide awake now, freed from the distorting fog of semi-consciousness, my brain distinguished the nightmarish booms for what they really were: nothing more than small but persistent taps on thin glass.

'Can I come in?' he smiled. 'I'm cold.'

I opened the window and Gavril clambered through, taking a blanket from the pile and gratefully falling to the floor. I turned to ask if he was OK, but his snores had already begun to match Joe's.

3

When my tinny alarm sounded its digital beep at 5 a.m. I was grateful. The last few hours had been those excruciating ones of the insomniac who tries every timeworn cliché to instigate sleep, only to find himself at the end of them more awake than before. As I dressed, yawning, I gazed back at the bed. It looked more inviting than ever.

The blog, the postcard, the letter home: they all extol the virtues of the sunrise and sunset. The travel book does not, because it tries to say something different and unusual, and what is different and unusual about a beautiful dawn or dusk? Those of us lucky enough to live above the poverty line, with our annual holidays or beach-side weekends or even stolen teenage nights of drinking until the stars disappear, we all have a score of photographs and memories of a score of sunrises and a score of sunsets.

But a clear-sky sunrise at Mount Everest – where the sphere emerges from behind you, first turning the plumes of spindrift base-red, then settling upon the 8,848 pinnacle and slowly painting the north face Tibetan orange and descending down it with a pencil-straight line – is surely the most remarkable sunrise in the world.

'This is important,' Joe, stood beside me, whispered. 'This is important.'

We stood and watched until all Everest was flushed with colour: its snow tangerine, its poking rock yak-brown.

'I need to come back here again,' Joe said. 'Everest. Tibet. I need to come back here again.'

We removed our hats, the sun warm on the back of our heads, our cheeks as blushing as Qomolangma before us.

Breakfast was a soup thinner than the yak-butter tea which complemented it. The cowpat stove had stayed on all night, and the room was toasty and comfortably stifling. Joe and Tanya shared a table by the small window. Tashi and Dawa played cards on another at the far end of the room. Gavril sat alone.

'Thanks for letting me in last night,' he said as I sat next to him. 'I thought I might die.'

'What happened?' I asked. My mind was a jumble of queries and incriminations. 'Why didn't you just stay with the rest of us? You weren't allowed that far! They could have shot you!'

Gavril nodded and took a slurp of his soup. 'Why did you come here, Charlie?' he asked over his spoon.

'To Everest?'

'To Tibet.'

'Dissatisfaction,' I said.

He snorted. 'That's a good answer. But dissatisfaction with what? With yourself?'

'No. With my ideas. I spent a lot of time in my youth calling myself a Tibetophile. It wasn't until my late twenties that I realised that everything I knew about Tibet came from outside sources. From the media. From Amnesty International and aid agencies and newspaper reports. I realised I was fundamentally ignorant about Tibet. And I hated that. I wanted to find out things for myself.'

'Do you want to know why I came to Tibet?'

Gavril was being uncharacteristically open, and it unsettled me. I knew him as the guy on the train who had sneered at my beers and soft-sleeper compartment and professed his need to spend time with the people. We had barely spoken since, though we had journeyed all the way along the Friendship Highway together. His travel-snobbishness had undermined my own, and I had resented that in much the same way as my friends do whenever I castigate their package holidays and loutishly describe my own hardships in Istanbulla train stations or upon Laotian buses. It is the curse of the backpacker: we revel in the tough journey, but when someone exceeds our stories with theirs, we meet them with nit-picking resentment. As a breed of tourist, we are insufferable.

'Go on,' I acquiesced.

'I am interested in Buddhism, but this can be found in India and across the world. I am interested in Tibetans and their history, but these can be found in India and across the world, as well. I am not a rich man – in Bulgaria, I make a living as a sculptor, and I work enough to feed me, to pay my rent, and to sometimes travel. To come to Tibet was very expensive, and it is a trip which normally I cannot afford. But I saved. Not to see Buddhism, not to see Tibetans. But to be here. At Mount Everest.'

I had been watching his spoon as it hovered over his bowl while he spoke, but it was the first time he looked at me, and I saw that his eyes were moist.

'I know what you think of me,' he said, his spoon hovering at his chest, the film of soup dripping from it on to the table. 'You didn't like what I did yesterday. You think I'm stupid, and that what I did was stupid. But I was only trying to get past those guards because I needed to get to the memory stones.'

'The memory stones?'

'I was told that, if you get to Everest Base Camp, you can see the memory stones. But they're not at the first hill, they're at the second, the one you're not allowed to walk to anymore. But I *had* to see them. Or, I had to see *one*.'

'All that,' I said, 'for some stones?'

Gavril's spoon crashed back into his bowl, sending a spray of hot soup up and out, which flecked over the table and my right hand. He pointed a finger at me. 'Not *some* stones,' he said. '*The* stone.'

I wiped my hand on the tablecloth.

'There is something I did not tell you, Charlie. About my journey. About why I am here. This year is the fifth anniversary of the death of one of my closest friends. He was an artist. Like me. We studied together. In 2004, he climbed Everest. He wanted to do it without oxygen. He climbed with two others: one, like him, did not have oxygen; the other did. They climbed faster than him and left him behind. Then they waited. He did not catch up. They went back to look for him but could not find him. Then a storm came in.'

He stopped for a moment to rub his beard.

'One of the climbers returned the next day, with oxygen, to look for him again, but he had to stop at 28,000 feet because of the bad weather. By that point, they suspected the worst. Camping at altitudes above 26,000 feet with nothing is almost certain death. A few days later, a Russian climber found him. He was sat down. He had taken one glove off. I think he stopped for a moment to rest. You know what this altitude is like. He was even higher than we are. Maybe he just fell asleep, just like that. He did not wake up.'

'I'm sorry,' I said.

'There is a pile of memory stones at Everest Base Camp. Each one has the name of a climber who died on Everest carved into it. Sometimes their fellow climbers do it, sometimes the Sherpas. I promised my friend's family I would find his memory stone and photograph it for them. But it was not where I expected it to be, on that first hill. I thought it would be OK to walk to the next hill. I only wanted to find the memory stones. But then the guards stopped me. You saw this.'

I nodded. 'They were mean bastards.'

Gavril laughed. 'I don't want you to think that, Charlie,' he said. 'Actually, I would like you to think something else. That is why I am telling you all this. Those guards, they were angry at first, but when they took me into the tent they calmed. We drank tea together. I explained to them everything I have now explained to you. It took me some time, but they understood in the end. We found our reconciliation, and they agreed to let me explore to the next hill. I was very touched by that. What's that phrase in English – the human spirit?'

I nodded.

'Well, their human spirit shone. They allowed me to search for the stone even though they did not have to. I am very grateful to them.'

'And did you find it?'

Gavril pulled his camera from his bag and turned it on, flicking through the images on the small digital screen until he found the one he sought. He showed it to me. There was his friend's memory stone, captured beautifully.

'It took me a long time to find it. A long time. But I did. Then I took some other stones – not memory stones – from the foot of Everest. They're here in my bag. I will take them home for my friend's family.'

I laughed. 'I thought your bag seemed empty when we were leaving!'

'Yes! It was to make room. I will carry them all the way home to Bulgaria.'

'But why were you so late?'

'I spent a long time beneath Everest. I thought of my friend.'

'I'm sorry,' I said again. Gavril nodded, and then smiled. We finished our soups.

'So, Charlie,' Gavril broke the silence. 'You told me you were dissatisfied. Now you have seen Tibet, are you satisfied?'

I thought about this for a while. 'No,' I said.

Gavril reached into his pocket and produced a tiny red pebble which he held out to me. 'I want you to have this,' he said. 'As a thank you for last night, but also something to remember Tibet by. It is red coral. Like jade, it is considered sacred here. Did you know all of Tibet once lay under a huge sea? The red coral reminds the Tibetans of the impermanence of things: once underwater, now the highest land on earth, one day underwater again. My grandfather tried to come here in 1955. He was stopped in Ladakh in India by the Chinese, but he bought a necklace of red coral from a Tibetan woman there. It was strung with thirty pieces identical to this. I have always carried them with me when I travel. I would like you to take a piece.'

He dropped the weightless stone into my palm as Tashi bustled through the room and told us it was time to head for the border. A monk who seemed older than Qomolangma herself hobbled towards us and wrapped a white *kata* scarf around each of our necks, muttering seamless syllables.

'He is thanking you for visiting Tibet,' Tashi said. 'He hopes you will return.'

That *kata* scarf hangs in my study today. Gavril's bead of red coral is woven into it.

chu-shi

Perhaps Lobsang was heartened by the fact that he had done it before, but leaving Tibet seemed far easier than entering it. A trail of names, started by Norbu who knew a friend of a friend who might help, led him deep into the Tibetan Quarter as one person suggested another who in turn suggested yet another. Finally, Lobsang found himself sat in a restaurant he never knew existed. This perturbed him. As a rickshaw driver, he thought he knew every place in Lhasa.

He was here to meet Tsering, or thought that was his name. His previous meeting on the Barkhor *kora* had been quick and quiet, and nothing had been written down. Tsering may not have been the correct name. This restaurant may not have been the correct address.

Lobsang heightened his anxiety with cups of strong, black tea. The owner was a tall and quiet man – possibly Khampa, Lobsang thought – who nodded when Lobsang asked if Tsering would be in soon. This meant nothing. Tsering was a common name. Lobsang could have been waiting for anyone. In fact, he realised, he *was* waiting for anyone: he had no idea who this Tsering was nor anything more about him save that he was a truck driver and might help him escape. But what was that based on? It was based on a few words by a hurrying monk who had been suggested to him by a man who could not walk properly who had been suggested to him by a street hawker with nauseating halitosis. These slim details were all he knew of each individual he had met over the past two days, but what did they know of him? They knew – for he had told them all – that he needed to leave Tibet. Not wanted, *needed*. They knew he was illegal, and they knew he was in trouble. What if just one of those men had been a spy? What if this Tsering was a spy or, worse, police? What if Lobsang had been directed to this unknown dive with thick curtains over its windows in the middle of the day because it was the perfect spot for a disappearance?

Lobsang slammed his empty cup on to the bar and hurried towards the door. It opened before he could reach it. A man entered: he had the face of a seventy-year-old but the lean and toned body of a man half that age.

'Hey, Tsering!' the owner called at him. 'This man's been asking after you.'

Tsering removed his cowboy hat. His head was almost entirely bald, and the few wisps of hair which draped over his temples were a translucent grey. Lobsang stared at his hands: smooth, soft, womanly even. Tsering barked at the owner for a beer, then stared at Lobsang, who demurely agreed that he would also like a beer. Together, they settled at a table in the restaurant's far corner.

'It's a thousand yuan,' Tsering said.

'What route do you take?' Lobsang asked.

'From here, straight to Zhangmu. No stopping. Then a twenty-four-hour break in Zhangmu. We get a hotel, two separate rooms. You'll pay for those, too. Then, the next morning, on to Kathmandu. I take that bit a lot slower, but you're free to get off whenever you want.'

'How will you get me across the border?'

'There's a little space in the back of my truck, kind of like a compartment. You'll fit if you stand up straight. It's not comfortable, and you can't let yourself out from the inside. You'll have to wait for me to cross the border then come and let you out once we're a safe distance. Could be three or four hours in there.'

Lobsang exhaled.

'It works, though,' Tsering continued. 'I've done this thirty, maybe even forty times before, and I've never been caught. One hundred per cent success rate.' He smiled and Lobsang could see that, in keeping with the rest of his prematurely ageing head, Tsering's teeth had all fallen out.

Lobsang met Yangchen on his cycle home and offered her a lift. Norbu was at home. Lobsang tried to explain the details of his escape to both, but neither would listen. 'If they arrest me again,' Norbu said, 'I will tell them everything.' Yangchen nodded. Lobsang restrained himself, and merely told them the day he would be leaving. The three spent the rest of the afternoon together, and it seemed to Lobsang that neither Yangchen nor Norbu could keep their hands off him. Palms rested on his legs, shoulders, patted the sides of his face and upper arms, tousled or ruffled his hair, and later, after *chang* had been imbibed, their fingers interlocked with his own and, for some time, the three sat quiet with linked hands while it grew dark outside.

Lobsang arrived at the truck stop exactly on time. Tsering had warned him to be neither early nor late. 'I don't want anyone seeing you waiting around for me. But I won't wait around for you, either. You got a watch?'

He saw Tsering smoking a cigarette and walked towards him. Making the slightest gestures with his hands but no eye contact, Tsering ushered him towards and behind a nearby truck which, Lobsang realised once he walked around it, had its back door left open.

'You don't have to go in the compartment until we leave Zhangmu,' Tsering had told him in the restaurant. 'You can stay in the back, but don't make yourself comfortable, don't *arrange* anything into a seat or a bed. Border guards look for that kind of thing. Just use the space. There'll be enough.'

Lobsang climbed in. Tsering had been right, there was not much here, just a few wrapped crates and pallets, but the smell was revolting, as if Tsering's last consignment had been to the waste landfill site and he had forgotten to clean out his truck since. Lobsang felt bile rising in his throat, and when Tsering suddenly appeared and slammed the door shut without a word, the smell intensified and the quantity of bile with it.

The truck started. Lobsang scurried about the floor, searching with his nose. He found a small patch of space above the fuel tank, where the rising fumes offset the nauseous smell somewhat, and there he was able to intermittently doze between sickly urges and toxic headaches.

Lobsang had brought little with him. He had a spare set of clothes (lighter than the ones he wore, for he remembered well the close heat of Kathmandu), some food and some water, as much money as he could carry, and three pieces of

Drolma's jewellery: a necklace, an earring, a bracelet. All of it fit inside a small rucksack, bought two days before on the Barkhor and already beginning to tear, and this he slung on to his shoulder as Tsering opened the door.

He did not know how long he had been in the back of the truck, but the sudden influx of light blinded him and he stumbled outside into sheets of indistinct whiteness. Tsering took him, not gently, by the arm and guided him towards the truck's front cab, where he pushed him in and then climbed in himself, starting the engine and pulling away.

'We've passed the last of the checkpoints,' Tsering said as Lobsang's eyes slowly began to accustom to the daylight. 'It's best if you're in the front with me when we enter Zhangmu. There's plenty of police and soldiers and border guards in the town, and they're all looking for someone climbing out the back of a truck.'

Lobsang could finally make out his new environment. The truck was slowly making its way down a long and curving road which wound along the edge of a wide crevasse. Trees grew from the cliff walls and Lobsang recognised their smell, alien in Tibet. This was the borderland. Soon, they would drop a mile or so in altitude, and everything would be different.

'Don't forget,' Tsering said as he pulled into Zhangmu and parked the truck at the side of the town's main road. 'We're getting two separate rooms, and you're paying for both. I also need the thousand now.'

'I'll give you five hundred now,' Lobsang said. 'You can have the rest when we get to Kathmandu.'

Tsering grunted, a clear negative. 'If we get caught on the border, I'll need it to bribe the guard, and I'll need it *all*.'

Lobsang said nothing.

'Then you can get out,' Tsering said with malice. 'You give me the full thousand now or you get out. That's your choice. You're still in China, you know.'

With reluctance, Lobsang reached for the rucksack which nestled between his feet and placed it on his lap, unzipping it and taking out his wad of yuan notes held together by an elastic band. He peeled a thousand off and then placed the rest back in his bag. When he handed the sum over, he noticed Tsering's gaze had followed the bag down to his feet. Tsering smiled another toothless grin as he took the yuan notes and folded them into his pocket, then he stepped from the truck and Lobsang followed him across the street and through the open door of a grimy hotel.

'Two rooms,' Tsering said, jerking his thumb over his shoulder in Lobsang's direction. 'He's paying.'

The rooms were stark and mildewy (Lobsang did not see Tsering's room, but Tsering had a long snoop around Lobsang's and confirmed that they were the same), dinner (paid for by Lobsang) was cold and the beers (also paid for by Lobsang) warm, but a mounting sense of excitement and purpose overrode everything else, and Lobsang decided that he could stand any squalor or discomfort if it got him closer to his goal of freeing Drolma. He felt as if valves were being plucked one by one from his body, a release of pressure with each – *psssh*, he would be in a free country soon; *pssh*, he would see his family; *pssh*, he would save Drolma, no matter how long or how much energy it took.

Lobsang bought more beers, insisting Tsering drink with him. They grew drunk together. Lobsang had not liked this truck driver at first, had found him surly and threatening, but he wasn't such a bad one, after all, as it turned out, and he was doing Lobsang a favour, he supposed, no, wait, he was doing Lobsang a *massive* favour, no supposing about it, and there was no way Lobsang would have ever made it over the border without him, not that they were over the border yet, still stuck in this filthy, depraved, miserable, stinking country, and when he said that he meant China, of course, not Tibet, no, never Tibet, but you couldn't call Tibet a *country* anymore, not unless you wanted your arms broken behind your back and your eyes held open while a guard pissed into them, which, did Tsering realise, was exactly what would have happened to Lobsang if he hadn't left Lhasa when and how he did?

Perhaps Tsering did realise, for when Lobsang woke the next morning – head ensconced firmly in the vice-like crush of a mean hangover – Tsering was not in his room. Nor was his truck outside. Lobsang turned from the window and looked about his own room, realising the man and the truck were not the only things missing. His bag was gone. Everything he owned – his clothes, his food, his money and Drolma's jewellery – had been taken, leaving him with nothing save the clothes he wore.

He stumbled out of his room and down the stairs.

'Your friend left this morning,' the receptionist told him. 'For Nepal, he said.'

'He robbed me,' Lobsang whispered.

The receptionist seemed not to hear him. 'What time will you be leaving?' he asked.

In a daze, Lobsang plodded out on to Zhangmu's main road. Traces of the previous night's jubilation, his excitement, his *purpose*, floated back to him, immediately supplanted by fear, paranoia and anguish, which seemed not to exist in his mind at all, but somewhere in his stomach. He noticed for the first time how many soldiers, police and guards strolled the streets, how many uniforms, and he did not like the way they looked at him. On the horizon behind and above the town – how far above? a thousand metres? two thousand? – the plateau began. It suddenly seemed as unreachable as Nepal, which itself was less than a mile away, beyond one of the most heavily armed borders in the world.

Lobsang did not eat that day, and he spent the night hidden beneath a truck, sharing his space with suspicious dogs who did not know whether to lick or bite him. The following morning, with the burgeoning desperation of the sleep-starved and hopeless, he entered one of Zhangmu's small bars in the hope of begging a cup of yak-butter tea. Nobody manned the bar: in fact, the whole place was empty except for one person who sat in the corner, sipping water, writing in a journal, his hat pulled low.

Lobsang edged closer and, as he did so, the man looked up from his journal and their eyes met. Lobsang was surprised to realise that the man was a Westerner, a European or American perhaps. There was only one reason why a Westerner would ever find himself in Zhangmu: he would be entering or he would be leaving Tibet. Lobsang, with a sudden and desperate hope that it was the latter, approached him, and sat at his table.

The
Friendship
Highway

I left Everest in the same manner as I arrived: over stone and ice. Dawa howled at the daymoon, stepped on the accelerator, and angled the Landcruiser out on to an ancient nomadic route between Everest and the small town of Old Tingri.

Navigating over the beds of long-ago-melted glaciers, through streams whose ice cracked beneath the tyres and up ferocious passes alongside terrifying valley-drops, we averaged perhaps 10 miles an hour. But the lethargic speed and the shin-rattling surfaces only heightened my excitement. My experience of twenty-first-century Tibet thus far had been irrevocably Chinese, at best a compound of two cultures. Even atop a pass or beside a lake or in the heart of a village or the cloister of a monastery, Chinese influence was present and inescapable: from the Chinese tourists to the Chinese signs in Chinese script to the Chinese pylons and Chinese roads. But out here, there was none of that. Even the latter, the roads, were absent, and I felt a swooping sense of elation as all about me became nothing but pure, rough, unpolished Tibet, though that euphoria dipped somewhat when I remembered that I was travelling through it all in a car which was, if not Chinese-built, then at least Chinese-bought and Chinese-maintained. How good it would be, I thought, to step from this Landcruiser, bid farewell to my companions, and walk the remaining miles to the border alone. But in this I was just as reliant on Chinese intervention as anyone else: to do as such would have killed me. I could not survive out here. No one could, except the Tibetans, and it was China's knowledge of this which had brought in the roads and the pylons, the signs and the hotels. If China had never annexed and then Sinicised Tibet, I realised, I never would have been able to travel it – me with my iPod and my sunscreen, my worn sandals and addictions, my thin legs and pot belly – and this thought made me angry, not at the Chinese for once, but at myself.

We passed through a village disconnected from any roads, just a smattering of decaying red and white houses circled around a pristine *chorten*, and children ran out in front of the car and stopped us. Dawa growled at them until a few men appeared, one revving the engine of his motorbike, and Dawa grinned at them, tapping his splintering sunglasses and placing his ten-year-old mobile phone against his ear, though he had not made or taken a call. He was posturing. He wheelspun the Landcruiser, sending up a plume of dust over one small boy who giggled and jumped in the shower of particles which matched his height twice over. I had thought of Dawa as the most Tibetan man I had met on my journey, but his boasts in that village – his sunglasses, phone and car – were all a product of China, and I knew then that, though I had crossed Tibet from its northernmost point to its southernmost, a land mass two-thirds the size of western

Europe and a quarter of China as a whole, I had barely scratched the surface of this country.

2

We rejoined the Friendship Highway at Old Tingri and stopped for lunch. I took my yak noodle soup out into the restaurant's grey and windless courtyard, stripping to my T-shirt and pants and then lying on my back on the gritty floor when I had finished. Fuck manners, I thought, this was my last taste of the high-altitude sun, and I knew I might never get so close to the star ever again. Soon, the road would take me down, back towards the sea level which my body had been accustomed to for twenty-nine years.

The plunge began at Nyalam, the penultimate town of Tibet, where we stopped for the security checkpoint. I walked to the side of the road, a six-foot drop with concrete embankments to the Bhote Kosi river, which was beginning its ferocious bursts of waterfalls and cascades down to the valley we were to follow for the next 20 miles or so to the border, and then halfway to Kathmandu.

Nyalam is said to be Tibetan for 'Gateway to Hell'. This is the very edge of the plateau's southern aspect, and one can imagine pilgrims staring down into the valley carved by the Bhote Kosi, often shrouded in low-hanging cloud, and only able to wonder what was down there. If Hell lies beneath us, or at the very ends of the flat earth, the road to it must be here. But it is not just the vertiginous heights which strike the senses: it is moreover the vegetation, and its colour. One notices an absence only in the subsequent presence, and I had not realised until Nyalam how bare Tibet had been of trees. The road ahead was cloaked in them, and the browns and oranges of Tibet were suddenly replaced by the green of the rest of the world. *Not so much a Gateway to Hell*, I wrote in my journal perched on that concrete embankment, *but a Gateway to Earth*.

We descended 6,500 feet in half an hour, following the river upon a thin stretch of road carved into the towering cliffs above it, and became oxygen-drunk. Giddy and giggling, I stared from the Landcruiser window out over the drop which edged the road, no fence to demarcate where the road ended and the drop began. We were still in Tibet, but this was woodland, was *green*, and I felt as if I had never seen anything like it before in my life. Waterfalls powered on to the road and bounced off down the sinews of the valley, and the birds which twittered from the trees looked like the sparrows and starlings of home, not the vultures and eagles of up there. Tibet was already *up there*: infinite and high, and my blood told me that, no matter how much I had loved Tibet, my place was here, in the forests, among the earth-dwellers. Mountains were a trip, but the trees were a fix. I suddenly missed the sea.

Two miles outside of Zhangmu, the road was blocked by workers on a resurfacing project. Tashi estimated we would be stuck there for at least two hours, and suggested we walk to Zhangmu and meet him and Dawa later. Holstering our daypacks, we set out on to the road, clambering down the cliff-face over precarious wooden planks roped to the tow bars of diggers, and sidling past the Chinese, Tibetan and Nepali labourers in their blue helmets to scale back up to the road again and continue downwards to Zhangmu. A shack built from sheets of corrugated iron sat on the edge of the road past the construction, and we bought cans of Everest beer from the sleepy Nepali manning it, delighting in the fact that, at this altitude, these beers alone would not floor us.

The last stop on the Tibetan odyssey, I entered Zhangmu on foot, tipsy on canned beer and oxygen, and fresh from an impromptu roadside waterfall-shower. Though this was still Tibet, it was no longer the plateau, and Tibet had effectively vanished with the high altitude. Zhangmu was a road: a single, winding road which zigzagged down the cliff-face, its homes and guesthouses and skanky late-night bars terraced on either side; its tarmac filled with blaring and honking *Tata* trucks endlessly importing and exporting; its valley-side descents caked in the rubbish and effluence of the thousands who passed through here every day, the entrepreneurial pioneers of the dragon and the elephant: New China and New India. Old Tibet and Old Nepal were just thoroughfares on this stop-off of the twenty-first-century Silk Road. Zhangmu was a border town, as modern and as ancient as any border town across the world, and it felt like, amongst these lorry drivers and travelling hawkers and border-crossers with their air and clothes of refugees, there was nothing local here, nothing permanent, only the transient.

3

There was a problem. It seemed we had hurried through Tibet quicker than our itinerary had demanded, and we were two days short of our visa expiration date: the date we had been due to cross the border. The rigours and red tape of Chinese bureaucracy as they are, we could not leave Tibet until the very day which had been prescribed. We were stuck in Zhangmu.

I went for a walk, determined to find a bar. There seemed little else to do in this dirty town but get drunk. Packs of yelping dogs fought about the wheels of the *Tata* trucks, chasing each other down the road and then losing their footing and sliding out of sight on their bellies. The sun was fierce but the flashing neon scriptures of the bars and clubs remained lit, and the faces of those who beckoned me into their buildings – whores, pimps and guesthouse owners – were never Tibetan, but Indian. There was a perceptible change of race here, and these were all folk of the subcontinent, not the plateau. The Himalayas are, it seems, an anthropological border, the kind China both covets and fears.

Nobody beckoned me into the bar I chose. That was why I chose it. I did not want to be propositioned or enticed. I wanted peace and a beer. The bar was open but empty – so empty, in fact, that even the bartender was absent. I did not mind so much. I could wait. Sitting at a table in the corner beneath a dim lamp, I pulled my journal and a bottle of water from my daypack, and settled in to complete my notes on Tibet.

The door swung open. I finished my sentence, and looked up. A young Tibetan man, filthy and harried, stood in the middle of the bar and stared hard at me. With a purposeful stride, he approached my table.

chö-nga

'I need you to help me to get into Nepal,' Lobsang said in English.

The Westerner understood, though he did not reply, and looked about the room in astonishment.

'No one can hear us,' Lobsang said, and then repeated: 'I need you to help me to get into Nepal.' The Westerner could have been a spy, a Chinese sympathiser, or even just a coward, but Lobsang did not care any longer.

'I… I'm not sure I…' the Westerner faltered. He composed himself with a sip of water. 'I don't think I can help you.'

'Can you listen?'

The Westerner nodded.

'Good. My name is Lobsang.'

'Charlie,' the Westerner replied.

'It is a pleasure to meet you, Charlie,' Lobsang said, extending his hand. Charlie shook it. 'But we should find a better place.'

'There's no one here,' Charlie said, gesturing around him at the empty bar.

'We should find a better place,' Lobsang repeated. 'For talking.' He turned and walked out of the bar. Charlie hesitantly followed.

The two men wandered through Zhangmu until they discovered a teahouse hidden beneath a massage parlour. Inside, an old Tibetan woman washed bed sheets in a large tub on the concrete floor. She stood up from her stool as they entered and walked towards the pot of yak-butter tea which simmered on an ancient stove. Lobsang asked for two cups and they were placed on a table in the corner. Lobsang sat at the table and then gestured for Charlie to do the same.

'This is better,' Lobsang said.

'How can you tell?'

'I don't know.'

'Can she understand English?'

'I don't know.'

Charlie was nervous. Lobsang observed the way his hand shook when he lifted the cup of yak-butter tea to his lips, the way he shifted uncomfortably on his stool, the way his left knee bounced up and down atop his fidgeting leg.

'So,' Charlie said. 'Nepal?' His semantic omissions betrayed his distrust of the old woman.

'If you like, we can talk about that later,' Lobsang replied. 'You said you would listen to me. Can I tell you a story?'

Charlie nodded, and a spark seemed to catch in his eyes. 'Of course,' he said. 'Would you mind if I... err... took some notes?' He pulled a tatty journal and a pen from his bag.

Lobsang's instinct told him to say no, but then he remembered why he had approached Charlie in the first place. He had nothing left to lose. Perhaps a record of their conversation would incriminate him if discovered, but the authorities already had enough detail to detain him for life. The scribblings of a foreigner could do no extra harm.

'OK,' Lobsang said, and Charlie took up his pen.

They spent the next seven hours in the teahouse together while Lobsang spoke and Charlie wrote. Lobsang's story spilled out with irrepressible fluency: a story which detailed Lhasa; Chogyal and Jamyang; the pilgrimage to Dorje; Kathmandu; 'long running'; the death of his mother; 'Little Panda'; a scholarship; Delhi; the fourteenth Dalai Lama; Drolma; Himalayan foothills; frozen mountain passes; Lhasa again; Norbu; rickshaw-riding; 'Stone and Ice'; a thieving truck driver; a story which started with the words, 'I felt my mother's fingers curl around my arm ...' and ended with '... and now I'm here with you'.

Charlie looked up from his journal, towards Lobsang and then at the small window over his shoulder. It was dark outside. The old woman had left the room hours ago, and nobody had come to replace her. Charlie had found it difficult to record everything Lobsang had said in his journal, especially during those times when he had been so entranced by the story that he had stared into Lobsang's eyes and listened to his words without penning a single letter. He wanted to hear the whole thing again, if only to capture it, to do it justice, for it was a story that, he felt, needed to be shared.

'I should go,' Charlie said. 'I arranged to meet my group for dinner. They'll be suspicious if I don't show up. But I can meet you again after.'

'When do you leave?' Lobsang asked.

'The day after tomorrow.'

'Then we can meet again tomorrow.'

'Where will you sleep tonight?'

'I will find somewhere.'

'I could sneak you into my hotel room once the others have gone to sleep.'

'No,' Lobsang said. 'If the police find me in your room, you will be in a lot of trouble.'

'You've asked me to smuggle you over the border,' Charlie replied.

Lobsang laughed. 'That is what we can talk about tomorrow. If you will still listen.'

Charlie nodded and the two men shook hands. Then Charlie left, leaving Lobsang behind in the empty teahouse. Lobsang walked to the stove and filled another cup of yak-butter tea.

The following morning, Charlie entered the teahouse to find Lobsang helping the old woman with a fresh stack of washing. She smiled at Charlie and then stood up to leave while Lobsang hung the sheets around the stove. Their two cups had not been cleared from their table, and Charlie swilled them in the stagnant water trapped in the sink before filling them with fresh yak-butter tea ladled out of the pot.

When they were both ready to sit, Lobsang asked Charlie if he had given any thought to his request.

'I told you I would listen,' Charlie replied. 'I've got nothing else to do today.'

'Good,' Lobsang said. 'That will give us time to make a plan.'

'I still don't know if I can do this.'

'But if you *could*,' Lobsang replied, 'how would you?'

Charlie sat back and thought, sipping from his cup until it was empty. He rose to fill another. Lobsang watched in silence. Charlie returned to his seat, blew ripples across the surface of the yak-butter tea and then, slowly, began to talk to it rather than Lobsang. 'Gavril would probably help. Joe and Tanya – maybe not. Tashi and Dawa would outright forbid it. But we could work around that. They wouldn't *have* to know. Every time we leave a place, it's always the same routine. We pack all our bags into the back of the Landcruiser and then Dawa insists we stop for breakfast a short distance away. And he always leaves the doors unlocked.'

Lobsang remained silent, but his eyes never left Charlie. Charlie's eyes, in turn, stayed on his cup of tea.

'The only problem, I guess,' he continued, 'is knowing *where* Dawa will stop for breakfast. But Zhangmu's small. There's nowhere beyond the town's limits to eat. I reckon you could easily follow us on foot and then, when we stop to eat, you could climb into the back of the Landcruiser and hide beneath the stack of blankets Dawa keeps in there in case of a mountain-pass breakdown. After breakfast, I'd get in the back, too. It wouldn't be unusual – it's where I usually ride. The others don't like to, so there's no risk of them getting in there and discovering you. So that would be OK. The big problem, though, would be the border. At the least, we'll all have to get out of the Landcruiser with our bags. That won't be a problem, because you'll be beneath the blankets. But they might want to check the vehicle itself.'

Charlie stopped to take a long draught of tea.

'You know what we should do?' he said. 'We should find Gavril. Ask his help.'

'Has he travelled across this border before?' Lobsang asked.

'No.'

'Then he cannot offer any new information for us. So does he really need to know?'

Charlie contemplated, and realised that, perhaps, he did not.

'Then you should not tell him. The less people who know the better. If I am caught, you must say you had no idea I was in the back. I will say I saw an opportunity and I took it. No one helped me.'

Charlie agreed, for it was believable enough. 'That way,' he said, 'the worst they'll do is deport us, and we're leaving the country anyway. But what about you? What will happen to you if you're caught?'

'If I'm caught on the border, then it's over. They'll find out about me being illegal, about my connection to Drolma and "Stone and Ice", everything. Prison for the rest of my life, and possibly execution. But it is no worse than if I were caught anywhere in Tibet. The same thing would happen. This is why I must leave.'

Such seemed fair, but Charlie could not dispel the dark speculations which revolved around Tashi and Dawa. What would happen to them if Lobsang was caught? Nothing as innocuous as deportation, that was certain. He mentioned this to Lobsang.

'What we are planning is unfair to them,' Lobsang said. 'They could get in a lot of trouble. Not execution, but prison certainly, perhaps for a few years. But it is a good plan, and I think it will work. If you can get me into the Landcruiser undetected, I think we can make it across the border.'

'How can you be so sure?'

Lobsang smiled, nodding towards the door the old woman had left through. 'I stayed here last night. The woman you saw, her name is Drolma.' Lobsang laughed. '*Drolma*! This building belongs to her. Her granddaughters run the massage parlour upstairs. She is very kind. She let me sleep on the floor if I helped with her washing. Last night, we drank some *chang* – not much – and she asked why a Westerner had spent the day writing my words. She thought I was famous! I told her the truth.'

'Was that a good idea?'

'I also told you the truth. Was that a good idea?'

Charlie smiled.

'She has crossed the border thousands of times. She buys food in Nepal because there is more and it is cheaper. She said she has seen tour groups of Westerners like you before. They all travel by Landcruiser. She said she has seen them at the border. She said it made her angry that every time she crossed the border she was searched, but she never saw it happen to a Westerner.'

'And what about the vehicle?'

'She said she has never seen one of them searched, either.'

Charlie's head swam within the reeling possibilities this statement evoked. Perhaps Lobsang noticed, for he continued building upon the plan with gusto. The border between Tibet and Nepal, he explained, was a river – the Bhote Kosi. It was far too dangerous to swim, and the only way across was the small, plain, iron Friendship Bridge. On the far side of the bridge lay Nepal. If Charlie could get Lobsang into the Landcruiser undetected, Lobsang was certain they could make it across the bridge. On the Tibetan side, the Landcruiser would certainly be stopped by Chinese immigration, and all six passengers would be instructed to step out of the vehicle with their luggage, identification and any relevant permits. But there were no guards or military at the far end of the Friendship Bridge; they simply did not exist on that side of the border. Drolma had explained to him that the only authority present was the visa office – a shack on the side of the dusty road – which was so nondescript that some Westerners had missed it and carried on into Nepal regardless.

From there, it was six hours by car to Kathmandu. Lobsang described the journey with breathless and mounting excitement: the Himalayas from the other side, congestion on the outskirts of Kathmandu, middle-aged women outside their shops with bare bellies bulging over their saris, confused but sedate cows holding up traffic and shitting in the middle of the road, humidity, sweat, and the pulsing headache of polluted, low-altitude air.

'Do you know which hostel you will be staying at?' Lobsang asked.

'Yes. Tanya's already booked ahead.' Charlie gave its name and Lobsang recognised it immediately. It was in the Thamel district, just a few streets down from his 'own' guesthouse. Lobsang lost himself for a moment in heady nostalgia: the taste of petrol in the air; the lingering aromas of cigarette smoke and frying chillies. He missed it. He thought suddenly of Jyoti. Lobsang wondered if he – or anyone from his childhood in Nepal, for that matter – would believe the life he had led since then.

The Kathmandu-past morphed into a possible Kathmandu-future. Lobsang mapped actions and directives out in his head, verbally outlining them to Charlie as the plan formulated itself step by potential step. The Landcruiser would stop at the hostel. Charlie would insist that the whole group – Dawa and Tashi included – head straight to the hostel bar for a celebratory beer. They could unpack later. All would agree, and Lobsang could slip out from beneath his stifling blankets, out of the Landcruiser's tailgate, and into the Kathmandu crowds. Lobsang would come back the following morning. He would show Charlie his Kathmandu, introduce him to his family, his old friends, offer him a place to stay even. But before that he needed to go home. To see his brother and his sister. To see his father. From the hostel, he could reach his home within an hour on foot. He could reach it quicker, he thought, if he ran.

Lobsang ended his monologue. Charlie thought he had never seen a man look so happy.

'I'm in,' Charlie said.

Somehow, Lobsang looked even happier.

They arranged to meet at the teahouse the following morning, one hour before Charlie's group were due to set off for the border.

'Now tell me your story again,' Charlie said, his journal back on the table.

'Why? So you can write it?'

'Perhaps.'

'I will only tell you again *if* you write it.'

Charlie removed the pen's lid with his teeth and spat it on to the table. 'Deal,' he said.

Lobsang was already there when Charlie arrived the next morning, washing more bed sheets with the old woman,

Drolma. When she heard the door open, she stood up and shuffled towards Charlie. One hand gently enfolded his own while the other tugged playfully at the wisps of his beard. She closed her eyes, muttered something in Tibetan, opened them again, dropped his hand, and left the room.

Lobsang hung the sheets above the stove, taking care to stretch out any creases. Then he poured two cups of yak-butter tea, offered one to Charlie and drained the other in three long, noisy gulps.

'So,' Lobsang said. 'Are you ready for this?'

'The days and nights will drag on slowly in suffering.'

|

And I replied: 'No.'

After leaving Lobsang the previous night, I had met my group for our last Tibetan supper. And there, in conversation with Tashi, some vital truths were revealed to me which scuppered my and Lobsang's plans in their entirety.

The truth was: our Landcruiser would not be crossing the Friendship Bridge.

The truth was: Tashi and Dawa were not allowed to cross the border themselves. Joe, Tanya, Gavril and I had to walk the bridge with our bags on our backs.

Here with Lobsang, other vital truths followed thick and fast.

The truth was: Lobsang asked me one final time to smuggle him over the border, and I said 'no' again.

The truth was: it would have been impossible, and we both knew it.

The truth was: Lobsang and I agreed on that final morning together that Zhangmu was perhaps the worst place for him to attempt to enter Nepal. The border there was too tightly controlled for anybody to slip through. I gave him the hundred US dollars I always keep with me when I travel in case of emergency, and he assured me, with a grace unmarred by the disappointment which must have ravaged his soul, that it would be enough to get him to Kathmandu. Noticing the journal which peeked out of my daypack, he pulled it out and opened it, thumbing through the pages of my, and then his, story.

'Will you write about me?' he asked.

'Can I?'

'Yes,' he said. 'Please.'

Then I left the teahouse and – the truth is – I never saw or heard from him again.

I spent my first day in Kathmandu walking the Tibetan area around the Boudhanath stupa, asking if anyone knew of a family with a Lobsang, a Jamyang, a Chogyal and a Norbu, but it was useless, and for myriad reasons. First, these are some of the most common names in Tibetan. Second, I knew no family name. Third, few could understand me, even when I tried Tibetan. And finally, it is highly likely that Lobsang may not have used real names. In my books, I never do.

2

'Tibet should be grateful to China,' the drunk American spat. He had invited himself on to my table in the Kathmandu hostel bar, interrupting my writing. He had grown increasingly inebriated and obnoxious as the evening wore on, and his girlfriend had gone to bed hours before. 'Trust me, I'm in IT. I've done the research. And I'll tell you this. If it weren't for China, Tibet wouldn't be like it is today.'

'Have you been to Tibet?' I asked.

'Of course not,' he leered, swaying away from and then back towards the table on his creaking stool.

I finished my drink, said good night and left.

The American was, of course, right. If it weren't for China, Tibet would be sovereign, self-governing, traditional. It would be Tibet, and not Xizang: China's Western Treasure. But such sentiments are immaterial, for within the American's words was a frank insinuation: that Tibet could never have modernised without Chinese intervention.

There is, in fact, an overwhelming amount of evidence which suggests that Tibet would have caught up with the rest of the world quite naturally. Even before the Chinese arrived, the thirteenth Dalai Lama had instilled a number of modernising reforms to the theocratic system of his independent country; a delegation of officials were sent on a world tour – taking in America, the Philippines, Hawaii and a number of European stops along the way – to set up trade agreements with the various countries; four young boys had been sent from Tibet to study at a private school in England in order to learn more about the Western way of life; and there were even a few automobiles up on the plateau. Heinrich Harrer notes that, in 1950s Lhasa, one could buy newspapers and magazines from all over the world, as well as American corned beef, Australian butter, Scotch whisky, gramophones, and even Bing Crosby's latest records to play on them.

That said, most of these international tendencies were localised to Lhasa, and much of the rest of Tibet was far behind those occidental countries we self-appoint as 'civilised'. But then, wasn't China just as backward at that time? It had itself only just thrown off the medieval shackles of ancient dynastic policies, and the few decades between that and Mao ravaged the country with wars, warlords and the ineffectual Chiang Kai-shek. And did Mao himself succeed in his intended modernisation of China? His Great Leap Forward and Cultural Revolution were, for the majority of the Han populace, gargantuan leaps backward, and it was not until the rule of Deng Xiaoping that China finally found its feet and started upon the path which would lead it to superpower status.

But there the question nags again. China *has* modernised. It may have taken some time, but it got there in the end, and it brought Tibet, kicking and screaming, along with it. But to suggest that Tibet would not have modernised anyway is to draw an illogical and unsound conclusion from an already shaky premise. For one must factor into the argument that which China conveniently negates: the fourteenth Dalai Lama himself.

Even in 1954, when he was still within Tibet, Tenzin Gyatso was making his own plans for reform in spite of the Chinese presence. In his autobiography, *Freedom in Exile*, he writes that at that time, 'I was determined to do all I could to propel Tibet into the twentieth century.' He began working on various plans: to install good and universal education across the land, to create a system of roads to improve communications across the vast country, and to remould the government into one which stemmed from democracy rather than theocracy. He was unable to drive any of these plans home, for he fled Tibet just five years later, but he did manage to install one quite revolutionary policy: abolishing the system of inheritable debt which had existed in Tibet for centuries, and writing off any government loans that could not be repaid. In doing so, the Dalai Lama freed an entire generation of his countrymen from a lifetime of repayments against debts their grandfathers had built up.

We shall never know how successful Tenzin Gyatso's reforms would have been, nor what would have happened to Tibet had China never marched on Lhasa, deposed him, and then set about installing their own reforms for the sake of Beijing's gain. But there are hints. In 1990, the Tibet-in-exile government's new Dharamsala cabinet was elected not by the Dalai Lama, but by – for the first time in Tibet's history – a democratic process. A year later, another landmark occurred when an article was introduced to the government's charter by Gyatso himself which stated that the Dalai Lama could actually be voted out of power. All these modernising reforms have been slow, not just because of the government's exile status, but because many Tibetans, even in the twenty-first century, resist them, for to them the absolute authority of the Dalai Lama is an unquestionable part of their faith. Nevertheless, twenty years later, in 2011, Tenzin Gyatso, at the age of seventy-six, publicly announced his intention to step down from the role of Tibet's political leader.

Those who claim Tibet would never have modernised without Chinese intervention are churlish and ill-informed, and many of them have never been to Tibet. What might have happened had China left Tibet to work things out on its own can only now be speculation, but we can make intelligent and rational conclusions, and many of them do not lead to that initial statement: that Tibet would never have modernised without Chinese intervention. It is better to say, in fact, what the American proclaimed before I left the table: *If it weren't for China, Tibet wouldn't be like it is today.* But such words hold too many pejorative connotations for Beijing, where the power of language is both understood and manipulated, and where Tibet was never invaded but 'liberated', and its people never colonised but 'freed'.

3

At the turn of the millennium, Jiang Zemin – then Paramount Leader of the People's Republic of China – took a world tour, meeting with a number of Western leaders. In America, he was reported to have told *The Washington Post*, 'China got rid of slavery long ago, except in Tibet, where it was not until the Dalai Lama left that we eliminated serfdom'; and when he and his wife met Prince Charles at Buckingham Palace, the Prince raised the subject of Tibet, only to be taunted with the repeated refrain, 'Northern Ireland, Northern Ireland, Northern Ireland'.

It was also during this visit to England that the police stopped the rising pro-Tibet demonstrations in London. When Jiang had visited Switzerland a few months before, his cavalcade had been interrupted by a number of pro-Tibet demonstrators, and Jiang reportedly told the Swiss parliament that Switzerland had just 'lost a good friend'. On hearing this, and doubtless scared of angering the emerging superpower which Jiang Zemin represented, the British authorities did everything they could to stop a similar incident occurring in London.

Such actions set a precedent for the twenty-first century. As China's global influence has grown, the Tibet issue has diminished at the same rate, and it seems that China can now stop pro-Tibet demonstrations both inside its own Middle Kingdom and outside. In 2008, China cancelled an EU-China Summit because the French president Nicolas Sarkozy met with the Dalai Lama; and, in 2010, when Barack Obama met with the Dalai Lama, he did so in the White House's Map Room rather than the usual Oval Office so as to suggest that this was merely a private meeting, not a political one. Still, disparaging reports grumbled out of the People's Republic at this meeting: the claims being that, through Obama's actions, the Americans were supporting China's new cardinal sin: *splittism*.

This word in itself is highly indicative of the new governmental rhetoric of Jiang Zemin, his successor Hu Jintao and the current Paramount Leader Xi Jinping regarding Tibet, for their policies have not really changed, it is just the language within which they exist which has. Today, in the twenty-first century, it is not the 'rightists' nor 'imperialists' nor 'running dogs' who are the enemy, but 'splittists' – that is, those who attempt to split and thereby destroy the unity and harmony of China and its newfound economic might. The enemy is, of course, still the same – it is only the terminology which signifies them that has been lexically softened and thus made more globally palatable: these are no longer political enemies, they are economic enemies, and such semantic safeguarding gives China a new angle by which to elude the pryings of the human rights watchdogs.

So important is this issue of splittism to China that there are now twenty-four separate institutions within the Party's bureaucracy dedicated solely to 'anti-splittism'. It was one of these groups which put a nationwide ban on the computer game 'Football Manager 2005', simply because there were separate teams for Tibet, Taiwan, Hong Kong and Macau. Defending their decision to ban the game, the Chinese authorities said that it 'threatened the sovereignty and territorial integrity of China' and that this 'seriously breaches Chinese law and has been strongly protested by our nation's gamers'.

When a mere computer game is outlawed because it gave Tibet its own football team, there is little hope for any meaningful discussion between Beijing and Dharamsala, and, as Tibet enters the second decade of the twenty-first century, such hope is dwindling further and further.

Granted, Tibet has accrued a number of positive developments thanks to its Chinese overseers. Its economy is growing exponentially, and China has recently poured over ten billion dollars into the region. The new railway and roads have caused controversy, but we must not forget that the fourteenth Dalai Lama, while he was still in Tibet, had planned the latter anyway, and it is fair to say that China has been able to construct them more cheaply and efficiently than an independent Tibet would have perhaps been able to. Both the ability to pay salaries and to levy taxes within Tibet is dependent upon the central government; without them the regional government would certainly struggle, if not descend into all-out economic recession.

But all of this has come at a very heavy cost. To date, Tibet remains as one of the most heavily militarised zones in the world, and there are few people anywhere who have to deal with such political oppression on a day-to-day basis. The heavy cost is, in a word, freedom, and even in our high-speed, broadband, smartphone, Wi-Fi, twenty-first-century world, the Tibetans remain as devoid of freedom as they have ever been since the Cultural Revolution.

It is in this Tibet that, on 5 September 2007, it was decreed by a new law that all incarnate lamas had to be first approved by the Beijing government before attaining their title, thereby placing important religious decisions into the control of an atheist government. Such a law, preceded by the Chinese handling of the nomination of the eleventh Panchen Lama, has chilling ramifications for when the fourteenth Dalai Lama dies, and the fifteenth is sought out.

It is in this Tibet that, on 30 September 2006, thirty-three unarmed Tibetans attempting to escape the country via the Himalayan Nangpa La pass were fired upon by Chinese border guards. One – a teenage nun – was killed by the bullets, and others were seriously injured. The survivors were arrested and imprisoned and, according to the testaments of some who were released, were tortured brutally for their 'crime'. There are some of that party who still remain unaccounted for. At first, China denied the event, but it was forced to concede when a Romanian mountaineer, Sergiu Matei, who had been climbing nearby and filmed the atrocity, released his footage to the international press.

It is in this Tibet that the lives of the nomads have been further interrupted and displaced by China's recent invitation to international mining companies to come and join them in reaping Tibet's wealth of underground resources from beneath the noses of her indigenous people.

It is in this Tibet that programs of 're-education' still exist, where monks and nuns are still forced into attending daily study sessions, forced to denounce the Dalai Lama, and forced to recognise the absolute rule of the Party.

It is in this Tibet that the laity, those outside of the monasteries, are given similar treatment, forced to sign and then abide by 'Conduct Agreements', which clearly detail their responsibilities as citizens of the motherland. These Conduct Agreements state that their signees must refrain from demonstrations or any other kind of splittist activity, that all their actions must instead be ones which show, above all else, their loyalty to the Party, and that, if they notice anyone else not abiding by their own Conduct Agreements, they must report them to the nearest official. To go against such rules is to go against the Conduct Agreement and, as a consequence, to break the law: risking arrest, imprisonment, and even torture.

It is in this Tibet that those three sanctions – arrest, imprisonment, torture – remain commonplace, often for offences as insubstantial as calling out 'Free Tibet!' in a busy street. The nun Pasang Lhamo did just that in 1994 and remained in prison for the next eight years. Once there, she was subjected to five-day-long re-education sessions, and then tortured with electric batons on the sixth day when she refused to agree that Tibet was and always had been a part of China. This would happen three or four times each year.

It is in this Tibet that religious freedom remains non-existent and religious persecution remains rife. Tibetan monasteries continue to be destroyed by the Chinese authorities, such as the Larung Gar Academy in Larung Valley, where the 1,700 buildings of the monastery were demolished in one day in 2001.

It is in this Tibet that intellectual freedom likewise remains non-existent. When the Tibetan writer Woeser published her *Notes on Tibet* in 2003, it was quickly banned for its praise of Tibetan Buddhism and the Dalai Lama, and Woeser herself was asked to undergo a series of 'self-criticism' sessions in Lhasa: a thinly veiled twenty-first-century rehash of the Cultural Revolution-era *thamzing* (struggle-sessions). The core of her self-criticism rested upon the tenet that she denounce the Dalai Lama and repudiate the praise she had laid upon him in her book. When Woeser refused, she lost her job, social security, medical and retirement insurance, and her home. Although barred from leaving the country, she managed to escape, yet another exile China is more than glad to be rid of.

It is in this Tibet that everyone, at all times, is under surveillance: from the ever-present military and police, from the clandestine spies, from those employed to examine all Internet and mobile phone usage, from random and legal house searches. It is in this Tibet that all speak with voices lowered and eyes shifting, in this Tibet that the borders remain closed for the best part of each year, and in this Tibet that, as I saw, most Tibetans from the bottom up scour out existences so devoid of any kind of 'liberation' as we might know it, that one wonders how Mao's terminology for his country's annexation of theirs could ever be justified.

It is, therefore, remarkable that the Tibetans' propensity for protest has succeeded in continuing from the 1959 Lhasa uprising to the present day. The most recent example, which put Tibet firmly back into the world's eye again, came with the 2008 Olympics, hosted by China and staged in Beijing. This was one of the most violent demonstrations the Tibetans have ever instigated, and a number of Han immigrants living in Lhasa were killed and their shops burnt down. The protest, aided by twenty-first-century technology such as email and text messaging, erupted across all Tibetan areas – including those outside the TAR – almost simultaneously, and then, aided by global media coverage, slowly extended across the world, following the Olympic torch on its grand tour. In Lhasa, the Chinese were quick to react, sending troops into the capital almost immediately, detaining thousands of citizens, and parading some of them through the streets in army jeeps. But still the demonstrations continued with student sit-ins and protests outside government offices. For perhaps the first time since 1959, these protests were not dominated over by monks, but came from something much more universal, with students, nomads, farmers and office workers at the forefront of the fray alongside their spiritual brothers.

It was due to this cross-section of involvement that the Chinese authorities decided, within their crackdown, to not just target the monasteries as they usually would, but to target everyone within the Tibetan Autonomous Region. The monasteries, of course, suffered – many were searched by the People's Armed Police and some were closed; a large number of monks were arrested or deported, and many of those left behind were ordered into re-education sessions – but, on a larger scale, everyone suffered. The borders were closed for the rest of 2008, arrests and property searches became more common than ever, and meetings were held in most public places – schools, colleges, government offices – where citizens were ordered to criticise themselves and, of course, the Dalai Lama. Even those Chinese outside the TAR who showed any sympathy for the demonstrations were kept under close scrutiny, and when a group of Chinese lawyers publicly offered to defend any Tibetans arrested in response to the incident, they were themselves arrested and told in no uncertain terms that, if they actualised their pledge, their licences to practise law would be revoked indefinitely.

When the government felt it had things under control again, it offered a statement justifying its harsh tactics, resorting to the same old scapegoat and saying among other things that 'there is sufficient evidence to prove this incident was organised, premeditated, and meticulously orchestrated by the Dalai clique'. Whatever this 'sufficient evidence' was, it has never been shown.

A couple of years after this, a year or so after I returned from Tibet, a series of revolutions spread across North Africa and the Middle East, leading towards a war in Libya. At around the same time, China closed Tibet's borders again, and, at the time of writing, they remain so. We do not know what is happening there now, and probably will not know for the next three or four years. Scant reports have leaked out of China featuring the disappearance of famous dissidents – such as the artist Ai Weiwei – but from Tibet itself little is currently known. All we can perhaps surmise is that the Party have sent out a very clear message to the Tibetans – *don't even think about it*. And we can perhaps surmise that Beijing's grip on its Western Treasure is tighter than it has ever been before.

As a result, the Tibet-in-exile government's position on Tibet has recently changed from one fundamentally ideological to one much more pragmatic. As the Dalai Lama steps down from his role as head of state, the campaign he began decades before continues – that is, Tibet should remain a part of China, but it should be allowed genuine autonomy, along the same 'one country, two systems' lines which have given Hong Kong and Macau the freedom to prosper and culturally evolve throughout the last decade. According to the policy of the Dalai Lama's stated campaign, the current exiled government in Dharamsala are still working towards the same 5-Point Peace Plan the Dalai Lama laid out years ago: that the Tibetan plateau should be demilitarised; that any nuclear testing or stockpiling there should be forbidden; that all Tibet be transformed into a National Park; that all regional policies be directed towards the promotion of peace and environmental protection; and that genuine human rights and genuine religious freedom be allowed in Tibet.

Each of these points, and all of them together, seem intuitive and genuinely workable. There is no call to arms there, no demands for sovereignty, no invocation of independence.

Within these terms, Tibet would remain a part of China, and China would continue to dictate its foreign policy and national directives. But the Dalai Lama wrote this 5-Point Peace Plan some twenty years ago, and still China has shown no inclination towards it in any way. In the twenty-first century, Tibet still exists purely on China's terms, and it seems that it will for the foreseeable future. Such obstinacy saddens me, for as long as China continues with the treatment of Tibet engendered over the last fifty years, the people of Tibet will continue to suffer.

During the Cultural Revolution, a prophecy written by the thirteenth Dalai Lama just before his death became actualised, and monks and nuns uttered it under their breaths in their cells between each struggle-session. On my first night home from Tibet, unable to sleep, I switched my bedside light on and began reading *Freedom in Exile*. I found the prophecy on page 36, and read it through clouding eyes. For all its tarmac roads and permafrost railways, its guesthouses and beers, its youths in expensive jeans and monks on motorbikes with mobile phones, this was the Tibet I had seen, the Tibet Lobsang knew intimately, predicted and put down on paper by an old monk twenty years before the Chinese invaded Tibet, and fifty years before my own birth:

It may happen that here in Tibet, religion and government will be attacked both from without and within. Unless we guard our own country, it will now happen that the Dalai and the Panchen Lamas, the Father and the Son, and all the revered holders of the Faith, will disappear and become nameless. Monks and their monasteries will

363

be destroyed. The rule of law will be weakened. The lands and property of government officials will be seized. They themselves will be forced to serve their enemies or wander the country like beggars. All beings will be sunk in great hardship and overwhelming fear; the days and nights will drag on slowly in suffering.

Postscript

In the years which have passed since I left Tibet, I have searched the Internet regularly, not for a 'Lobsang from Tibet' (try locating a 'John from the UK'), but for the *Free Drolma* campaign which I know Lobsang will spearhead the moment he escapes Tibet. So far, I have found nothing remotely similar. I continue to look.

Acknowledgements

As welcoming, as forthright, as genuine as the Tibetans, and indeed many of the Chinese, I met on my journey were, they could only, under their circumstances, tell me a small portion of the story of Tibet. For the rest, I am indebted to a number of authors whose wonderful books have littered the floor of my study since I returned from Tibet. Foremost among them are Tsering Shakya and Jonathan Fenby, whose histories – Shakya's *The Dragon in the Land of Snows* and Fenby's *The Penguin History of Modern China* – have been my mainstays. Both tomes are as well-thumbed, spine-cracked and battered as any of the Dickens novels I've ever taken on my travels, though their deterioration results not from months sat at the bottom of a backpack, but from constant and unremitting perusal. For their objectivity, their unsurpassed research and their sheer bulk of good, factual information, I remain ever thankful to the writers of these two books. Others which I annotated, reread and referenced nightly, and which I feel must be name-checked here, are:

Bennett, Joe: *Where Underpants Come From*
Buckley, Michael: *Heartlands*
Chang, Jung: *Wild Swans*
Chang, Jung and Halliday, Jon: *Mao*
Chatwin, Bruce: *What Am I Doing Here*
Craig, Mary: *Tears of Blood*
Demick, Barbara: *Nothing to Envy*
French, Patrick: *Tibet, Tibet*
Gyatso, Palden: *Fire Under the Snow*
Harrer, Heinrich: *Seven Years in Tibet*
Harrer, Heinrich: *Return to Tibet*
His Holiness The Dalai Lama: *Freedom In Exile*
Karko, Kate: *Namma*
Laird, Thomas: *The Story of Tibet*
Le Sueur, Alec: *The Hotel on the Roof of the World*
Matthiessen, Peter: *The Snow Leopard*
Min, Anchee: *Red Azalea*
Palin, Michael: *Himalaya*
Scobie, Claire: *Last Seen in Lhasa*
Seth, Vikram: *From Heaven Lake*
Shakya, Tsering and Lixiong, Wang: *The Struggle for Tibet*
Stewart, Rory: *The Places in Between*
Shuyun, Sun: *A Year in Tibet*
Theroux, Paul: *Riding the Iron Rooster*
Thubron, Colin: *Behind the Wall*
Thubron, Colin: *To a Mountain in Tibet*
Xinran: *The Good Women of China*
Xinran: *Sky Burial*